FOREVER
YOUNG

FOREVER YOUNG

by

JONATHAN COTT

For David

With incessant admiration

From Jonathan

December, 1977

Random House New York

Grateful acknowledgment is made to the following for permission to reprint previously published material:

George Allen & Unwin Ltd.: An anonymous Japanese poem from *Japanese Poetry the Uta* by Arthur Waley.

Robert Bly: Poem from *The Book of Hours* by Rainer Maria Rilke translated by Robert Bly. Copyright © 1976 by Robert Bly.

E. P. Dutton and Faber and Faber Ltd.: Excerpt from *Lawrence Durrell and Henry Miller: A Private Correspondence*, edited by George Wickes. Copyright © 1962, 1963 by Lawrence Durrell and Henry Miller.

Grove Press, Inc. and Calder and Boyars Ltd., London: Excerpts from "Into The Night Life" reprinted from *Black Spring* by Henry Miller, pages 156–157. Copyright © 1963 by Grove Press, Inc.

Estate of Walter Lowenfels, Manna Lowenfels-Perpelitt, Literary Executor: Excerpts from *Walter Lowenfels: The Poet in the Flying Suit* by Walter Lowenfels.

New Directions Publishing Corporation: Excerpts from *The Book in My Life* by Henry Miller. Copyright © 1969 by New Directions Publishing Corporation; excerpts from *The Cosmological Eye* by Henry Miller. Copyright 1939 by New Directions Publishing Corporation; excerpts from *The Wisdom of the Heart*. Copyright 1941 by New Directions Publishing Corporation; excerpts from *Remember to Remember* by Henry Miller. Copyright 1941 by New Directions Publishing Corporation.

Persea Books, Inc.: "Some Advice to Those Who Will Serve Time in Prison" by Nazim Hikmet, translated by Randy Blasing and Mutlu Konuk. Copyright © 1975 by Randy Blasing and Mutlu Konuk. Reprinted by permission of Persea Books, Inc., P.O. Box 804, Madison Square Station, New York, N.Y. 10010.

G. P. Putnam's Sons and Peter Owen, London: Excerpts from *Henry Miller: Letters to Anaïs Nin* by Anaïs Nin. Copyright © 1965 by Anaïs Nin.

Stonehill Publishing Co., N.Y.: Poem from *The Wishing Well*. Translated by Howard A. Norman.

Grateful acknowledgment is made to the following for permission to reprint photographs:

Deacon Chapin: A photograph of Stéphane Grappelli © by Rolling Stone.

Columbia Records: A photograph of Glenn Gould.

Nancy Crampton: A photograph of Maurice Sendak © by Nancy Crampton.

New Yorker Films: A photograph of Werner Herzog.

Betty Freeman: Photographs of Henry Miller, Harry Partch, and Jonathan Cott.

Eric Lindbloom: A photograph of Walter Lowenfels.

Maurice Sendak: A Fantasy Sketch.

Foto Torrini: A photograph of Oriana Fallaci.

Library of Congress Cataloging in Publication Data

Cott, Jonathan.
Forever young.

1. Artists—Interviews.   2. Arts—Psychology.
I. Title.
NX165.C67   700'.92'2   [B]   77-5963
ISBN 0-394-41655-4
ISBN 0-394-73398-3 pbk.

DESIGN BY LILLY LANGOTSKY

Manufactured in the United States of America

2   4   6   8   9   7   5   3

First Edition

IN MEMORY OF

MY GRANDMOTHER, FANYA CAHAN
RALPH J. GLEASON
DR. ABNER STERN

WHO STAYED FOREVER YOUNG

"Those who wonder shall reign,
and those who reign shall wonder."

Preface

I have always liked to think that the first interview took place in the Garden of Eden. Having eaten of the fruit of the tree of knowledge and hearing the sound of the Lord God walking in the cool of the day, Adam and Eve hid themselves among the branches. "Where art thou?" the Lord asked Adam, who replied: "I heard thy voice in the garden, and I was afraid, because I was naked; and I hid myself."

To an all-knowing God, of course, Adam's answer may seem superfluous, but in its expression of guilt, fear, and vulnerability, it is a true uncovering. On a deeper and more personal level, we may understand—as scriptural exegetes have suggested—that God's question directs itself to our own sense of self-realization: "Where am I in my world?" But on both levels, God's question and Adam's answer, taken together, present a paradigm of the interview's form and purpose—attempting to reveal what is concealed—as well as a model of an internal dialogue that all of us, at some time, have with ourselves.

When an interview transcends its simply pragmatic function of eliciting information (e.g., job interviews, "background" interviews for news articles), it can in fact move into the realm of conversation and dialogue. "Dialogue between mere individuals is only a sketch," Martin Buber once wrote; "only in dialogue between persons is the sketch filled in." And in the interviews I most admire, this is exactly what occurs: A person is allowed gradually to fill him- or herself in; the process by which this takes place is a dramatic interchange resulting in a realized embodiment of the meaning of personality.

If one thinks, as I do, of Boswell's *Life of Johnson,* Eckermann's *Conversations with Goethe,* and the works of Oscar Lewis and Studs Terkel as quasi-interviews, one is enlarging the meaning of the word—but not, perhaps, as much as one might imagine. The word "interview" itself is derived from the French *entrevoir* (to see between), which conveys the meaning of "to foresee, to glimpse, to sense, or to have an idea or feeling of."

In the stories of Adam and of Odysseus—who, upon returning home, delayed recognition of his identity—we are reminded that in order to see clearly, one must be seen through. Certainly in an interview—in the enlarged definition of the word—the act of glimpsing and sensing requires, on the part of both interviewer and interviewee, a delicate balance between "seeing through" and "seeing between," a balance between openness and a respect for the mysteries and boundaries of personality.

Needless to say, you cannot engage in this kind of interchange without admiring and delighting in the person to and with whom you are speaking. In an era when the sententious anecdotes and platitudes of late-night talk show celebrities—hardly disguising a pandemic sense of *tedium vitae*—dominate not only television but also the publishing media, it sometimes becomes hard to notice the multitude of men and women around us doing innovative and inspiring work—among them the eight persons in this book. All of them share a childlike aliveness to the feelings of the world and to the world of their feelings, all of them persevering, in spite of shifting fads and fashions, in the belief in and the exploration of that mysterious area where, in the words of the painter Joan Miró, "creation takes place and from which there flows an inexplicable radiance that finally comes to be the whole human being."

As Rilke, in the translation by Robert Bly, powerfully wrote to those of us on the edge of stupor and sleep:

> Already the ripening barberries are red,
> and the old asters hardly breathe in their beds.
> The man who is not rich now as summer goes
> will wait and wait and never be himself.
>
> The man who cannot quietly close his eyes
> certain that there is vision after vision
> inside, simply waiting until nighttime

to rise all around him in the darkness—
he is an old man, it's all over for him.

Nothing else will come; no more days will open;
and everything that does happen will cheat him—
even you, my God. And you are like a stone
that draws him daily deeper into the depths.

Jonathan Cott
September 1977
New York City

Acknowledgments

Most of the conversations in this book were first published, in slightly different form, in *Rolling Stone* magazine between 1974 and 1977:

> Harry Partch: April 11, 1974 (#158)
> Glenn Gould: August 15, 1974 (#167)
>   August 29, 1974 (#168)
> Henry Miller: February 27, 1975 (#181)
> Oriana Fallaci: June 17, 1976 (#215)
> Werner Herzog: November 18, 1976 (#226)
> Maurice Sendak: December 30, 1976 (#229)
> Stéphane Grappelli: May 19, 1977 (#239)

I am inestimably grateful to the editors of *Rolling Stone* who worked on and improved these conversations: Christine Doudna, Barbara Downey, Sarah Lazin, Marianne Partridge, Paul Scanlon, Vicki Sufian, and Robert Wallace. I want especially to thank Susan Bolotin, Cordelia Jason, and Jann and Jane Wenner, who made this book possible.

Contents

ORIANA FALLACI

The Art of
Unclothing
an Emperor

Little man whip a big man every time if
the little man's in the right and keeps a'
comin'.

—Motto of the Texas Rangers

W hen Oriana Fallaci went to in-
terview Ethiopia's Haile Selassie, the emperor's two pet Chihuahuas,
named Lulu and Papillon—sensitive antennae of the monarch's auto-
nomic nervous system, geiger counters registering the presence of
friend or foe—stopped dead in their tracks. And after this interview
(in which the emperor sounded "sick or drunk") was published in
Italy, the Ethiopian ambassador in Rome was recalled to his home-
land, and no word of or from him was ever heard again.

It is not uncommon for political repercussions to result from a
Fallaci interview. Her uncomplimentary portrait of Yasir Arafat attracted scores of threatening letters and letter-bomb scares. The original tapes of her conversation with Golda Meir, Fallaci claims, were
stolen by agents of Libya's Colonel Qaddafi. Her interview with Pakistan's Ali Bhutto delayed a peace agreement between Pakistan and
India. And Henry Kissinger paid Oriana Fallaci one of her greatest
compliments, saying that his having consented to an interview with
her was the "stupidest" thing he had ever done.

Like the child in "The Emperor's New Clothes," and like the
"Plain Dealer" of Restoration comedy, whose unremitting rudeness
signified to the audience that this stock character was being true to
himself, Oriana Fallaci has, simply with a tape recorder, exposed the
inanities and pretensions of those contumelious rascals and fat-hearted
popinjays who pose and act as the powerful leaders and manipulators
of the world's destiny.

After years of interviewing "vacuous" movie stars, this slight (in stature), passionate, and mettlesome woman—who speaks in a candent, husky tone—has become the greatest political interviewer of modern times. The Oriana Fallaci Tape Collection is now housed in humidified shelves at Boston University. And just this month [June 1976] Liveright is publishing *Interview with History*—a book consisting of fourteen of Fallaci's extraordinary interviews with persons such as Kissinger, President Thieu, General Giap, Golda Meir, the Shah of Iran, Archbishop Makarios, and Indira Gandhi. As an international correspondent for the Italian magazine *L'Europeo*, she has become a star throughout Europe—where her articles, interviews, and books appear regularly in translation—and has attracted a devoted following in this country through the publication of her interviews in magazines and newspapers such as the *New Republic*, the Washington *Post*, the *New York Review of Books*, and the *New York Times Magazine*. Her most recent work—a spare, annealed dramatic monologue entitled *Letter to a Child Never Born*—has sold almost a million copies in Italy and was published by Simon and Schuster in 1977.

Oriana Fallaci claims that she prepares herself for her interviews "as a boxer prepares for the ring," but it is as a "midwife"—as she defines her role in the following interview—that she has drawn from her subjects many astonishing revelations. Through her gentle ministration, Kissinger finally explained the reason for his abiding popularity: "Well, yes, I'll tell you. What do I care? The main point arises from the fact that I've always acted alone. Americans like that immensely. Americans like the cowboy who leads the wagon train by riding ahead alone on his horse, the cowboy who rides all alone into the town, the village, with his horse and nothing else. Maybe even without a pistol, since he doesn't shoot. He acts, that's all, by being in the right place at the right time. In short, a western."

From the Shah of Iran, Fallaci received the following remarks concerning the role of women in his life: "Women, you know. . . . Look, let's put it this way. I don't underrate them; they've profited more than anyone else from my White Revolution. . . . And let's not forget I'm the son of the man who took away women's veils in Iran. But I wouldn't be sincere if I stated I'd been influenced by a single one of them. Nobody can influence me, nobody. Still less a woman. Women are important in a man's life only if they're beautiful and charming and keep their femininity and. . . . This business of feminism, for instance. What do these feminists want? What do you want?

You say equality. Oh! I don't want to seem rude, but. . . . You're equal in the eyes of the law, but not, excuse my saying so, in intelligence."

From the tortured leader of the Greek Resistance, Alexandros Panagoulis, Fallaci elicited his haunting description of how it felt to rediscover space after years sequestered in the darkness of prison: "I made a terrible effort to go forward in all that sun, all that space. Then all of a sudden, in all that sun, in all that space, I saw a spot. And the spot was a group of people. And from that group of people a black figure detached itself. And it came toward me, and little by little it became my mother. And behind my mother, another figure detached itself. And this one too came toward me. And little by little it became Mrs. Mandilaras, the widow of Nikoforos Mandilaras, murdered by the colonels. And I embraced my mother, I embraced Mrs. Mandilaras." [Alexandros Panagoulis was killed in Greece on May Day, 1976.]

And at the conclusion of her conversation with the ill-fated President Thieu, Oriana Fallaci presented the following dialogue that extends the interview form into the realm of the greatest comic farce:

THIEU: *Voyez bien, mademoiselle,* anything I do I like to do well. Whether it's being converted, or playing tennis, or riding a horse, or holding the office of president. I like responsibility more than power. That's why I say that power should never be shared with others. That's why I'm always the one to decide! Always! I may listen to others suggest some decision, and then make the opposite decision. *Oui, c'est moi qui décide.* If one doesn't accept responsibility, one isn't worthy to be the chief and . . . *mademoiselle,* ask me this question, "Who's the chief here?"
FALLACI: Who's the chief here?
THIEU: I am! I'm the chief! *Moi! C'est moi le chef!*
FALLACI: Thank you, Mr. President. Now I think I can go.
THIEU: Are you leaving? Have we finished? Are you satisfied, *mademoiselle?* Because if you're not satisfied, you must tell me. *Mademoiselle,* I hope you're satisfied because I've hidden nothing from you and I've spoken to you with complete frankness. I swear. I didn't want to in the beginning. But then . . . what can I do? That's the way I am. Come on, tell me. Did you ever expect to find such a fellow?
FALLACI: No, Mr. President.
THIEU: *Merci, mademoiselle.* And, if you can, pray for peace in Vietnam. Peace in Vietnam means peace in the world. And sometimes I feel as though there's nothing left to do except pray to God.

At their best, Oriana Fallaci's brilliantly theatrical interviews remind us of the aims of historians and playwrights such as Thucydides and Ben Jonson, in whose works history and human relations are seen as nothing less than moral drama.

Interviewing Oriana Fallaci is an instructive and reassuring experience. She approved of the kind of cassette recorder I use (she has the same model) and, as well, my 90-minute tapes (120-minute tapes jam up, as interviewers learn not soon enough). And throughout the interview, which took place in February 1976, she positioned the machine and checked the battery indicator, turned over the tapes while remembering and repeating the last words of her unfinished sentences on the new side, then numbered the tapes for me. She suggested that I learn how to ask one question at a time instead of rambling and ranging over a series of suggestive ideas, and turned the recorder off when she wanted to say something off the record. "Only Nixon," she once stated, "knows more about tape recorders than I do."

It wasn't so long ago that advice-to-the-lovelorn columnists used to suggest that all a woman had to do to get a man interested in her was to cajole him gently into talking about himself all evening, thereby flattering him and bolstering his sense of self-importance. In your interviews you seem, almost unconsciously, to have taken this piece of folk wisdom and pushed it very far down the line, using it in order to expose your grandiloquent subjects for what they really are.

I've never thought of that. Neither in my private nor my public life have I ever thought in terms of "seducing" somebody, using what are called the "feminine arts"—it makes me vomit just to think of it. Ever since I was a child—and way before the recent feminist resurgence—I've never conceived of . . . I'm very surprised by what you say. There might be some truth here, but you've really caught me by surprise.

What you're talking about implies a kind of psychological violence which I never commit when I interview someone. I never force a person to talk to me. If he doesn't want to talk, or if he talks without pleasure, I just walk out; I've done that many times. There's no courting or seducing involved. The main secret of my interviews lies in the fact that there's no trick whatsoever. None.

You know, there are many students who write about my interviews—in Italy, France, and America, too. And they always ask me how I go about it and if I could teach them to do it. But it's impossible, for these interviews are what they are, good or bad, because they're made by me, with this face, with this voice. They have to do with my personality, and I bring too much of myself into them to teach them.

When I was reading Interview with History, *I began thinking of the great Enlightenment author Diderot, who, it's been said, had an "instinctual" urge to expose what was concealed. And it seems to me that one of the underlying impulses of your work—along with your unmediated hatred for fascism and authoritarianism—is exactly this instinctual urge to expose. Do you feel that this is true?*

All right. You must give me a little time to answer, as I do with the people I interview. It's a difficult question, very difficult. As I told you before, I bring myself into these interviews completely, as a human being, as a personality; I bring what I know, what I don't know, what I am. Oriana is in there, as an actor. And I bring into these encounters all my choices, all my ideas, and my temperament as well. So, being at the same time very antifascist and very passionate, it's very difficult for me to interview the fascist, in the broad sense of the word. And I say it with shame, since I'm perfectly aware of how ridiculous this is. If I am, as I claim to be, a historian as much as a journalist (I claim that a journalist is a historian of his time), how can I reject at least half of humanity? Because at least half of humanity is fascist.

And when I happen to be interviewing a fascist, and if he really "counts" in history and the interview is going well, I get fascinated. I want so much to know *why* he's a fascist. And this "fascination" on my part then leads to what Socrates called *maieutica*—the work of the *midwife*, whose role becomes especially interesting when I have in front of me someone like Thieu. You see, I think that *power* itself is in some sense fascist by definition (I'm not speaking here of the Mussolini-type of fascism but am rather referring to it in the philosophical sense of the word). And I almost always end by being captivated by it.

I say "almost," because I did once walk out during an interview with Giorgio Almirante. Almirante's that nice gentleman whom the Americans invited to Washington, the man who's reconstructed the Fascist party in Italy. And I really did violence to myself when I asked to interview him. He received me immediately, he was happy to see me, of course; an interview with me is always publicity, even if it's negative. The more negative, the better for Almirante! So I went to see him, and he was immensely polite, most intelligent, and I started with my *maieutica*. And my *maieutica* was working *so* well that at a certain moment he said, "Oh yes, sure I was a Fascist, sure I was, I'm very proud of it." And I said, "Well, listen . . . Mussolini, what about Mussolini?" Believe me, I was very nervous, I was suffering like hell, I was hiding my head and suffering. And he said, "I *love* Mussolini, I loved him, I still love him." And I got up and said, "That's enough! I refuse to stay one second more. This *bullshit*—you don't think I'm going to *publish* this!" It was such a wild thing. Almirante first became pale, then red, then green, and all he could say was "I'm sorry, you're not going, you're not really. . . ." Argh, argh, argh! And after that, for five years, Almirante has tried to see me again, to be interviewed by me. He wrote me a letter; I didn't answer. He sent me messages through two people: "You know, he would like so much to be interviewed by you. You can do the nastiest of interviews to him, he doesn't mind. He's so sorry that you walked out like that." And I believe he would like that, sure he would like it. But I'm not going to do it, I'm not going to give him an interview.

He's obviously suffering from an unrequited interview.

Unrequited interview! [Laughing] That it was. And it happened again with Mujib Rahman, the man who was martyred in Bangladesh. I started the tape recorder, and all at once he started behaving so badly. He was so arrogant and so stupid—one of the most stupid men I've ever met in my life, maybe the most stupid. So I said: "Listen, Mujib, I'm not going to go on like this, you know. If you're not polite, I'm not going to do this interview." Argh, argh, argh . . . he started yelling. We both yelled, there was a big fight, and he said: "Get out of my country, don't come back again, leave my people, leave us alone, leave us alone!" And I yelled back: "Be sure I'll leave you alone!" It went on and on and on like that. The Mukti

Bahini—the guerrillas—almost lynched me because of that, and I was only saved by two Indian officers.

Another interview that ended tragically was with Muhammad Ali. I'd previously done a very bad interview with him. Some people say they liked that one, but I didn't. (Usually, the interviews that people like, I don't.) So I'd gone to see him again in Florida and found him in front of an enormous watermelon which seemed to disappear in his mouth with one bite—like one of those Mickey Mouse movies. And when I asked him a question, he just belched. I asked him again—it was a question about the Vietnam war—and again . . . a few belches. At that point, I got so furious that I took the microphone and threw it at him and shouted: "You think that I came to Florida to be insulted by you?" Things like that. And then a Black Muslim started to approach me. And I was really scared. I kept yelling, because when you're scared, the only thing to do is to attack. . . . So these "unrequited" interviews, as you call them, are always very dramatic and always end tragically because I'm passionate and I'm not able to control myself sometimes.

In your book you often talk about your desire to "remove the veils" masking the politicians you're interviewing. And when you've done that, what often appears before you and us are characters straight out of Alice in Wonderland *or* Ubu Roi. *(I'm thinking here of your interviews with Kissinger, Thieu, and the Shah of Iran.) But with persons such as Helder Camara—the leftist archbishop of Brazil —and Alexandros Panagoulis—the jailed and tortured head of the Greek Resistance—you are clearly presenting portraits of two unalterably heroic human beings.*

You see, I think that each of us is Dr. Jekyll and Mr. Hyde. But with Dom Helder and . . . Panagoulis . . . well, maybe I didn't want to look for that in them. I am the judge, I am the one who decides. Listen: if I am a painter and do your portrait, have I or haven't I the right to paint you as I want? It's my interpretation. I've seen the last portrait that Annigoni painted of Queen Elizabeth, and it's really cruel. I said: "Annigoni, how could you do that, she's not like that!" And he said: "Yes, maybe she's not." "Then why did you do it like that?" "Because that's the way I saw her." So if this is permitted to a painter, why shouldn't it be permitted to us? I saw Dom Helder as a saint, and I portrayed him as one; Panagoulis as a hero, and I portrayed him as a hero. By the way, they *are* two very decent people. [Laughing] It's not my fault. But I'm sure that they have their Dr. Jekyll and Mr. Hyde sides, too, which I didn't look for. Maybe Dom Helder goes around in the nighttime stealing the virginity of the girls of his village. I doubt it very much. But I saw him as a saint.

Improbable as it might seem, might there have been a saintly side to someone like President Thieu?

Thieu is very far from being a saint. I interviewed him when Kissinger had just taken him by the nose. And Thieu was damn right when he realized that Kissinger only looked at the world in terms of global strategy. "I give you Russia, you take China, I go to America, add a little salt and then some onion, a little of Guatemala, and then some parsley, and maybe some Brazil." That's the way Kissinger cooks the destiny of people. And Thieu said: "I'm not that. If Kissinger cooks like that, I'll fall immediately. I'm Vietnamese, I'm small, if they give me a slap—boom—I fall. I'm left here with 300,000 North Vietnamese and their tanks inside South Vietnam. What kind of an armistice is that?" And he was right! He was a victim of Mr. Kissinger, of American power, of American arrogance—as much as the people of Hanoi were victims of American bombings. And naturally I pointed that out.

But in the introductory essay to your Thieu interview, you finally judged him harshly, saying: "Almost every time that I have tried to give compassion and respect to a government leader, almost every time that I have tried to absolve even partially some famous son of a bitch, I have later been bitterly sorry." And I wanted to ask you about your unmitigated sense of justice and your inevitable judgmental assessments. It's obvious that you view people in strict moral terms—almost as if they represented physiological humors like choler, phlegm, or black bile.

Yes, you're right, and that's terrible. It's very Protestant. I guess it's the destiny of atheists to become moralists. And the more they age, the more moralistic they become. I think that it helps to dramatize things, but I don't do it because of that, unfortunately. I'm *really* a moralist. It's a defect I have, and it limits freedom, it limits *my* freedom. Imagine, I don't feel free to go and interview a son of a bitch, I suffer when I do it. But I am a moralist.

Your criticism of Arafat, however, was couched in aesthetic rather than moral terms, accusing him of lacking "originality and charm."

I think that the interview demonstrates well enough that he also lacked intelligence. As for lack of "charm" . . . maybe the translation isn't very happy. In Italian, when you say that someone lacks charm, you mean that the person's arrogant and impolite. It's too "charming" in English. Arafat was shouting all the time and was watching my photographer, whom he liked very much, maybe a little too much. He wasn't sincere. The interview with Arafat has the value of a document, nothing more. I didn't get to the soul of Arafat— maybe because there was no time, maybe because there was no soul.

Do you know Lenin's dictum: "Ethics will be the aesthetics of the future"?

No I didn't. That's interesting, but my moralism is not of the Leninist kind. I'm too much of a liberal to see things—

You really are full of contradictions—an anarchist in spirit, a socialist in theory, a liberal—

Listen, Jonathan, in my most recent book, *Letter to a Child Never Born*, I have brought to such a paroxysm exactly what you're saying—a book that's the apotheosis of doubt. Every time the female character says something, she soon thereafter says the contrary of that, and then the contrary of *that* without denying the original statement. And it goes on in this way. Antithesis and synthesis occur here at the same time, all at once. The woman keeps contradicting herself, keeps being controversial with herself, and in the end she is terribly human.

Speaking of the "terribly human," I was struck by a moving moment during your interview with Mrs. Gandhi when you talked about "the solitude that oppresses women intent on defending their

*own destinies." You mention that Mrs. Gandhi, like Golda Meir, had
to sacrifice her marriage for her career. And I got the feeling that here
you were somehow also talking about your sense of yourself.*

The first difference between me and them is that I never give
up. Marriage is an expression that to me suggests "giving up," an
expression of sacrifice and regret. I never wanted to get married, so I
didn't make that sacrifice—it was a victory for me. The solitude I was
referring to wasn't a physical solitude. Nor was it, for instance, for
Indira Gandhi, because everybody knows that at the time I interviewed her she wasn't alone at all. She likes men, thank God, and she
makes use of that. It was an internal solitude that comes about from
the fact of being a woman—and a woman with responsibilities in a
world of men.

That kind of solitude is a victory for me, and I've been searching for it. Today, you are interviewing me in 1976. If you had interviewed me in '74 or '73 or '65, I would probably have answered a little
differently—but not too much. Like a photograph, an interview has to
crystallize the moment in which it takes place. Today, I need that
kind of solitude so much—since it is what moves me, intellectually
speaking—that sometimes I feel the need to be physically alone.
When I'm with my companion, there are moments when we are two
too many. I never get bored when I'm alone, and I get easily bored
when I'm with others. And women who, like Indira and like Golda,
have had the guts to accept that solitude are the women who have
achieved something.

You must also consider that, in terms of the kind of solitude
we've been talking about, women like Golda and Indira are more
representative because they are old. A person of my generation and,
even more so, a woman younger than myself, really *wants* that solitude. Golda and Indira were victimized by it, since they belonged to a
generation in which people didn't think as we do today. They were
probably hurt, and I don't know how much they pitied themselves.
Golda cried at a certain moment during the interview. When she
spoke of her husband, she was regretting something.

As for myself, in the past I felt less happy about this subject. It
was still something to fight about inside myself, trying to understand
it better. But today I'm completely free of it, the problem doesn't exist
any more. And I don't even gloat over the fact that what could have
been considered a sacrifice yesterday is today an achievement. We

must thank the feminists for this, because they've helped not only me but everybody, all women. And young people, both men and women, understand this very much.

Golda spoke of having lost the family as a *great* sacrifice—she was crying then. But to me, the worst curse that could happen to a person is to *have* a family.

That's not a very Italian attitude, is it?

You'd be surprised. We know about Marriage Italian Style. But people in Italy today are getting married less and less. We have an unbelievable tax law that makes two persons who are married and who both work pay more taxes than they would if they were single. So they get separated or divorced. And there's nothing "romantic" or "Italian" about this. No, the family, at least morally and psychologically, is disappearing in Italy, as well as all over Europe.

What should exist in its place?

Free individuals.

But no community.

You ask me too much. If I could answer you I would have resolved the problem. If you said to me: "All right, socialism as it's been applied until now hasn't worked. Capitalism doesn't work. What should we do?" I'd have to respond: "My dear, if I could answer these questions, I'd be the philosopher of my time."

In the introduction to your interview with Golda Meir, you comment on the resemblances you noticed between Meir and your own mother, writing: "My mother too has the same gray curly hair, that tired and wrinkled face, that heavy body supported on swollen, unsteady, leaden legs. My mother too has that sweet and energetic look about her, the look of a housewife obsessed with cleanliness. They are a breed of women, you see, that has gone out of style and whose wealth consists in a disarming simplicity, an irritating modesty, a wisdom that comes from having toiled all their lives in the pain, discomfort, and trouble that leave no time for the superfluous."
And in the introduction to your interview with Henry Kis-

singer, you tell how you were immediately reminded of an old teacher of yours "who enjoyed frightening me by staring at me ironically from behind his spectacles. Kissinger even had the same baritone, or rather guttural, voice as this teacher, and the same way of leaning back in the armchair with his right arm outstretched, the gesture of crossing his legs, while his jacket was so tight over his stomach that it looked as though the buttons might pop." It's at special moments like these in your book that I get the sense of a little girl looking at the world so clearly because she remembers so much—a sense one usually finds in the best literature and films, but almost never in interviews.

Do you understand now why I can't teach someone how to make these interviews? Do you understand now why they are what they are because I do them? Kissinger was sitting on this raised arm-chair, having asked me to sit down on the sofa. So he was up there and I was down here, and it was like seeing . . . Manchinelli was his name, that professor of physics and mathematics. He was a real bas-tard who used to sit up high and mighty at his podium like God, judging us instead of teaching us, and from there cursing and re-proaching us, making us suffer. He made me suffer particularly because I was the only one who answered him back. Oh, I was terrible in school. Poor people, poor professors, I made them suffer so much. Because I was very clever, I was always first in my class, but I was terrible. Because if they said something wrong, I didn't keep my mouth shut. Anyway, when I saw Kissinger sitting like that—poor man, he wasn't aware of it, of course, and he didn't do it on purpose; he is what he is and was showing what he is—I said: "Oh, God. Here we go with Manchinelli again."

I associated the two things, and I always do. I always go back to childhood. But do you know why I make these comparisons? Not only because they come spontaneously to me but because I like to be simple when I write, I want to be understood, as I used to say, by my mother when I write about politics. How can my mother understand me? And my audience is made up mostly of people who have not been to university. So in order to simplify things, I use everyday facts, "human" facts—that word is overused, but I'll use it here again. So you associate Kissinger with a nasty old professor, or Golda with your mother—the same wrinkles, the same irritating modesty. And then people understand. My use of associations is a result both of spon-taneity and tactics.

I didn't start writing about politics until fairly recently—until Vietnam, in fact. But I've always been a very politicized person because of the family I was born into—I'll come back to this in a minute—and because of my experiences. I was a little girl during the Resistance—and a member of the Liberal Socialist party—and I spoke in public the first time when I was fifteen at a political rally. I'll always remember—I had pigtails and was trembling: "PEOPLE OF FLORENCE . . . A YOUNG COMRADE SPEAKS TO YOU. . . ."

And I kept saying to my editors: "I want to write about politics, I want to interview politicians in the same way that I interview actors. Because it's boring when we read politics, it must be done in another way." But they didn't let me do it because I was a woman. (There we go again.) And only when I demonstrated that I could be a good war correspondent in Vietnam did they allow me to do interviews with politicians in the same way that I'd done them with astronauts, soldiers, and actors.

Do you think that your forceful way of doing interviews was in any way determined by the humiliation and contemptuousness you might have felt being a girl growing up in a world of political men?

Absolutely not. I can't complain too much about men because, number one, I had the luck to be born into a feminist family—they didn't know it, but indeed they were. To begin with: my father. He always believed in women. He had three daughters, and when he adopted the fourth child, he chose a girl—my youngest sister—because . . . he trusts women. And my parents educated me with the attitude of: you *must* do it because you are a woman. It was, for sure, a challenge, which implies the recognition of a certain reality. But they never thought that I couldn't do it.

In the beginning I wanted to become either a surgeon or a journalist. And the only reason why I didn't choose medicine was because we were too poor to afford six years of medical school. So then it seemed obvious for me to get a job as a reporter when I was sixteen. I gave up medicine because I was poor, not because I was a woman. What I never forget is that I was *poor*. And this is probably at the roots of my moralistic attitude that we were speaking about before. Not the fact that I was a woman.

I noticed that you dedicated your book to your mother. Was she a strong influence on you?

She pushed me. She pushed all of us. But my father did, too. I dedicated it to her more than to him because she's dying from cancer, but I should have dedicated it to both of them, because the person who gave me my political ideas was my father. I've changed my mind about many things, but not about my belief in freedom, social justice, and socialism—*that* came from him. And when we get to this point, it doesn't matter whether one is a man or a woman.

We were speaking before of Golda and Indira. The feminists are wrong to say: "Ha, ha! Indira behaves the way she does because she lives in a society of men." No, sir. She does it simply because she's a person of power who wanted more power. She wasn't ready to give it up and she acted as a man would have acted. At that point, it was the moment of truth—*el momento de la verdad*, as the Spanish call it. She could have said goodbye, sir, thank you very much. *That* means democracy to me. But instead she became a dictator, she demonstrated that being a woman makes no difference, she was no better because she was a woman. . . .

I want to return to something I spoke to you about earlier—about my obsession with the fascist problem and how it relates to my family experiences. I've just said that I come from an antifascist family, and this was important for me because, to me, being fascistic means making *anti*politics, not *politics*. The fascist—as I once told an interviewer—is someone who resigns, who obeys, who doesn't talk, or who imposes himself with violence and avoids the problematic. The antifascist, on the contrary, is a naturally political person. Because being antifascist means to fight through a problem by means of a discussion that involves everybody in civil disobedience. And this atmosphere of disobedience . . . I've breathed it since I was a little girl. My mother's father was an anarchist—one of those who wore a black ribbon and the big hat. He was a deserter in World War I, and I remember my mother proudly saying: "My father was a deserter in the Great War"—as if he had won some kind of medal. In fact, he was condemned to death because he was a deserter, but they couldn't catch him. And my father's father was a Republican follower of Mazzini, when being that meant one was an extreme leftist. And my father was a leader in the Resistance. It's really in the family.

What you're saying reaffirms what I find most inspiring in your work—the fact that you stand on the side of those who have been abused and humiliated. As you state it so movingly in the introduction to your book: "I have always looked on disobedience toward the overbearing as the only way to use the miracle of having been born."

That's socialism, Jonathan. Being a socialist, or wanting socialism, doesn't mean just the distribution of wealth. It *should* work, but it doesn't in the so-called socialist countries. And for sure not in the capitalistic regimes. Socialism means much more to me. One of the great victories has been what we call the *spirit of socialism*, with its sense of equality. When I was a little girl, the reality of hierarchy was so strong—the teacher above the pupil, the rich above the less rich, the bourgeoisie above the proletariat. In Europe we had it, we still have it, but we have it much less. And this was brought about by socialists and is why, for me, socialism is synonymous with freedom.

Socialism *is* freedom. When I say this, I imagine that if I were a peasant of Chianti and you were a landowner, I'd look at you like this [fearless and skeptical look] because of my belief in socialism, in freedom. And this spirit has such deep roots in me that when I go to interview a person of power, the more power this person has—would you believe me?—the more I intimidate him. And inevitably, this personal attitude of mine is transferred mentally and technically in the interview. So I undress them. I say: "Come on, come on, maybe you're better than you look, or maybe you're worse."

This is interesting: I've noticed that when a person goes to interview someone, he often sees himself in a position of inferiority. It's a nuance, it's very subtle, it's difficult to explain. And this feeling increases when this someone being interviewed is a person of power. If you're observant, you can see the eyes tremble and something in the face and the voice changing. That's never happened to me. *Never.* I'm tense, I'm worried because it's a boxing match. Oh ho! I'm climbing, I'm going into the ring, I'm nervous. My God, who's going to win? But no inferiority complex, no fear of the person. When someone starts acting superior, then I become dangerous, then I become nasty.

In a recent interview with Jean-Paul Sartre on his seventieth birthday, he stated: "I believe that everyone should be able to speak of his innermost being to an interviewer. I think that what spoils relations among people is that each keeps something hidden from the other, something secret, not necessarily from everyone, but from whomever he is speaking to at the moment. I think transparency should always be substituted for what is secret."

I don't believe it. He's not sincere, he's acting. Noble, intelligent, yes; he's playing the philosopher. But I can't conceive for a second that he means what he's saying because his daily life is the contrary of that. He's an arrogant man, often proud, and he can be very cruel and cold to people. He never forgets to be Sartre.

You want to know what I think of his idea? You cannot deny a human being his right to his privacy, to his secrets, to himself. When I speak of socialism, I don't mean that. I am mine, and to hell with the others: at a certain point I have the right to say that. What he's saying is pure intellectualism. If he had said that to me, I would have replied: "Come on, that's enough of that bullshit, you don't believe that. Come on, now."

You're obviously more Shakespearean—knowing that if you conceal something, you reveal it at exactly that moment, while letting it be known when and how this occurs.

What have you studied, politics or English literature? You studied it well, huh? Did you finish? Bravo. I'm very surprised, I'm fascinated—now I would like to interview you! But anyway . . . to get back to Sartre. I really believe so little in what he says. You know, there's always a moment during an interview, during my research into the soul of the person, when I stop. I voluntarily stop. I don't want to go on, I haven't the guts to invade further the soul of that person.

Listen, I'll give you an example. I've had two moments of great embarrassment. Not superficial embarrassment, because I'm a tough person, but here, inside. One was with Golda, when I asked her about her husband and she cried. And I felt—I'll make a confession now—a sort of shame. It was far from the vulgar way that journalists put questions, you know: "Tell me about Mr. So-and-so." I'd done it very sweetly, very elegantly, but all the same I felt ashamed of myself when she was crying. And the other moment was with Thieu, when he started crying while talking about being just a little man. And God knows, I was against everything he represented, but I saw a man, a person, and again I felt a sort of shame.

There are moments when I listen with an internal embarrassment that you'd never notice, but I have it very deep. For instance, with Kissinger—when we got to the problem of women, he was like that, he didn't want to talk about it. But I didn't want to either. Even with Hussein, when he spoke of the fear of his being killed, I felt uncomfortable, uncomfortable.

I think it's important to make a distinction between "mystification" and "mystery," and I feel that you respect the latter.

Ah, you see how coherent I am for once in my life? The way I reacted to Sartre . . . well, the explanation is here. Because I wouldn't like them to do it with me. I wouldn't.

The duty of a journalist is to reveal everything that's possible. Not to leave any interrogation point. To wipe out all curiosity. But I'm not a journalist 100 percent. I'm a writer, and I bring that into the journalism. I much prefer to have something well written, well built from a literary and a dramatic point of view, so that it can be read as a piece of literature—and this necessarily includes the *mystery*. I'm more interested in doing that than in telling everything as a good journalist should.

And when I'm asked, "What do you prefer to be, a journalist or a writer, and what is the difference between them?," I reply that there is no difference for me. And I mean that. My approach is to see the president of Angola, for example, as if he were a character in a novel rather than just an important name mentioned in the *New York Times*.

It might sound a bit far-fetched, but while reading Interview with History, *I was reminded of Plutarch's* Lives—*though I know that you are hardly a propagandist for the ancient Roman senatorial caste or Spartan despots.*

Don't forget that they've broken my balls with Plutarch for years in school. It's part of our culture. And they tortured us with Herodotus, too. But listen, these idiots who want to get rid of these things from the school curricula—it's nonsense. It was good to study Plutarch, Herodotus, and even Cicero.

A lot of the things from my book that you've liked and quoted to me today come out spontaneously, but they come out that way because we have a "classical" culture. Thank God you studied literature! You should listen to Panagoulis when he talks. One day he was in

Bologna for a speech, and he hadn't prepared it. And I said: "Oh, God, what are you going to do now?" And he replied: "Something will happen." So he went up to the platform and he began: "I did not want to kill a man. I cannot kill a man. I wanted to kill a tyrant, and I can kill a tyrant." And I complimented him: "My God, it was great when you said that." "Ah, come on!" he retorted, "we say it in school when we're children." Another time, at a rally in Florence, he said: "Freedom has no country. The country of freedom is each of us." "You prepared that, didn't you?" I asked him. "No, I didn't," he replied. "I hadn't the slightest idea what I was going to say." "But how did it come off so well?" "Because . . . because I felt it, no? Because I say things like that on other occasions." You see, he has classical culture. This is a richness that you don't have much of in the United States. I agree that it's good in high school to learn how to drive a car. I'm still not able to drive a car because I'm too lazy to learn, and I would like to have been in a school where they taught me how to drive. However, a little Plutarch when you're thirteen, fourteen, fifteen years old, it's not bad. And I defend our Italian school system, which is going to be destroyed because they want to follow the American style. I think they're committing a crime. Maybe we'll have better drivers and more technicians, but we'll have fewer poets and writers—and also, which counts more, fewer people with the sense of history. I know that I have this sense. When I see things, when I judge a situation—personal and overall political situations—I always see it as if I were at a window very far away in space and time. I have a sense of perspective.

I had a discussion the other day with an American about the Communists coming into the Italian government and, in the end, taking over power in Italy. We don't want, I kept saying, American tanks in the streets of Rome, like the Soviet tanks in the streets of Prague. The first stage of the discussion was passionate, and I was saying these things, and yelling. The second part of the discussion was quieter, and I told my friend: whether you like it or don't like it, whether I like it or don't like it, it has to happen. It's the normal development of history. They have to take power, it's their turn. You've been very stupid in not understanding the importance of Italy these past years. Italy was never on the front page of the *New York Times*. Now it is, not for the right reason, but because you're scared and angry. But if you'd looked at us with more intelligence and less ignorance, you would have seen that things were developing that way, inevitably. And that in Italy something was going to happen that would be terribly important, not only for Italy but for the rest of Europe and, therefore, for the world. I don't mean it's good or bad. But it will happen. And then it will begin in France, it will spread all over, and will be as important as the French Revolution was in France.

So I see things in perspective, and when I perform my work as a journalist, I do it in that way. And this is another secret of these interviews: being able to see people from afar. I always say when I ask for an interview: "I need time, I'm not looking for scoops, I'm not looking for sensationalism." If I ever went to Brezhnev, who'll never see me, of course, I wouldn't go with the idea of asking him: "What will you discuss tomorrow with Dr. Kissinger?" I want to do an interview which will be interesting in ten, possibly twenty years.

Are you going to continue doing interviews?

It's becoming more and more difficult for me and I'll tell you why. First, I've launched a fashion and now everybody does it, or tries to do it. There are more people requiring those interviews and so you see more of them around. And second, it's become more difficult because people are stupidly scared of me. They're worried. And if they decide to do an interview with me, it's because they think the moment is good for them—I'm a good vehicle for publicity. And then they act too nice. I have one to do soon, and when I telephoned yesterday, the people said: "Oh, Oriana Fallaci—we're *so* honored," and I thought: "Oh, no, *Madonna mia.*" Others like Qaddafi, for example, don't want to see me. (I accused him of having stolen my Golda Meir tapes—which is true.) Some persons really don't have the guts to see me.

In the preface to your book, you regret that no one had tape recorders during the time of Jesus, in order to "capture his voice, his ideas, his words." Were you being hyperbolic or serious? And if serious, what would you have asked Jesus if you had had the chance to interview him?

I meant it seriously. For sure! Today we think and speak of Jesus as he's been told to us. So now, after 2000 years, I'd like to know how important he was at the time or find out how much he was built up. Of course, I reject the concept of Jesus as God, Christ/God. I don't even pay attention to that for one second. But as a leader, was he that important? You know, he might very well have been a little Ché Guevara.

And a deeply enlightened person.

He might have been, but not the only one. Because many of those people were crucified just as he was. We make all this fuss about him, but it would be like saying, "Jesus Christ has been executed by Franco!" What about the others? For Christ's sake, how many people have been executed in Spain? *La garotta!* What about Paredez Manot, called Txiki—one of the five Basques who was executed in the fall of 1975 in the cemetery of Barcelona, in front of his brother Miguel. He's the one who died singing, "Free, free the country of the Basques," smiling all the time and singing, then waving goodbye to Miguel. And that was Txiki. But there were four others who were executed, and hundreds of others all these years. So I don't know if Christ was that important later on.

One of the first things I would have asked him is "Where have you been all those years, where have you been? Did you go to India?" Oooh-la-la! That would have been the first question. Then I would have asked if he really behaved chastely or if he had women, if he slept with women, if he went to bed with Mary Magdalene, if he loved her as a sister or as a woman. I would have asked that. And I would have loved to have found the grave of Jesus Christ—that would have been good *reportage.* And those who had stolen the corpse and reported he had flown to heaven: "*Who* told you to do that? For *whom* did you do that?"

That might have ended Christianty then and there.

It might have been a good thing.

I imagine that you'd have one question to ask the Virgin Mary.

[Laughing] Certainly one.

This is getting a bit sacrilegious.

Well, why be scared of that?

Don't you think it's possible that Jesus was an avatar?

Listen, I don't know how much about Jesus is just the image created by Mark, Luke, Matthew, and John. They were so damn intelligent, those four. And I'm afraid . . . Listen, Jonathan, do you know how many times I make people more interesting than they are? So what if Mark or Matthew did the same thing with Christ, huh? What about if this Jesus Christ was much less than Luke or John? I have no evidence, I have no tapes. . . .

I guess you don't believe in miracles.

Oh, no, come on, come on. You must be very religious, no?

I believe that some people have certain special powers. And I've always loved the simple and radiant view of the miraculous as depicted in films like Rossellini's The Miracle *and* The Flowers of St. Francis.

Well, remember Kazantzakis' book on Christ and that scene where Christ dreams of making love with Martha and Mary, the sisters of Lazarus!

Who else in history would you have liked to interview?

Julius Caesar, very much. And the Emperor Augustus, because he was such a damn fascist Nazi. He was a real Nazi, that man. Unbearable. And Cleopatra. Ahhhh! *Simpatica! Che simpatica,* Cleopatra! Intelligent. I'm sure she was extremely intelligent, with enormous culture.

You don't think that she was like Mme. Chiang or . . .

Those are puppets, little puppets. Just think of what Cleopatra did with the library at Alexandria! She put together . . . I mean, it would take the National Library in Florence and your library. . . . My God, she did marvelous things. Think of the scientists she called upon.

And although she was obsessed with her own beauty, she had people who studied cosmetics. *Nothing* was banal in that fantastic woman.

Then, of course, there's Joan of Arc. With Joan of Arc, however, I would have gotten myself in trouble. Because I would have forgotten my duty as a journalist—that is, as a historian—and I would have tried to free her. The moment she was condemned to death, I would've done everything to free her. This is the way I feel. I am not able—and *this* explains my interviews, all of this explains my interviews, of course—I am not able to see things in a cold way. Looking at things from afar doesn't mean looking at them coldly.

For instance, when I was in Bolivia—Torres was the president at that time until your CIA got him out—there were three brothers named Peredo. Two had already been killed. The third and youngest one was leading a group of guerrillas in the center of Bolivia, and the group was surrounded and caught. So the students of the opposition whom I was interviewing and working with came to me and said: "Fallaci, Fallaci, they've caught Chato Peredo." And I started working like hell. I went looking for a certain Major Sanchez, who was Torres' man, and with him I went around to the presidential palace to get the news to Torres, who stopped the execution. I wasn't thinking a second of the newspapers I was writing for. Afterward, I wrote up the story, of course, but at that moment I got very much involved. . . . And I would have tried to save Joan of Arc.

But just to go back in time for a minute: I would have loved to interview St. Paul—I almost forgot him. He's responsible for everything. . . . And Dante, for sure. Not as an artist, but as a politician. You know, Florence of that time seduces me. I'm Florentine, and that was the very first experiment in democracy—in the commune at Florence, not in Periclean Greece.

How about Dante's Beatrice?

Who cares about Beatrice? . . . But you don't have to go so far back, because I've missed some recent ones. I missed Chou En-lai because the Chinese never gave me a visa, they didn't want me. I almost cried when he died. He was the person of our times whom I wanted to interview more than anybody else. And he died without seeing me. Oh, God, he shouldn't have done it to me! They were too intelligent to invite me because they knew I'm too unpredictable. If I arrived there and I saw all those red this and red that, I would have really started carrying on, giving them problems. . . . And so I lost Chou En-lai. And of course I can't see the Pope, but I would have loved to interview John XXIII. Ahhh, another one.

You'd be the person I'd choose to interview the first being we met from outer space.

And I would do it like a *child*. That's the secret. . . . I'll tell you something. During the first moonshot, there was a press conference just before the launch. There was a group of Very Important American Journalists there, and, thank God, there was also my dear friend Cronkite among them. And Cronkite sent me a note—we were in the same room because the press was interviewing the astronauts via TV—asking me if I wanted to ask them a question. "Put a question to them? Thank you." And I wrote down my little question—three words—and sent it to Cronkite.

The other questions went on and on . . . about the fuel and not the fuel, about the gas and the starter and the trajectory. . . . I didn't understand anything being said. You know, I wrote a book about the conquest of the moon and I still don't know how and why a rocket goes up. I'm very proud of that. And I didn't understand the questions of the journalists, who were extremely pompous. Everybody was pompous. And then Cronkite said: "I have a question here from Oriana Fallaci." Pause. And he didn't ask the question. (He was marvelous, he was a real actor.) Then, dramatically: "The question is: *Are you scared?*"

Well, after discussing it with Aldrin and Collins, Neil Armstrong was elected to take the walk: "Well," he hesitated, "you know, the adrenalin goes up." "Ah, bullshit. Say you're scared!" I yelled out loud to everybody in the pressroom. "Who cares about the adrenalin! Tell me, tell me, fear, *fear!* Walter, ask them about *fear!*"

And that was the question of the child. If you asked my youngest sister to put a question to the astronauts, she'd say: "Are you afraid going to the moon?" Of course. That's what she'd want to know.

GLENN GOULD

The Pianist's Progress

PART I

"The nut's a genius," the conductor George Szell once remarked after attending a performance in Cleveland by the Canadian pianist Glenn Gould. Since 1947, when he first publicly performed Beethoven's Fourth Piano Concerto at fourteen, Glenn Gould has been amazing audiences and critics. He has been called a musician of "divine guidance" and the greatest pianist since Busoni. He has also been called the Bobby Fischer of the piano and has been castigated for: (1) his unconventional performing mannerisms—loping onstage like a misplaced eland with unpressed tails, sometimes wearing gloves, playing almost at floor level on a sawed-down, short-legged, wooden folding chair (facilitating an almost on-the-floor, nose-on-the-keys slouch that has driven Victorian church-pew piano teachers into a state of total stupefaction), and conducting, humming, singing, combating and cajoling and making love to his piano as if it were Lewis Carroll's Snark ("I engage with the snark/ Every night after dark/In a dreamy, delirious fight"); (2) his uncompromisingly imaginative choice of repertoire (William Byrd, Bach, Hindemith, and Schoenberg instead of Chopin and Rachmaninoff . . . and more Rachmaninoff); (3) his obsessive search and preference for a light-actioned piano, meant to facilitate a musical approach that emphasizes clarity of definition and textures and a rarely equaled analytical subtlety and acuity (the pianist Sviatoslav Richter, oboist Heinz Holliger, and cellist Janos Starker seem to me to be Gould's few peers in this regard)—as well as for certain startling but revelatory interpretations of "standards" like the Brahms First Piano Concerto. When

Gould first performed this piece with Leonard Bernstein and the New York Philharmonic, Bernstein actually got up before the audience to disassociate himself gently from Gould's approach, which featured slow tempi and a profound structural design that, for the first time I can remember, truly revealed the work's pent-up emotional rapture.

And, finally, Gould has been criticized for his supposedly eccentric and hermetic lifestyle (the pianist refuses to fly, likes taking trips by himself to the far north of Canada), for his bizarre get-up, e.g., wearing gloves, mittens, T-shirt, shirt, vest, sweater, coat, and scarf in warm weather—and, to cap it all off, for his having retired, at the wizened age of thirty-two, from any and all public concert recitals.

Gould's retirement, in fact, has allowed him to make good his claim that the functions of concerts have now been taken over by electronic media—that it is the recording medium itself that allows for an unparalleled analytic clarity, immediacy, tactile proximity, and catholicity of repertoire. The "analytic dissection by microphone" enables Gould to present the music from a "strongly biased conceptual viewpoint," just as it allows the music to emerge—as in unrepressed bodies and souls—with an untrammeled force and luminescence. As Gould's performances demonstrate, structural clarification always releases new energy.

Since his retirement in 1964, Gould has continued to produce one extraordinary recording after another. (As of 1977 he has made about sixty-five albums for Columbia Records.) And he has interspersed his unsurpassed Bach realizations with "first" recordings of Richard Strauss's *Enoch Arden* (accompanying the actor Claude Rains, who reads Tennyson's sentimental, drawing-room poem), the Lizst piano transcription of Beethoven's Fifth Symphony, Bizet's *Variations Chromatiques*, a debut piano realization of virginal pieces by Byrd and Gibbons, and an astonishingly beautiful piano transcription of Wagner's *Siegfried Idyll*. Gould composes as well. Some of his works include a string quartet Opus 1, written between 1953–55 and recorded by the Symphonia Quartet. It is a romantic composition showing Gould's *fin-de-siècle* predilection for the works of Bruckner and Richard Strauss. He has also composed *So You Want to Write a Fugue* for vocal and string quartets, a brilliant, jocular piece which was recorded by the Juilliard String Quartet for a plastic insert record in *HiFi/Stereo Review* some years ago.

In addition to his recording career, Gould has produced and

made six programs of "contrapuntal radio" for the Canadian Broadcasting Corporation (using voices in trio sonata form and employing the sounds of a train and the sea as a basso continuo); has narrated and performed on CBC television programs (a Beethoven bicentennial concert, for example) and has made four films about music and technology for the French ORTF; and has completed the first four of a series of programs that examine music in our time decade by decade: *The Age of Ecstasy (1900–1910)*; *The Flight from Order (1910–1920)*; *New Faces, Old Forms (1920–1930)*; *The Artist as Artisan (1930–1940)*.

Gould also continues to write brilliant and provocative magazine articles and self-interviews on subjects like: the forger as hero of electronic culture, Artur Rubinstein, Petula Clark vs. the Beatles, the analytical importance of the "flip-side overlap"—the four-minute demarcation points at the ends of 78 rpm records—and of Beethoven as an exemplar of a composer whose "professional developmental skills" conflicted with an "amateur's motivic bluntness."

These articles are an extension of Gould's dazzling and witty liner-note extravaganzas in which, like the eighteenth-century *Spectator* and *Tatler* newssheets, the pianist advises and warns his listeners, informs us of the state of health of his piano, and analyzes (usually brilliantly), comments on, and theorizes about a wide range of musical matters. On his Lizst-Beethoven Fifth Symphony album, Gould prints four "reviews" of his Beethoven interpretation from Sir Humphrey Price-Davies of *The Phonograph* magazine, from Professor Dr. Karlheinz Heinkel of *Munch'ner Muskilologische Gesellschaft*, from S. F. Lemming (M.D.) of the North Dakota Psychiatrists Association, and finally from Zoltan Mostanyi of *Rhapsodya, Journal of the All-Union Musical Workers of Budapest*. Gould was awarded a Grammy in 1974 for his liner notes on *Hindemith: Three Piano Sonatas*.

And for his recording of Bizet and Greig piano pieces, Gould informs us that Greig was a cousin of his maternal great-grandfather, thus affording him a not-to-be-begrudged interpretative authority. And the pianist goes on to advise his critics that, since no previous recordings of the Bizet works exist, "for those of you who greet the release with enthusiasm, I should like to propose a phrase such as '—vividly and forcefully, as only a first reading can, it partakes of that freshness, innocence, and freedom from tradition that, as the late Artur Schnabel so deftly remarked, is but a "collection of bad habits." ' On the other hand, for those in doubt as to the validity of the interpretation involved, I venture to recommend a conceit such as '—regrettably, a performance that has not as yet jelled; an interpretation that is still in search of an architectural overview.' "

Glenn Gould lives, records, and works in Toronto, and he keeps in touch with friends around the world by means of the telephone. He does not give personal interviews at his home or office. The following interview was edited down from a two-part, six-hour telephone conversation, Toronto to New York, that took place in late June 1973. It was revised, emended, and expanded by the pianist and myself in a series of phone calls in March 1977.

The publication of this interview celebrated the Tenth Anniversary of Glenn Gould's retirement from the concert stage (March 28, 1974). And knowing Gould, one would have liked to imagine that he might have honored the day by showing up at some local northern Ontario bar on March 28, sitting down at the cocktail piano and quietly beginning to play Bach's *Goldberg Variations*—the first work he ever recorded for Columbia Records in 1955 and still one of the splendors of the record catalog—for an unsuspecting audience caught unawares by this music which—as Gould described it (and, I like to think, his own playing as well) in his now twenty-two-year-old liner notes—"observes neither end nor beginning, music with neither real climax nor real resolution, music which, like Baudelaire's lovers, 'rests lightly on the wings of the unchecked wind.' It has, then, unity through intuitive perception, unity born of craft and scrutiny, mellowed by mastery achieved, and revealed to us here, as so rarely in art, in the vision of subconscious design exulting upon a pinnacle of potency."

Writing about the works of the late-Elizabethan composer Orlando Gibbons, you once observed: "One is never quite able to counter the impression of a music of supreme beauty that somehow lacks its ideal means of reproduction." You've also talked about the "idealized aspects of the works of Bach." And this emphasis on the idea of "idealization" really seems to me to define your approach to music. . . . But perhaps I'm starting off on too abstract a note.

No, it's marvelous, it's an interesting point, and I suppose that if one fed it into a computer, probably that phrase—"ideal means of reproduction"—or some variant of it would turn up very frequently in what I say and write. I hadn't realized it before, but it *is* a preoccupation, and I think it would be interesting to explore why it is. . . .

But let me start out on a very practical level and proceed from there to something more abstract. I was recently talking to a group of educators about the problems concerning the teaching of pianists in institutionalized technical "factories." You see, I think there's a fallacy that's been concocted by the music teachers' profession, to wit: that there's a certain sequence of events necessary in order to have the revealed truth about the way one produces a given effect on a given instrument. And I said: Given half an hour of your time and your spirit and a quiet room, I could teach any of you how to play the piano—everything there is to know about playing the piano can be taught in half an hour, I'm convinced of it. I've never done it and I never intend to do it, because it's *centipedal* in the Schoenbergian sense—that is to say, in the sense in which Schoenberg was afraid to be asked why he used a certain row in a certain way, saying he felt like the centipede, which doesn't want to think about the movement of its hundred legs because it would become impotent; it couldn't walk at all if it did think about it. And I said: Therefore I'm not going to give this half-hour lesson, but if I chose to, the physical element is so very minimal that I could teach it to you if you paid attention and were very quiet and absorbed what I said and possibly you could take it down on a cassette so that you could replay it later on, and you wouldn't need another lesson. You would then have to proceed along certain rather disciplined lines whereby you observed the correlation of *that* bit of information with certain other kinds of physical activity —you would discover there are certain things you can't do, certain kinds of surfaces you can't sit on, certain kinds of car seats that you can't ride in.

And by this time I was getting a great laugh—they regarded this whole thing as a routine, which it was *not*. I was trying to make quite a serious point, which was: that if this were *done*, you would be free of the entire tactile kinetic commitment. No, *correction*—you would not be free, you would be eternally bound *to* it, but so tightly bound to it that it would be a matter of *tertiary* interest only. It would be something that could be "disarranged" only by a *set* of circumstances that would confuse it.

I once talked about such a "set." It involved a time in Tel Aviv—the fall of 1958, in fact—and I was giving a series of concerts on an absolutely rotten piano, the manufacturer of which shall be left unnamed [laughing]. Israel was, after all, a desert country, as they kept explaining to me, and they had desert pianos, understandably enough. I was playing I think eleven concerts in eighteen days, which for Isaac Stern would be like nothing, but for me is very difficult— *was* very difficult, I should say—and I think eight of the eleven were given on this monstrosity.

In any event, one day I was switching programs, which was a real problem, because till then I'd coasted on a kind of tactile memory based on the experience of playing the earlier repertoire, and now suddenly I had to change. I had to do a little practicing, and it was at that moment that things began to run downhill. So on the afternoon of the first of that series of concerts, I'd gone through a miserable rehearsal at which I really played like a pig because this piano had finally gotten to me. I was playing on *its* terms. I had "put it on," as Mr. McLuhan would say, and I was really very concerned because I simply couldn't play a C-major scale properly. I was incapable, apparently, of responding on any terms but those which were immediately presented to me through the medium of that piano.

So I had a car, rented from the Hertz agency in Jerusalem (the idea of which delights me), and I was in any case staying about fifteen miles outside of Tel Aviv at a place called Herzliyya-by-the-Sea (it's an American colony where there are rather nice hotels and you feel as though you're in the San Juan Hilton). And I went out to a sand dune and decided that the only thing that could possibly save this concert was to re-create the most admirable tactile circumstance I knew of. And at that time *that* was in relation to a piano which I still own, though I haven't used it in many years, a turn-of-the-century (about 1895) Chickering—supposedly the last classic piano built in America—classic by virtue of the fact that it had a lyre that looked as if it were off the cover of the old B. F. Wood edition—short, stubby legs and slightly square sides. This piano was the prototype of the piano that I now use for my recordings and the other one that I have in my apartment as well, in that I discovered a relationship of depth of touch to aftertouch, which admittedly had to undergo a considerable amount of modification for a Steinway. It couldn't just be transferred across the board (no pun intended), and both of the pianos that I own were modified along the lines of this turn-of-the-century Chickering.

So I sat in my car in ye sand dune and decided to imagine

myself back in my living room . . . and first of all to *imagine* the living room, which took some doing because I'd been away from it for three months at this point. And I tried to imagine where everything was in the room, then visualize the piano, and . . . this sounds ridiculously *yogistic*, I'd never done it before in precisely these terms . . . but so help me it worked.

Anyway, I was sitting in the car, looking at the sea, got the entire thing in my head and tried desperately to live with that tactile image throughout the balance of the day. I got to the auditorium in the evening, played the concert, and it was without question the first time that I'd been in a really exalted mood throughout the entire stay there—I was *absolutely* free of commitment to that unwieldy beast. Now, the result, at least during the piano's first entrance, really scared me. There was a minimal amount of sound—it felt as though I were playing with the soft pedal down, which at times I often do, but without the intention of creating quite so faint-hearted a piano tone.

I was shocked, a little frightened, but I suddenly realized: Well, of course it's doing that because I'm engaged with another tactile image, and eventually I made some adjustment, allowed for some give-and-take in relation to the instrument at hand. And what came out was really rather extraordinary—or at least I thought so. And so, apparently, did a couple of elderly souls who wandered backstage after the concert. One of them was the late Max Brod—the Kafka scholar, who at that time was living in Tel Aviv and who wrote for the Tel Aviv German paper. He came backstage with a lady, whom I took to be his secretary, and made a few nice sounds, and the lady in question, whose name I didn't catch, came up to me and in a rather heavy German accent said—bear in mind I'd just played Beethoven Two—and said [conspiratorial half-whisper], "Mr. Gould, ve haf attended already several of your pairformances in Tel Aviv, but tonight's, zis vas somehow, in some vay, somesing vas different, you vere not qvite one of us, you vere—you vere—your being vas *removed*." And I bowed deeply and said, "Thank you, madam," realizing of course that she had in fact put her finger on something that was too spooky to talk about even, and I realized that with her obviously limited English there was no way I could convey what I'd really done. But then she finished it off by saying, "Yes, I haf just been saying that zis was unquestionably ze finest Mozart I haf ever heard" [laughing], and of course it was Beethoven.

When you were sitting in the car in the desert, were you performing the piece in the air or on the dashboard, or . . .

Neither, neither. The secret is that you must never move your fingers. If you do, you will automatically reflect the most recent tactile configurations that you've been exposed to.

Is there a difference between imagining a total performance of a piece and performing it in your imagination? Were you simply imagining a performance of the piece in your mind?

No. That is something profoundly to be wished for and not necessarily contradictory to what we've talked about, but at a certain point there is an overlap, and odd bits and pieces stick out, and I think we should define those bits and pieces. There *is* a difference, and the difference is something like this: I don't know if you've ever experienced it—and certainly they're not going to try it on me—but some years ago they discovered a remarkable method of local anesthesia which was employed in dentistry. The method was that of taking a patient who, for some reason, was reacting badly to Carbocaine or Zylocaine or whatever-ocaine, and giving him two dials, one of which contained white noise, while the other controlled possibly a radio or a cassette or record player, on which was a piece of musical information with which the patient was familiar—Mantovani or Beethoven—whatever he knew. It had to be something he could "pull in," so to speak. Now then, that meant that his reaching out to that source had to be impeded in some way, there had to be an area of *blockage*, and that area of blockage was represented by the dial which controlled the white noise. It was arranged in various ratios, but at all times the ratio of white noise to actual sound had to be in favor of the white noise, so that you had to fight through that sound barrier, quite literally, in order to pull out remnants of a remembered sound. And it was discovered that without exception this was the most effective local anesthetic they'd ever employed in dentistry. They had a remarkable success with it . . . except that there were very few people who were willing to have it tried on them [laughing]. But the reason for its success, I think, is quite obvious: if you are forced to concentrate totally on some object that is other than that which concerns you most deeply at the moment, there's an element of transcendence implied in that concentration.

To give you another example of the same sort of thing: years ago I was playing for the first time Beethoven's Sonata no. 30, Opus 109. I was about nineteen at the time and I used to try out pieces that I hadn't played before in relatively small Canadian towns, and this one fell into a program that I was giving about 120 miles from Toronto—a university town called Kingston. I never bothered to practice very much—I now practice almost not at all—but even in those days I was far from being a slave of the instrument. I tended to learn the score away from the piano. I would learn it completely by memory first, and then go to the piano with it afterwards—and that, of course, was another stage in the divorce of tactilia from expressive manifestations of one kind or another. No, that's not quite accurate, because, obviously, certain expressive manifestations were built into the analytical concept, but the tactile assumptions were not.

Now, Opus 109 isn't a particularly difficult or strenuous piece, but there is in it one moment which is a positive horror, as you perhaps know, and that is in the fifth variation in the last movement—a moment which is an upward-bound diatonic run in sixths. It's an awkward moment, not only in terms of black-versus-white note fingerings but also in terms of that break in the keyboard around two octaves above middle C where problems of repetition most often show up. For at that point you have to change from a pattern in sixths to a pattern in thirds, and you've got to do that in a split second. I had always heard this piece played by people who, when that moment arrived, looked like horses being led from burning barns—a look of horror would come upon them, and I always wondered what was so intimidating about it.

Anyway, about two or three weeks before I was to play the thing for the first time, I started to study the score, and about a week ahead of time I started to practice it (which sounds suicidal, but that's the way I always operate). And the first thing I did, foolishly—very bad psychology—was to think in terms of: Well, let's try the variation, just to make sure there's no problem—it had never *seemed* to be one when I sat down and read the thing through when I was a kid . . . but better try it, better work out a little fingering system just in case, you know. And as I began to work out my system, one thing after another began to go wrong. Before many minutes had elapsed I found that I'd developed a total block about this thing. And three days before the concert, the block, which I'd tried to get rid of by all kinds of devious means—not playing the piece at all, for instance—

had developed apace, so that I couldn't get to that point without literally shying and stopping. I just froze at that particular moment.

I thought, something's got to be done about this—I've got to change the program or delete the variation or pretend that I know something about the autograph that they don't. So I decided to try the Last Resort method. That was to place beside the piano a couple of radios, or possibly one radio and one television, turn them up full blast—that's really in effect the experiment that years later I was to read about re Non-Anesthetic Dentistry—turn them up so loudly that, while I could feel what I was doing, I was primarily hearing what was coming off the radio speaker or the television speaker or, better still, both. I was separating, at this point, my areas of concentration, and to such an extent that I realized that *that* in itself would not break the chain of reaction. (It had already begun to make its mark, the problem had begun to disappear. The fact that you couldn't hear yourself, that there wasn't audible evidence of your failure, was already a step in the right direction.) But I realized that I had to do something more than that.

Now, in this variation, the left hand has at that moment a rather uninspired sequence of four notes, the third of which is tied over the bar line. There's not too much you can do with those four notes, but I thought—all right, there are, we'll say, in terms of accent and so on, maybe half a dozen permutations that would be possible [sings several of the permutations], and I played them as unmusically as possible. In fact the more unmusical the better, because it took more concentration to produce unmusical sounds, and I must say I was extremely successful in that endeavor. In any event, *during* this time my concentration was exclusively on the left hand—I'd virtually forgotten about the right—and I did this at varying tempi and kept the radios going, and then came . . . the *moment*. I switched off the radios and thought: I don't think I'm ready for this . . . need a cup of coffee, made a few other excuses, and then finally sat down. The block was gone. And now, every once in a while, just for the hell of it, I sit down and do that passage to see if the block's still gone. It still is, and it became one of my favorite concert pieces.

Now, the point is that you have to *begin*, I think, by finding a way to any instrument that gets rid of the whole notion that the instrument presents you with a set of tactile problems—it does, of course, but you have to reduce those problems to their own square root, so to speak, and having done that, adapt any kind of situation in relation to that square root. The problem then is to have a sufficient advance and/or extra-tactile experience of the music so that anything that the piano does isn't permitted to get in the way. In my own case, my means toward this is to spend most of the time away from the piano, which can be difficult because you occasionally want to hear what it sounds like. But a certain analytical ideal (which is somehow contradictory, I can't quite think how—I'm a bit stupid today, but anyway . . .), an analytical *completeness*, at any rate, is theoretically possible as long as you stay away from the piano. The moment you go to it you're going to diminish that completeness by tactile compromise. Now, at some point that compromise is inevitable, but the degree to which you can minimize its effect is the degree to which you can reach out for the ideal that we were talking about.

A number of pianists have talked about their anxiety dreams in which they continually saw themselves walking out onstage naked or sitting down to find themselves unable to play, like Sparky and his Magic Piano, which refused to perform at the necessary time.

I only have one dream of that kind, which one would think would have abated the moment I stopped giving concerts, but it didn't. I simply transferred it to other media, and I now have it in relation to recording sessions. The dream always makes me aware of the fact that the repertoire that I think I'm doing is not the repertoire I'm really doing. Now in order to make that practical it's never there-fore a solo performance; it's usually an orchestral recording, and I've had many variations on this dream.

The most elaborate variation, in fact, took place in an opera house. I was backstage in rather cramped dressing-room quarters, and while wandering around, I saw someone come up to me—at that time it must have been the equivalent of Rudolf Bing or Rolf Liebermann —and he came rushing up to me, saying: "Mr. Gould, you're just the man we need!"

It turned out that they were going to give a performance of some Bellini opera with Mme. Callas, and the lead baritone had fallen ill or lost his voice, and I was supposed to go on. "This is absurd, I'm no singer." "Of course you are," the man replied, "I mean, you can read a score. You have an innate grasp. . . ." And they threw this score into my hands, and I quickly looked through it, hoping just to grasp the idiom. They told me that they'd describe, as I came offstage, what the next scene would be, and for the rest of it, I'd just have to obey my musical conscience.

Well, I couldn't let them down, could I? I was told that when Mme. Callas was kneeling before an altar—I was at this point standing in the wings—I was to enter stage left, she would greet me, and we'd go into a duet. I surmised she would open it, and she started [Gould sings florid coloratura passage] or something like that. And then I responded with sixths and thirds, "Ya dum, ya da la da leeee da la . . . ," and we were going along *magnificently* with superb euphony. But all of a sudden, a diminished chord, which I thought was heading back to E major, decided to veer off and go to G—as diminished chords have a tendency to do [laughing]. And I was left hanging there. . . . So you can add this dream to your collection of naked moments.

In your striving for the ideal performance, you can often be heard humming and singing, turning some of your solo piano recordings into lieder recitals. I've always felt this was a compensation for the inflexibility and imperfectibility of your instrument. If you could, though, would you try to eliminate this "additional" poltergeist on your recordings?

Oh yes, and if I could find an equalization system that would get rid of it, which I obviously haven't to date—if it occurred at only one frequency, a frequency that would be expendable in terms of the piano—I would cue it out in a second; to me it's not a valuable asset, it's just an inevitable thing that has always been with me. In fact, when I was a kid—really a kid, nine or ten years old, playing my star pieces at student concerts—people said exactly the same thing as they now say about my latest records—so it really doesn't make any difference, I've never been able to get rid of it.

It wasn't until about 1966 or '67 that we started putting a baffle beside the piano, and that has helped a bit. I think if you "a" and "b" any record done now with a record done prior to that time, there's a noticeable improvement. But the other problem, of course, is that since we've moved the whole operation to Toronto we have a drier hall than the one we used in New York, and consequently I think it exaggerates my voice. *Because* it's a drier hall we decided to capitalize on that quality, and we've gone in very close—we always did mike closely, we've never made use of your ideal Deutsche Gram- mophon concert hall pickup. But in Toronto we've gone in even closer, which I think gives it a very lovely and very clear sound, but it does necessarily augment the voice a little. So there has been a slight increase in the vocal disturbance the last two years [laughing], but it would still not be up to the great old days of pre-1967.

I heard that for one of your first recordings you actually wore a gas mask during the session.

No, I didn't, that was a joke. Somebody brought one in and I put it on, just for the hell of it, and pretended I was going to keep it on. I think Howard Scott, my first producer at Columbia, picked it up at a war surplus store as a gag.

Your posture at the piano has been the occasion of many jokes —slouching position, sitting on a chair hardly off the floor, conducting with your left hand while the right hand is playing, your nose on the keys, swooning into space, your whole body totally involved in the musical situation. Would you change this aspect of your playing if you could?

No, if I didn't do that there would be an absolute deterioration in my playing. That is an indispensable component, and for the life of me, I've never seen why anyone should concern himself with it. The other thing about my singing is genuinely objectionable for people who lay out their $5.98 or whatever and say, "Gee, do I have to listen to that? It may be interesting as a document, but it's annoying as sound." Well, I would feel exactly the same way. In fact, I was just listening the other day to one of the last records Barbirolli made, the *Pelleas und Melisande* of Schoenberg (which is a magnificent perfor- mance, by the way), and he obviously got carried away several times. It doesn't bother me, really, but I can well imagine that some people will be bothered by it, as they are by Casals' records, for that matter. I do think it's a valid objection. But the other business is surely a private matter between my left hand and my right, and I can't see why it's of concern to anybody.

There's another thing, of course, that you have to remember, and that is that the caricature of my playing is that of someone whose nose is touching the keyboard. Now, in point of fact that happens only under optimum circumstances in terms of repertoire. It does not happen as a general rule—not that I sit the rest of the time like Wilhelm Backhaus or whomever. I discovered early on that there are certain keys to the kingdom in terms of manipulating the instrument which are not those of the Prussian school, obviously. The special circumstances in terms of repertoire have to do with situations that do not demand a widening of the hands—say, Bach or Mozart or pre-Bach. But you cannot, you simply cannot play Scriabin in that position, for the simple reason that the leverage required to support a widening of the hands is such that you have to be further away from the keyboard, you couldn't be that close. But you *can* play Bach that way, and should, because by so doing you refine the sound, you minimize the pianistic aspects of it, and you increase your control—I don't want to be dramatic and say "a thousandfold," as one of the senators did today (I've been watching the Watergate hearings all day—I don't know which senator it was, oh, yes, it was Gurney), but certainly by a considerable measurement.

And the other factor involved is the nature of the piano that you use. If you use a piano with a conventional heavy action and/or a deep action, you're obviously going to have to make certain adjustments. This brings us, of course, to another fallacy that piano teachers like to spread about: there is a notion abroad in the land that you in some way benefit by learning to play on a difficult instrument, the theory being that if you play on a heavy piano, by the time you get to a light one your task will consequently be easier. This is as sensible as saying that by learning to play on a piano it will make you a good harpsichordist. I mean it does *not*—it does exactly the opposite; it means that the harpsichord is, in fact, more difficult to play precisely because you're used to what is, in harpsichord terms, *overkill*.

In my case there's no problem because I use only one piano and have for the last fifteen years. The piano that I do all my recordings on since 1960 is a piano built in '45 but reconditioned by me in '60 and many times subsequently, including last year, when it had to be completely rebuilt—it was dropped by a truck. Anyway, the long and the short of it is that this piano has a very light action, as indeed all pianos that I prefer do. Many people say it's tinny and sounds like a harpsichord or a fake harpsichord or God knows what. Maybe it does. I think it has the most translucent sound of any piano I've ever played—it's quite extraordinary, it has a clarity of every register that I think is just about unique. I adore it. But, as I've said, it happens to have a very light action. Now if it had a different system of leading, if the draft of the key (which means the fall from top to bottom) were different, if the relationship of the after-touch to the kickback point when you're depressing a key were different—if any or all of those things were different, one would not be able to sit at that piano as you do. You would have to exert a different leverage and sit further back, of necessity.

But because this conventional wisdom, the origin of which I do not know, began to travel abroad in the early years of this century, it was assumed that the great classic pianos were in some way heavy pianos. The Mason & Hamlin, for instance, was regarded at one time as a classic piano. . . . It *was* a very heavy piano, with beautiful qualities, but it wasn't a piano with the kind of action that I find appealing. That sort of instrument, and/or any other kind modeled after it, poses problems of leverage that would make it very difficult for me to adopt the posture that I would like to.

You haven't only released piano recordings. There are harpsichord performances by you of four of Handel's Suites, as well as a wonderful organ performance of the first part of Bach's Art of the Fugue. *And I've noticed, in these recordings, that you seem to work against the grain of the predominant temperamental characteristics of each instrument. For instance, on the harpsichord, where you can't easily duplicate the arched line and sustained legato of the piano, you seem to aim for just those two qualities. In your piano recordings you aim for the immediacy of attack provided more easily on the harpsichord. And on the organ, you produce a sense of spriteliness more characteristic of both the piano and harpsichord.*

Yes, I think you're absolutely right, there's a kind of cross-fertilization involved here. I'll let you in on a secret, however, in regard to both the organ and the harpsichord records: both of them were done literally without practicing on those instruments at all; my preparation for both was on the piano exclusively. I don't own a harpsichord and never have, and there's only one harpsichord in the world that I can play, and that's one that many pro-harpsichordists turn up their noses at—the Wittmayer—simply because its tactilia, and particularly the width of its keyboard, is as close to the piano as one can get. I love it, however, and the particular Wittmayer that I used was owned by a choirmaster here in Toronto who just has it for his own amusement. It's the equivalent of a baby grand, a five- or six-foot instrument, and it lacks certain amenities such as a lute on the four-foot, which I would dearly like to have and which any self-respecting harpsichord offers. Anyway, the registrations for that record were worked out movement by movement as the sessions progressed. I did exactly the same thing with the organ record. Of course, I was somewhat more experienced as an organist because I had played the organ as a kid, but I hadn't played it *since* I was a kid, and again I set up registrations only at the last minute.

It's part and parcel of the anticipatory syndrome that I've often talked about in relation to conducting. With the harpsichord, of course, one deals with a particular set of tactile problems and a more or less immediate response to their solution, whereas when one conducts, the tactile problems are, in a sense, imaginary, and the response to their solution is delayed—but there are certain parallels nonetheless. On the harpsichord, for example, it's very easy to achieve the sort of secco, pointillistic, détaché line that I've always tried to produce on the piano with varying degrees of success. On the other hand, having achieved it, you can't influence it dynamically and you're left, so to speak, beholden to the generosity of the ear which is sometimes prepared to read dynamic implications into rhythmic alterations. But this introduces another set of problems, because, on the harpsichord, you have a choice between rhythmic inexorability and its converse, which is infinite rubato, a kind of sound-world which really never comes to rest on any bar line. I was determined to try and find a way around that problem. And I thought, well, the best solution would be to pretend that I'm not playing the harpsichord at all [laughing], because if I do otherwise, I'll fall into exactly the same trap. And I found as the sessions wore on that that danger was very real indeed because it's very, very difficult to play a straight, square eight bars on the harpsichord without making some rhythmic alterations in lieu of dynamics. Sometimes indeed I *had* to do that; sometimes there simply was no other way to shape a phrase. In very chromatic writing like the beginning of the Variations of the big D-Minor Suite, you have to do something of the sort. And again in the cadenza-like Prelude of the A-Major Suite, you've got to differentiate between all those scales and runs—otherwise it really does sound like a sewing machine. But that aside, once having hit the stride of a certain tempo, I would like to be able to hold it almost as tightly as you can on a piano.

Don't certain harpsichord pieces need exactly this kind of ru-bato approach, like the works of Couperin, for example?

Oh, yes. I'm sure that's true. But Handel, at least to me, is a very regal figure and needs a certain kind of straightforwardness and uncomplicatedness, essentially, as well as an almost deliberate lack of sophistication, and that would not be true of Couperin. In any case, the rubato that one applies to Couperin has more to do with social grace than structure.

Mozart's nonpolyphonic style would seem to be least suited to your temperament, and in fact your version of the C-Minor Piano Concerto has been criticized for your addition of embellishments and a number of continuo passages. You've also released three albums of Mozart piano sonatas—and a fourth is just coming out [since the interview, Gould recorded a fifth album]—and when I first heard them I thought they were a put-on. In fact, they seem to have gotten progressively wilder as the series progresses—Alberti base lines smashing out, manic or depressive tempi. And then I began to think that perhaps you were taking a Brechtian approach to these works—distancing them in order to get away from the typical emotive type of performances we're used to hearing. But this is a pretty perverse way to deal with Mozart, isn't it?

You're absolutely right, I think, and I'll take it point by point (I can't get John Dean out of my head: "I'll take it point by point if I may, Mr. Chairman"). Let me deal first of all with the C-Minor Mozart. It's the only Mozart concerto that I've recorded because it's the only one that I sort of halfway like. My objection to that record is that I didn't do nearly *enough* continuo-izing. First of all, those who commented on the things that I added are just plain wrong: It's documentable fact that Mozart himself made it up as he went along, we know that. Not only that, he took it for granted that everybody else would, too. You've got to remember that Mozart was still much-influenced by the concept of figured bass. The Haydn concerti, after all, are full of figured bass ideas, and all other differences to the contrary notwithstanding (differences of orchestration, of length, and so on—the major difference between let us say the earliest of Haydn's concerti and the latest of Mozart's . . . and the C-Minor is one of the late ones) would be that in the Haydn, the soloist was still doubling as a continuo player. Or, he might sit at one harpsichord and do his thing, and the conductor would sit at another harpsichord and support him with some doodlings based on figured-bass notations which amplified the harmonic texture but which were not in themselves absolute.

Now, after thirty years or so, by about 1785, say, the role of the conductor *has* become absolute, or at any rate if not that, the role of the soloist has been at least consolidated into that of one person. But the Mozart keyboard style, in the concertos anyway, is still tied to the preconception of a continuo-style support for the solo instrument. And the solo textures consequently are very thin, very undernourished in the Mozart concerti, they're really very badly written. The unaccompanied moments are beautiful, they're gorgeous, one couldn't have a more beautiful cantilena than the opening of the A-Major Concerto's slow movement—that's a magnificent moment of keyboard writing. But it just so happens that once the orchestra enters (Mozart is a right-handed composer), he literally does nothing with the left hand. And the reason for that is very simple: he was still thinking in terms of that type of concerto, twenty years back, in which the conductor had given continuo support.

Now we get to the sonata recordings. I had more fun with those things than anything I've ever done, practically, mainly because I really don't like Mozart as a composer. I love the early sonatas—I love the early Mozart, period. I'm very fond of that period when he was either emulating Haydn or Carl Philipp Emanuel Bach but had not yet found himself. The moment he did find himself, as conventional wisdom would have it, at the age of eighteen or nineteen or twenty, I stop being so interested in him, because what he discovered was primarily a theatrical gift which he applied ever after not only to his operas but to his instrumental works as well, and given the rather giddy hedonism of eighteenth-century theater, that sort of thing doesn't interest me at all.

There is, as you know, a tradition in Mozart-playing—and you described it beautifully with the word "emotive"—a tradition in which one played with the masculine-feminine "opposites" within the first and usually the last movements of the sonatas. Well, you know the sort of thing I mean: one had that which was stern, that which was melting, that which was commanding, that which was seductive—in opposition to each other. Now, that's all very well and good, except that that whole concept had just begun to go around the symphonic world at the time when Mozart wrote those sonatas. Now, again I seem to be leaning heavily on historical argument, which I don't like to do, because, as I say, I defy it so often that I could be hoisted on my own petard; it's not a safe ground in court for me. But in view of the fact that I lack any other argument at this moment, I will have recourse to it nonetheless.

The plain fact is that the Haydn sonatas, for instance, which are much more extensive in the canon than the Mozart—there being fifty-something to seventeen or eighteen—are also more interesting as pieces, as pieces and as experiments, musically. It's the only late-night music that I've sat down and really played for myself in the last year—well, occasionally Wagner or something like that—but otherwise it's Haydn sonatas, the early ones especially, the baroque-ish ones. They are *so* beautiful and in every case so delightfully innovative. One never gets the feeling that any two are cut from the same cookie stamp. I do get that feeling in Mozart, I'm afraid. I get the feeling that once he hit his stride, they're *all* cut from the same cookie stamp. I think that as Mozart became relatively successful as a theatrical craftsman, his instrumental compositions declined in interest very rapidly.

Now, coming back to what I said about the idea of "opposites": The coalition of opposites was by no means fully developed at that time—it was only in its first stages. (By the time you get to Beethoven, of course, the earliest sonatas already exhibit it in a much more full-blown state, though even there there are some reservations.) But the point is, I think, that if you examine Haydn about the same period, you find that Haydn—who was after all Mozart's god in many ways, certainly in instrumental writing—was not developing this idea as a consistent phenomenon, but in fact toward the end of his life was getting further away from it, so that on occasion, the second theme is also the first theme—there's a kind of Lisztian consistency in the later Haydn sonatas in that a rhythmic configuration will be lifted, from the tonic to the dominant, say—just as Bach might have done in a rondeau or something like that.

But the psychological argument for the arrival of a new moment—a new key, a new theme, whatever—is that one must slow down or soften down or make the phrases legato, as opposed to upright and nonlegato previously, if that's what they were—in other words, a change of heart and temperament. And this doesn't seem to me all that justifiable in the Mozart sonatas.

Indeed, I think the proof of the fact that these developments hadn't *fully* infiltrated the music Mozart wrote in mid-career is that Mozart never really did learn to write a development section, because, of course, you don't have to write a development section unless you've got something to develop. I'm not being flip about that. I mean, literally, that the development section in the classical sonata was there in order to crystallize the potentialities of opposite forces, and it was precisely Beethoven, whose structural notions were based on the coalition of opposites, who wrote developments until you begged for the return to some kind of sobering tonic reaffirmation. And, of course, Haydn also wrote much more extensive developments than Mozart, even though, as I've said, Haydn was not terribly interested in the masculine-feminine coalition. In any case, I really think that the notion that one must start a Mozart sonata with a firm, upright kind of tempo and steady beat and then relax into something that is slurpy and Viennese, and then return to a hint of the original pulse just before the double bar and follow that with a bridge passage and so on, is pretty silly. It's simply not borne out by the music, it really isn't. As I say, I'm reluctant to situate the argument so firmly on some sort of historical pedestal, because I normally am prepared to argue much more eccentrically for the things that I do, but in this case I really can argue that way.

Which brings me to why I had fun with it. I had fun with it precisely because you can play the damn things in the most deliciously straightforward manner, never yielding at a cadence, never giving up for a moment, just going straight through to the end with baroque-ish continuity, if you will. And this has nothing to do with tempo per se. You can do it just as successfully with a slow tempo as with a fast one. Well, not quite as easily perhaps—a slow tempo just by the weight of its duration makes you want to make more curves in the music, that's certainly true. But in any event, such structures can, I think, be made to work without regard to the tempi that you choose.

Now, the horror and the outcry that resulted from my Mozart recordings—I think it was the critic Martin Mayer who said about Volume 2: "Finally, this is madness!" or something to that effect—is to me terribly funny, because all the critics are really responding to is a denial of a certain set of expectations that have been built into their hearing processes. I'm not saying that one can or should try to develop this theory ad infinitum, but there is one thing that's instructive to remember, and that is that if you listen to any decent conductor, and give him the same material appropriately orchestrated, he's not going to stop at the dominant modulation and go into a whole new tempo. He may soften the strings or change their bowings a little, but he isn't going to change the tempo.

I wanted to ask about the famous red herring that almost anyone who doesn't like your playing immediately uses against you— the question of tempo. To me, it seems that the emotional content and structural form of a piece isn't so much determined by a fast or slow tempo, but rather that, in a qualitative sense, whatever tempo you choose creates, within that tempo field, a certain level of tensions and relationships. So that the tempo appears, in a way, like a container into which a liquid is poured.

I couldn't agree more and can't begin to top that in terms of expressing it so well. The best example of that, if we talk about just the classical literature, is Artur Schnabel. I think that Schnabel, and I'm not exactly saying anything new, was probably the greatest Beethoven player who ever lived. I find myself more genuinely drawn to the essence of Beethoven in Schnabel than I ever have been by anybody. I mean, you may not particularly care for the way he did certain things, but by God, he knew what he was doing. There's a sense of structure that *nobody* has ever really caught as he did in most of the Beethoven things. And this is especially true in the early works, where he does something that I suppose was very revolutionary for the time, and something that's in contradiction to everything I've just argued for, because I don't do it at all. I'm very *aware* of constant pulse—Schnabel was aware of the pulse of the *paragraph*. He was certainly aware of the interior pulse as well, but he chose to let it ride through the paragraph, as if he were dictating a letter with a certain series of commas and semicolons, and I don't think anyone else ever played the piano using *that* system successfully—other people have tried, but nobody else ever really got it.

I'm thinking of one gorgeous record, Opus 2, no. 2, in which you really are not aware of the bar line, and in which the structure of the piece could not be more plastic—it's *utterly* clear—but there's no sense of the sort of vertical tension that I, for example, would automatically try to bring to the piece. I would play with very firm, very tight rhythmic features. But Schnabel doesn't. He makes you feel that you're floating through an entire paragraph, and that when you get to the end of that paragraph, no momentum has been lost. Sometimes in the later works I'm not so convinced by some of the things he does; but in those early pieces, as far as I'm concerned, Schnabel could play fast, slow, or in between—it wouldn't make any difference.

And I would like to think that, similarly, I could . . . well, as a matter of fact, perversely enough, my two recorded versions of the Mozart C-Major Sonata, K. 330 employ two very different tempi—one is very slow (the one done in 1958), and the other is of course very fast.

Yes, I agree with you about tempo, I've never understood why it's such a big deal, you know. It's always seemed to me that tempo is a function of so many relatively extraneous things. For instance, my tempi have noticeably slowed down in the last year, because I'm playing on a piano newly rebuilt, which eventually will assume the characteristics that it had before, I hope and pray, but which at the moment has a heavier action. And one by-product of that heaviness is a certain quality of legato which I would frankly like to get rid of—I'd like to get it right back to its nice secco quality that it had before it fell off a truck. But a new piano with new hammers hitting new strings is going to give you *innately* more legato. Now, you can go one of two ways. You can fight it, which I've tried to do to some degree. We have a new record coming out of Bach's first four French Suites [Gould has since recorded an album consisting of the fifth and sixth Suites and Bach's Partita in B Minor]—in fact it's the first thing we did make after the piano was restored—and they're just as deliberate and dry as any Bach I've ever done. But they are played more slowly, because one way you can function within a somewhat thicker sound is obviously to slow down. The articulation, if you adopt the tempo that you might otherwise have done, *is* going to be less clean. So the instrument determines it, as does the hall to an extraordinary extent.

Do you consciously, in your own performances, try to comment on other musicians' interpretations—for instance, playing a Bach work intentionally different from the way Landowska or Edwin Fischer do it?

No, I can honestly tell you that . . . well, I knew many of the Landowska recordings when I was a kid, but I don't believe I've heard any of them since I was about fifteen, and Edwin Fischer I never knew at all. Rather than the playing of people like that, I was much more familiar when I was growing up with the recordings of Rosalyn Tureck, for instance, than I ever was with Landowska. In fact, really I didn't like Landowska's playing very much, and I did like Tureck's enormously—Tureck influenced me.

That's strange. I've found that some of her performances are a bit stiff and artificially terraced.

Well, I think that she and I have very different notions about the music, perhaps. I think that what you've just said about the *strata*, the emphatic terracing in her playing, is partly true. But back in the forties, when I was a teenager, she was the first person who played Bach in what seemed to me a sensible way. In those days, being fourteen, fifteen, sixteen, I was fighting a battle in which I was never going to get a surrender flag from my teacher on the way in which Bach should go, but her records were the first evidence that one did not fight alone. It was playing of such uprightness, to put it into the moral sphere. There was such a sense of a repose that had nothing to do with languor, but rather with moral rectitude in the liturgical sense. Whereas the Bach "specialists," the people who had really brought him to the attention of the many—Casals, Landowska, and so on—played with enormous amounts of rubato. In fact, their whole approach is based on the way in which the Romantic sensibility could be welded onto the baroque, and I think that's really what made their playing very attractive to that generation. Not that it wasn't great playing—it was fantastic playing; perhaps, as playing, better than the people we've been talking about—but nevertheless it, to me, was not really Bach.

Casals has a moment in a documentary I've been working on—it's a line that he always uses, and he used it again with me—in which he talks about the fact that his playing of the Bach Suites for unaccompanied cello was only regarded as revolutionary because, as he put it, the Germans didn't understand him and didn't understand Bach—they didn't understand that Bach was a human being. But I don't agree with him, because—well, I don't know how you feel, but to me the most interesting Bach orchestral performances that I know of on records have come out of Germany—notably Karl Richter's.

But to me, Tureck was a revelation in terms of the way in which Bach could be adapted to the piano. I would think the original recordings that Munchinger made of the *Brandenburgs* must have had much the same revelatory impact. I'm sure this was true for most people of my generation who, shortly after the war, were coming out of a conservatory system which put a premium on expressivity, wanted or not. There was, we were told, something cultivated and cultured about producing a *langueur*, though there were limits of permissibility. For instance, in playing Chopin—which I was never deemed to be able to do, though I had great fun a couple of years ago when I played the B-Minor Sonata on CBC, the only professional Chopinizing of my career—I was always chastened for forgetting about such things as the de-emphasis of the top note in an upward-bound progression. You were supposed to super Bellini's conventions on Chopin's thematic ideas. There were certain expressive conventions of the sort that were supposed to be taken into account, and it wasn't considered good taste to turn these conventions on their head. Above all, it was important that one find some sort of 1945 *Zeitgeist*, and apply it to everything. To play Bach with no pedal at all was just not done. And the models for the teachers of that generation certainly were Casals and Landowska and Fischer. None of those people influenced me in the least; and the one who really did was Tureck.

The composer and pianist Busoni once wrote: "All composers have drawn nearest the true nature of music in preparatory and intermediary passages (preludes and transitions), where they felt at liberty to disregard symmetrical proportions and unconsciously draw free breath." And as examples of what Busoni called the "boundlessness of this pan art," he cited the transition to the last movement of Schumann's D-Minor symphony and the introduction of the fugue of Beethoven's Hammerklavier *Sonata. I wanted to apply this fascinating idea to what seems to be your interest in transitional, fin-de-siècle composers like Orlando Gibbons, Max Reger, and Richard Strauss.*

Well, I think you've put your finger on something that I had never really thought about very much—but you're absolutely right—and that is that the repertoire that I'm fondest of tends to emerge from the pens of *fin-de-siècle* men. I can't think of anybody who represents the end of an era better than Orlando Gibbons does, and Gibbons *is* my favorite composer—always has been. I mean, I can't make a case for him being a better contrapuntist than Bach—obviously he wasn't, and obviously he wasn't as gifted a word-colorist as Wagner. There is, however, a spiritual attachment that I began to feel for his music when I was about fourteen or fifteen and first heard some of the anthems; I fell in love with them, and consequently all my life I've wanted to make a Gibbons album of some kind. Unfortunately, there are very few keyboard pieces of quality—his best work is for the voice and not the keyboard—whereas the William Byrd stuff . . . well, I said in my notes on that album that Byrd relates to Gibbons as Strauss to Mahler, and I think the parallel is a valid one. Byrd is both an extrovert and a nostalgist, and that combination is not just effective—it's absolutely irresistible.

But to get back to your point about *fin-de-siècle* composers: It occurs to me that there might be a parallel with my enthusiasm, or lack of it, for nineteenth-century repertoire. I am, as you know, absolutely hooked on all the late-Romantics, or at any rate all of those in the post-Wagnerian tradition—Strauss, Schoenberg in his first style, etc.—but I do find it very difficult to muster any enthusiasm for the early Romantics. Schumann, for example, is a composer with whom I have very little patience, though Mendelssohn, on the other hand, especially when he's not writing for the piano, appeals to me enormously.

But then, Mendelssohn was probably the most disciplined and classically oriented of the early Romantics.

Exactly.

On the other hand, you play the late Brahms Intermezzi *so beautifully.*

Well, I'm fond of many of them; in fact, I really have great affection for some of them. But I have to be very frank and say that when I sit down and play late-nineteenth-century things for my own amusement, Brahms doesn't often figure in the picture. I'm much more likely to play a Strauss tone poem in my own transcription, or something of the sort. . . . By the way, did I tell you I'm doing my own transcription of *Meistersinger* this weekend?

You're kidding! How many records is that going to take?

Oh, no, not the whole opera [laughing], just the Prelude. You know, I've always sort of sat down at night and played Wagner for myself, because I'm a total Wagnerite—hopelessly addicted to the later things especially—and I thought it would be fun to make my own transcriptions. But I tried to avoid what Liszt does, which is to be very faithful to the original. I preferred to go, if not all the way, then a long way toward a realization rather than a transcription. Anyway, the album will consist of the *Meistersinger* Prelude, which will probably open it, followed by *Dawn* and *Siegfried's Rhine Journey*, and on the flip side the most Germanic (and for "Germanic" read "slowest") performance of *Siegfried Idyll* since—God, what's the name of that man? Knappertsbusch—and which absolutely fits the piano . . . well, can be made to fit the piano, rather as if it had been thought up by Scriabin in his earliest years.

The piece is inherently pianistic—I always thought it would be. I wondered at first about the advisability of a piece that had *so* much repetition, that was so given to sequences of [sings] four bars of that, and then [sings again] four bars of that, but I found that it could be done by changing the emphasis, the accents on one voice or another. And, in the process, I've developed a thesis about transcription. The whole area is one that really irritated me before, because as a kid everybody was playing the Bach-Liszts or Bach-Tausigs or Bach-Busonis or Bach-something-or-others, and I never did, I didn't like them. I played those things on the organ, and they sounded much better that way.

The Liszt transcriptions, on the other hand, whether of Beethoven or Wagner, tend to be relentlessly faithful, in that if the orchestral texture is thick, Liszt will reproduce that thickness on the piano, and of course a thickness on the piano doesn't sound good, let's face it. If the drum roll goes on for sixteen bars, there will be a tremolando of sixteen bars in the lower octaves of the keyboard, which is impossible pianistically. Now, there are certain places where the timpani have a theatrical role, as in the beginning of the *Rhine Journey*, and where you just can't avoid it. But apart from such moments I took a solemn oath that there wouldn't be anything other than the occasional punctuation from the timpani and that I would try to re-create the pieces as though somebody like Scriabin, who really knew something about the piano, as Wagner did not, had had a hand in it.

The *Meistersinger* is not a problem because it's so contrapuntal that it plays itself, although I must say it's the only place where I'm going to have to cheat, because I'm going to have to put on earphones for the last three minutes, when he brings back all the themes which, if you want to represent them properly, need three hands at least, and preferably four. I've played it as a party piece all my life, and you can usually get through the first seven minutes without incident, and then you say, "O.K., which themes are we leaving out tonight?" So I will do it as an overdub. I've already played the *Siegfried Idyll* on the CBC as a kind of tryout, so I know that *it* works, and what I did there was horizontalize the sound through arpeggiated chords and similar devices. I took the position that one of the things that goes wrong when you transcribe a work faithfully, especially a work that has a predominant string texture, as the *Siegfried Idyll* does, is that the doubling of contrabass and cello should be either an intermittent feature or one which is used to widen the spectrum of the sound, as indeed it does in the orchestra, without adding to the percussiveness of the sound. So what I did, except in the biggest climaxes, throughout the entire *Siegfried Idyll*, was to have the contrabass always enter on the off beat, much as the timpani in Sibelius' symphonies tend to come in more often than not just before or just after the beat. And that was the prototpye for several other little inventions along the way. For example, Wagner frequently sits for six bars or more on an E-major chord, and there's simply no way you can do that on the piano without losing all sense of momentum. Now, Liszt usually falls back on a tremolando, which is just so turn-of-the-century I can't stand it. So what I did—and if you think my Mozart sonatas upset people, wait till the Wagnerians get hold of this—what I did was to invent whole other voices that aren't anywhere in the score, except that they are convincingly Wagnerian. For instance, there's a moment quite near the beginning of the *Siegfried Idyll* where an F-sharp major chord is held for four bars, and over it the violin has the figure [sings]. Now, I just sang it at about twice the tempo at which it is normally played, and if you imagine that played twice as slowly on the piano, you'll realize that the lower notes are bound to be inaudible by the end of the phrase. You can reinforce it, you can hit it again, but I chose not to. What I did, rather, was to invent a dialogue between two offstage horns, one in the tenor and one in the alto, that try to mimic each other [sings the two horns], and they go on like this between themselves, and it's gorgeous . . . forgive me for saying so, but it's gorgeous!

[*We hung up on this ecstatic note. A week later Glenn Gould called me to continue and finish up the interview.*]

PART II

In the intervening period, Gould had gone to the studio to record the Prelude to Wagner's Die Meistersinger, *the last three contrapuntal minutes of which required him to overdub another four-handed primo and secundo dialogue. I asked him how his duets with himself had come out.*

It just went swimmingly, to be immodest about it. At the end of the *Meistersinger* Prelude, the chap doing the primo stuff kept indulging in all sorts of strange rubato conceits, and I had to study his rather eccentric tempo notions for quite a while until I got with it [laughing], but once I did, on my secundo part, it was enormous fun. I had staged the primo fairly cannily—the overdub runs only about three and a half minutes anyway—so that at all times the primo consisted of at least two elements—one that involved something that was continuously in motion, a sort of perpetuum mobile texture, or at any rate, whatever figure was fastest. In addition to that, whichever bass figure was most prominent—not necessarily lowest, but most prominent—was given to primo, so that I could hear it over the earphones rather easily.

Which of the two performers—primo or secundo—did you prefer?

Oh, I wouldn't want to play favorites, though the secundo somehow represented all the challenging material, and the primo, by comparison, all that was rudimentary. But it really is rather odd, you know, because the moment you attempt to telegraph an upcoming accelerando or ritard in an overdub, then there's trouble. There's some little switch that goes "click" inside your head a half-second before you arrive at that spot, and it's at that fatal moment that the notion of adjusting a dynamic level or adjusting a tenuto that will service the telegraphy takes shape. And if you're charging along in the secundo, to put yourself into the posture, so to speak, of the primo is no easy task. In fact, we made them on separate nights, so that I had to think back twenty-four hours ("Where was I, what was I thinking about at that moment? When is it going to happen?"). And those were the troublesome moments, but they really could be counted on the fingers of one hand; there weren't more than four or five that were that difficult—it wasn't anything like the marathon I thought it was going to be.

I wanted to ask you about the extension of this Doppelgänger *syndrome as it appears in your radio and tape experiments. You've made several little tape-dramas in which you impersonate a number of "personalities" who seem to inhabit your mind. And I'm sure that if I were a structuralist, I'd be able to identify at least four of these archetypal personages. . . . There is the little tape you made for Columbia Records to explain how you perform a Bach fugue, and you introduce three characters who sit around and confabulate with you. First, there's an elderly, slightly dotty BBC-type pedagogue named Sir Humphrey. . . .*

[Oxbridge accent] Yes, that's right . . . Price-Davies, I think.

Then there was some kind of erudite German musicologist.

Well, he usually is, yes . . . I would not have him if he were not entirely skilled . . .

From north or south Germany?

[Herr Gould]: Zat depends entirely upon vether or not you vant him to be civilized or somevat *astringent.* . . . In this case it was a gentleman, as I recall, from south Germany and he spoke with a very *shrill* accent indeed.

Then you had a hippie pianist named Teddy Slotz who plays at the Fillmore and who sounds a bit like a takeoff of Lorin Hollander.

Theodore Slotz, yeah. Everybody kept guessing who this was based on, and you know who it was based on? . . . *Nobody*. Well, no, that's not quite true—there was in my mind a Theodore Slotz, but he was based on a New York taxi driver, whom I met on the occasion of the 1966 off-year elections. I was coming from the 30th Street studio up to my hotel, and the chap who was driving suddenly turned around—I hadn't even thought of it as being election day, it just hadn't occurred to me—and he said, "So, who do you think's going to do pretty good in the election, Mac?" And I said, "Well, I don't know, I guess the governor's got a pretty good chance"—Rockefeller was running for reelection—and he looked at me (*he* had initiated the subject) and said, "Yah don' expect me to talk politics wit yah, do yah, Mac? I mean, like, there're two things I don't never talk about in this cab, one's politics and the other's religion, know what I mean? I never talk about that, man. No offense to you personally, man. I don't know if you're a Democrat or a Republican." "Well, I'm Canadian, so I'm not really either of those things." "Well, I don't care where yah come from, Mac, but yah can't trust people these days, yah know what I mean? Like I'll tell yah a story, Mac, like just last week I had a guy in the cab—he was from Venezuela, yah know—and he says to me, he says, 'What do yah think about Rockefeller?' So I says, 'Aw, that s.o.b.,' yah know. Well, it turns out them Venezuelans are really hot on the Rockefellers. Now, I didn't know that, how's I supposed to know that? This guy got so mad I don't get no tip. 120th Street! 120th Street, man, I don't get no tip." At that moment Theodore Slotz was born.

And from that moment on, whenever I wanted to do an American hippie, that taxi driver came into my mind; but I really didn't have any musical archetype in mind at all.

What's fascinating about all of these routines is the fact that you touch on really interesting ideas—about Bach's evolutionary approach to composition, for example, as you talk about it on that tape.

This whole idea of impersonation reminds me of one of your articles in which you talked about Van Meegeren, the famous forger of Vermeer paintings, and suggested that the forger is the hero of electronic culture. I can't help but relate this Doppelgänger *idea to your series of impersonations. There's something of the trickster in all of this, isn't there?*

It's a very interesting tack you're endeavoring to take. I would love to go along with it; I'd have to think about it a bit and maybe call you back in a month and say, "Yes, you're right." I am fascinated with the fact that most of our value judgments relate to an awareness of identity; we tend to be terribly frightened of making judgments if we're not aware of the identity of whoever is responsible for a piece of art. And I am fascinated with that idea—in fact, my most joyous moments in radio, as opposed to my most creative ones, perhaps, are those when I can turn to impersonation. As a matter of fact, Theodore Slotz turns up fairly frequently on my programs as a sort of intermission guest, and he usually has something unkind to say about my performances. On one occasion, he caught a few people off guard, I guess, although the context should have made it quite clear that this was a put-on, but the switchboard lit up with abusive calls—"How dare they let this idiotic young beat critic tear our local talent apart?"

To be serious, though, I'm absolutely convinced, despite the old saw about the fact that a good novelist is someone who does not need a *nom de plume*, that a certain part of your persona operates efficiently within the structure of a certain lifestyle, a certain name, while another part may operate best only providing you change those factors. I, for instance, was incapable of writing in a sustained humorous style until I developed an ability to portray myself pseudonymously. I started this in the mid-sixties. I wrote a few articles for *High Fidelity* in which I turned up as a critic named Herbert von Hochmeister who lived in the Northwest Territories. The reason for that metaphor was that Herbert could thereby survey the culture of North America from his exalted remove, and pontificate accordingly. The character was also vaguely based on Karajan: Von Hochmeister was a retired conductor and was always spouting off about Germanic culture and things of that nature. At least, that's how I got into the character. Once having got into it, I had to make him sufficiently aware of other and more recent innovations so that he could speak of them with some authority. But in any event, once I did that, I found it no problem at all to say what I wanted to say in a humorous style. Until then, there was a degree of inhibition that prevented me from doing so. But then the floodgates were open, and subsequently I developed a character for every season.

I wanted to ask you about your experiments with quadra-phonic sound. I know you tried recording a Bach fugue, playing each of the four musical lines separately and then allocating each to its own speaker.

First of all, the results, in terms of performance per se, were appalling. They weren't expected to be otherwise, because nobody thought that I was going to turn into the First Piano Quartet over-night. It was an in-house demonstration, purely and simply that, and in fact it came up literally at the last minute. We had a couple of hours left over in the session and somebody said, "Will you do this for us," so I did it. But the whole question of quad, it seems to me, is interesting at the moment because it's going through so many sea changes—it's still on its shakedown cruise, really.

Well, take the quad recording of Bartók's Concerto for Orchestra, which features "surround" sound, so that you hear it as if you were sitting in the middle of the orchestra. It's an interesting idea, but this is one of Bartók's more traditional and formally "classical" works, and what this quad approach does is to analyze that piece and then refashion it in a sonic and structural perspective which seems to go against its grain—much as it would with a Mozart and Beethoven symphony.

If one thinks in terms of a proscenium stage, as one does for classical music, it certainly does. I've argued this point with my producer, Andy Kazdin, and others at Columbia with some vehemence, because I basically argue from *your* point of view when we're talking about things like Beethoven symphonies, or whatever.

I assumed you automatically preferred "surround" sound. You once gave an interview in which you criticized the ambient coughing-in-the-back type of quad recording . . .

No, I don't, that's not at all true. Because in that case I'd never look at a black-and-white movie. On the contrary, I prefer mono sound for certain kinds of things. I think that there are certain works that don't benefit even by left and right separation. Quadraphony is not necessarily about Bach trio sonatas or Beethoven symphonies at all.

Now, when for Gabrieli they station four brass choirs around the room, then, of course, that's perfectly feasible. There's a piece by a Dutchman, a contemporary of Beethoven's, whose name I can't remember, for four string quartets and orchestra—really anticipatory of Elliott Carter—which is quite an extraordinary piece. Phillips recorded it fairly recently, and I saw the score. That's a natural piece from the classical period for quad. But there aren't many such things, and unless you want to do something very radical with the repertoire —maybe these words will come back to haunt me—I can't really see that the bulk of the classical repertoire is designed for quad.

I think that I've probably moderated my views about rear-end ambience since I gave that interview. I see nothing really wrong with it, as long as it doesn't assault you with the notion that you are back in the concert hall, because after all that's precisely what the recording got you out of. To put you back there and say that *that's* the ultimate achievement seems to me to defeat the purpose of the recording. But if indeed the added ambience does something to enhance the presence of the acoustical environment overall, that's something else again.

Color can be an enhancement of black-and-white, but it doesn't have to be, and there are lots of things that work much better in black-and-white: I mean, I would not want to see *Woman in the Dunes* in color. Let me take another example: think of *Miss Julie*, for instance. Implicit in the structure of the play, which is a very tight structure, is the notion of light—northern light, as it happens—light that barely goes below the horizon and never altogether loses its power, and which in the end is much stronger than when the play opened. Now, presumably some hot-shot director could come along with a new angle on Strindberg and say that *Miss Julie* should really be set in Bolivia. In that case, we'd have sudden blackouts come sundown, and I'm not at all sure that that wouldn't work. But if it worked, you'd have to rethink the characterization, you'd have to restructure the whole relationship of Jean and Julie and Christine so that the matriarchal triangulation reflected a tropical as opposed to a

Nordic culture. I think that's as good a parallel as any that I can think of—*that* notion of *that* action taking place on Midsummer Night was not accidental. It was absolutely indigenous to the structure of the play and to the sense of the importance of hesitancy in class inter-relationship—that was the whole point of that play, really. Set that in Bolivia, and it isn't going to work—unless you change the characters. That isn't to say it would be a less compelling creation, it's just that it would be a different creation, and I think you have to start from scratch. So, I suppose by the same yardstick you could design an experience around a classical work that would work in quad.

Would you give an example of how you'd go about doing this?

I have in the can an eight-track version of a Scriabin sonata. Now, of course, this was overkill in relation to any pianistic needs, obviously: Four-track would already be overkill, but this was quadruple overkill. It was done, however, with the idea, as yet un-realized because unmixed, that it would be interesting to see what would happen if you opted for the notion that a piano was not a piano was not a piano, that it didn't have to be locked into one acoustic environment from first groove to last. By which I don't mean that it was being pan-potted all over the place.

Pan-potting?

"Pot" in the sense of potentiometer and "pan" as in panning across. . . . Pan-potting is a way of precisely rather than organically—that sounds like a contradiction but I'll explain what I mean by it in a minute—moving one or more sound sources about a room.

Let me give you an example—this is just a parenthesis, we'll eventually get back to what we're talking about: If, for instance, I have a voice on my tape recorder, such as that of Maestro Casals (with whose voice I've been living for the past few weeks, since I'm making a documentary about him), and if I want to move it across from the left speaker to the right, I can do that in one of two ways. I can start it off full left, gradually open the right channel and move it to a center screen, or, if I simultaneously close the left pot, full right. But if I want to take that source and—in the process of a complicated mix involving, let's say, two or three other characters speaking at the same time perhaps, and music on another couple of tracks—confine it to one track as opposed to two tracks, then the only way in which I can move it is by pan-pot. It's like a swing of the audio camera, but it provides for a degree of precision in terms of repositioning the sound source that would be hard to duplicate via the two-track, left-versus-right movement that I described first.

Anyway, as that voice moves across the room towards center stage, it will appear to have gone up towards the ceiling, rather than to have moved in a straight line. This doesn't, generally speaking, affect orchestral placement, because we've grown inured to the idea that strings are on the left, which seems all wrong to me as a pianist. I mean, everybody knows that high notes are played by something that's on the right, right? [laughing] But this simulated elevation is a disadvantage which one can turn to good account on occasion. For example, in my documentary on Newfoundland, I positioned an elderly minister in such a manner as to suggest a pulpit-like location.

However, this kind of advantage is greatly outweighed by the fact that as you move sound sources about, the nature of that particular vertical triangulation does distort the sense of line that's inherent in the image. Now, in the same way, when, in quad, you listen to sound coming at you from four corners of a room, you're also dealing with the business about who sits where and who gets the best view in the house—in Germany the father would; in America the mother would; and in France, I suppose, the mistress would. You're dealing with multiple triangles and not with the absolute, razor-sharp, pinpoint accuracy that you want for character placement.

I think that a possible solution is to fill out the space with many more speakers, but to use them in order to flatten the surface, to minimize the multiple triangulations we were talking about, which I think constitutes the great drawback of quad at the moment.

I really think that quad has a much greater potential for the spoken word than for music. I mean, if you were going to represent the Shakespearean theater in the round, how else than by quad? That would be magnificent—utterly magnificent. But anyway, I don't think that you can deal with a Haydn string quartet and simply treat it as you would Elliott Carter's—I don't think that's what it's all about. And there I come right back to your corner.

End of parenthesis. Now, what we did with the Scriabin was to record the piece with four different mike perspectives—my conventional perspective, which is for most people's taste too close and too tight and too taut and which is usually about five feet away from the instrument, then a somewhat more discreet, more conventionally European pickup, perhaps eight or nine feet away, again with a rank of three mikes. Those were respectively the second and third ranks. Rank number one was the sort of pickup that you might have used for Art Tatum twenty years ago—the mikes were right inside the piano, almost lying on the strings, ultrapercussive. But, curiously enough, not at all unsatisfying. It had a kind of whiskery quality that was very pleasant—you could feel every note bristling, and that was very nice.

The final perspective, or nonperspective, consisted of two mikes pointing at the far wall—pointing *at* the wall, and not at the piano, so that they were picking up the ambience. And the Scriabin sonata in question, which was the fifth one, starts with a trill in the lowest octave of the piano, supported by a tritonic passage played as a tremolando, and in the course of about ten seconds this trill plus the accompanying tritone moves up the keyboard, octave by octave, until it gets to the very top, at which point the score unrealistically asks for fortissimo, and, of course, you can't play fortissimo at the top of the piano. Anyway, it moves theoretically from pianissimo to fortissimo, and it also moves from octave to octave with the same set of quasi-magic-chord notes. What we did was to record the whole piece with these four perspectives and decide that at some time in the future it would be nice to choreograph it, to look at the score and decide what it might offer in terms of a cinematic projection, what opportunities it might afford for long shots, tight shots, two-shots, dissolves, hard cuts, jump cuts, whatever. If you thought of it in those terms, how would you design this piece for sound cameras?

Well, we managed to excite some very blasé engineers by experimenting with the place I've just described—starting off with the hindmost mikes, those that faced the wall, and which picked up sort of a distant rumble, which was really quite an unearthly sound. I'm just trying to equate it with what listeners might think when they first heard it—for one second it would sound God-awful, and they'd think, "What is that?" Anyway, with each octave, as it moved up the piano, we'd kick in another rank of mikes, but never so many that the sound lost its basic clarity. For instance, as rank two came in, four went out, so we then had two and three combined. As one came in, three went out, and so on. We finally ended up on the topmost notes, those that Scriabin specified as fortissimo, but which can't be played fortissimo, with the Art Tatum pickup (or the Oscar Peterson pickup or whatever you want to call it).

Like a zoom.

Right, it was a zoom, it was a ten-second zoom right to that *thing*, and it was one of the most dazzling audio effects I've ever heard. At that point in the score there's a pause—a fermata—then an eighth-note rest, and then Scriabin starts his main theme, if you can call it that, at which point we pull back to perspective two, our conventional pickup, and the movement proper begins. Now, that kind of thing, if you extend its implications to quad, could, I think, produce some really interesting results.

You could also theoretically move that sequence around the room topologically from one corner to the other. That would be another kind of "shot."

Absolutely. But I think, again, that if you did that, you might prefer to have recorded it in a different way. I mean, we recorded it with the idea in mind that we were locked into left-right stereo, even though quad was a known quantity at the time: Now, what would that difference be? I don't really know. Perhaps it wouldn't be so much a question of recording it differently as of presenting it differently. [The above techniques are embodied in Gould's November 1977 release of Sibelius' *Three Sonatinas*, Opus 67, and *Kyllikki*, Opus 42.]

There's a moment in the radio documentary I made about Stokowski which is, I think, quite magical. It's a moment, prior to which, for some ten minutes, Stokowski had been talking about his experience with recording in the early days of his association with the Philadelphia Orchestra, beginning in 1917. He talked about making records in the twenties and his experiments at the Bell Lab and the fact that they built a research studio for him under the stage at the Academy of Music in Philadelphia. During this sequence the only possible illustration I could think of was Stokowski's own 78rpm catalog, and we managed to use a number of brief excerpts from his recordings of that era, employing a deliberately primitive, monaural style of stereo. Obviously we *were* in stereo, we couldn't deny that, but I took these 78s and fed them alternately to left and right speakers at a fairly snappy pace, and with each example succeeding the preceding one by three or four years, so that within a space of seven or eight minutes we moved from about 1917, with the *Rienzi* Overture, to about 1934, with his first recording of Wagner's "Good Friday Spell." And in so doing, I used nothing but hard cuts, whereas my natural inclination in treating Stokowski to a sound portrait was to use dissolves, because he's a dissolve man and not a hard-cut man—he cries out for a Visconti and not a Bergman.

Anyway, at the end of the sequence I faced a real problem, because somehow I had to get him back to time present, if only because he was about to say something elegiac—I can't remember the exact line, but I think it was "Today it is much better than in the past, but I believe we can do better still"—in that delightful tone of his. And so I had to find a way of suggesting this betterment, and at the same time bringing us back into the present, because by this time we were forty minutes into the show and we'd spent thirty of those minutes with contemporary stereo sound. And I discovered that he had remade the "Good Friday Spell" in 1960.

And just on a wild chance I got out the record, timed various segments—his views about the work hadn't changed to any great extent at all over the years—and found one segment, of no less than twenty-five seconds, which ran within three quarters of a second of the 1934 version. So what we managed to do was to have the 1934 version going in the left speaker—I used probably fifteen or sixteen seconds of it solo—and then, also in the left, began to super, note by note, the 1960 version, to which we applied a good deal of compression so that the frequency response would not at first sound appreciably different from the earlier recording. Then, gradually, we opened the right channel and moved the stereo version across the screen. The 1934 version suddenly appeared to move, to grow, to creep out of the left wall, to become almost incandescent. But the effect was that during the phrase "Things are better than they were," the sound was not yet so good that you wanted to say, "Whoopee." On the contrary, you wanted to say with him, "Yeah, it could be better than that . . . but how the hell do they do that!" It's a moment I'm very proud of.

*Many people don't know much about the several radio documentaries you've made for the Canadian Broadcasting Corporation. You've spoken about your dissatisfaction with the linear quality of radio—the over-to-you-and-now-back-to-your-host wrap-up approach. Two of your programs—*The Idea of North *and* The Latecomers—*are*

both about the idea of solitude as it affects people living in northern
Canada and Newfoundland. And in these programs you used all sorts
of contrapuntal effects—trio sonata, fugal counterpoint, and basso
ostinato forms—in structuring and displaying the voices of the per-
sons heard on the programs. Now, you've also talked about the idea of
the media in relationship to sensory deprivation. How does this idea
relate to your ideas about radio?

That's a huge question, so let me try to tackle it one point at a
time. The first point that you mentioned was the fact that both those
programs deal to some degree with solitude. In fact, so do all of the
major documentaries I've made. There are six programs thus far that
have taken three or four hundred hours of studio time each. Number
one was, as you mentioned, *The Idea of North*, two was *The Late-*
comers, three was *Stokowski*, four is the one that we're just mixing
now about Casals (*Casals: A Portrait for Radio*). Five, a fantasy-
documentary on Schoenberg which is intended for his centennial next
year (*Schoenberg: The First 100 Years*). And there's one other program which has lain around now for a year and a half, it's been ready
for mixing for a year and a half and hasn't been yet. It's a program on
the Mennonites which is called *The Quiet in the Land—Die Stillen in*
dem Lande is what they call themselves—and that is the ultimate in community isolation. So next I want to do a comedy about an isloted man,
because I'm sick and tired of these profound statements [laughing].

To some extent or other, all of the subjects that I've chosen
have had to do with isolation—even the musical ones. I mean, certainly Stokowski is not exactly a mainstream figure; he's a man who
has deliberately decided to go his own way, as has Casals, for other
reasons. In any event, all six programs have had to do in some way
with isolation, and most particularly, of course, the three that have
been about groups of individuals. Because the first group were people
who had for one reason or another chosen to isolate themselves in the
north—all of them at this stage in their lives are out of it. But precisely because of the success of that program, one person has changed
his life: programs, you know, have a funny way of changing people's
lives, as the *American Family* is only too well aware. But in any event,
that program put together a group of individuals and compared their
individual experiences.

The Latecomers dealt with a subject for which I didn't feel the
same sense of sympathy at all, because the whole idea of the herd

gathering—no matter how splendid and remote the rock on which they isolate themselves—doesn't really appeal to me. The subject of the program was nominally the viability of outport life. Outports are simply villages devoid of conveniences, and geographically isolated from the outside world—villages not serviced by a main highway or something of the sort.

The village we talked about—though it wasn't where most of the people involved came from, I just pretended that they all came from there—was a village called St. Joseph's, which is a ghost town now, and our chief spokesman, our narrator, who is at present the dean of the faculty of arts at the university down there, had come from this village. A few months before I made the program, he had been back to see the community pulling up stakes, quite literally, and he had to escort his father, who had been the last of the village to leave. It was a very touching story as he told it, and it made sense to me to unify the program and suggest that all these disparate characters were in some way involved with that village. And in order to do that I then had to sketch imaginary family relationships and to create quasidramatic exchanges between the main characters, which would lend credence to those relationships.

Marshall McLuhan once wrote that radio is a "hot" medium, television a "cool" one. I've always felt the opposite. Radio always seems to allow you to turn inward—into your own solitude—and to contact your fantasies, whereas television just zonks you out and doesn't really let you participate in much of anything.

I agree, and I think that he made that distinction not so much in deference to what he thought or didn't think about radio—I have the sneaking suspicion that Marshall doesn't listen to that much radio, frankly—but that he was *aiming it*, structuring it, so that he could eventually distinguish between film and television, which was never a distinction that convinced me either.

I admire McLuhan very much—at one time he was a neighbor, as a matter of fact, but he's moved since—and I still see him once in a while; he's a dear and wonderful man. But I always felt that he would have been better off without that sort of trendy terminology that he got off on in *Understanding Media*, and that we would have understood him better without it. I never did really try to figure out what it meant, though I remember arguing endlessly with him one time, which is an exercise in futility in itself: You do not argue with Marshall, you wait for a *probe*; there's no guarantee that his answer will relate in any helpful way to your question. The answers will be illuminating and exciting and animating, but they will not necessarily be in response to your questions. So there's no possibility of an argument. But in any event, I tried to suggest to him that at a time when the medium of television was gobbling up films at a great rate and putting them out at all hours of the day—not just for the late, late viewer, as had been the case maybe two decades ago—that it was futile to try and make that distinction.

Take the idea of radio as a metaphor for solitude. It's a much more private experience. Why do you think you're so interested in this inward-turning medium?

I'd like to deal with this as sensibly as I can, because it's a big question, it's an important question. I don't know what the effective ratio would be, but I've always had some sort of intuition that for every hour that you spend in the company of other human beings you need X number of hours alone. Now, what that X represents I don't really know; it might be two and seven-eighths or seven and two-eighths, but it's a substantial ratio. Radio, in any case, is a medium I've been very close to ever since I was a child, that I listen to virtually nonstop: I mean, it's wallpaper for me—I sleep with the radio on, in fact now I'm incapable of sleeping *without* the radio on, ever since I gave up Nembutal [laughing].

Does it affect your dreams?

Sure, in the sense that if there are newscasts on the hour, I pick up the bulletins and use them as the subjects for my dreams. In the morning, if there's been a boat that's just gone down, I'll think, "Gee, that was an odd dream about the *Titanic* I had last night," and then pick up the paper at the door: "*Lusitania* Sinks," and I will, of course, have concocted my own dream variation on the story already.

I've never conceded any real contradiction between the assumption that one can have a rather solitary existence and the fact that one can supportively have radio in the background at all times. I mean, we talked last week about a purely physical demonstration of its power—you know, its power to block out mental impediments; we talked about Beethoven's Opus 109. I'm totally incapable of understanding people who get upset with any kind of Muzak. I can go up and down on endless elevators and never be bothered by it. No matter how insipid the stuff may be, I really don't care—I'm utterly undiscriminating.

Maybe your feelings about solitude come from the fact that you've got a Nordic temperament.

That certainly is part of it. It's an ambition of mine, which I never seem to get around to realizing, to spend at least one winter north of the Arctic Circle. Anyone can go there in the summer when the sun is up, but I want to go there when the sun is down, I really do, and so help me I'm going to do it one of these times. I've said this now for five or six years, and every year the schedule gets in the way.

What would you do about playing the piano up there?

I don't need to play it. But I'm sure the local bar has got a piano I could noodle on if necessary. Well, to be truthful, once a month or so I've literally got to touch the piano or I stop sleeping properly. That really is true. I was in Newfoundland last summer, just as a tourist, and after about a month I found that I was getting by on three and four hours a night, which seemed ridiculous, because I was doing reasonably energetic things like wandering up and down cliffs and beaches and cuing the surf for all sorts of imaginary documentaries . . . and this was insane, because I was getting more and more tired every day. And finally I realized that what was missing was the fact that I *did* need contact with a piano just for an hour or so. And, literally, that will do me for a month; that's all that's necessary. As it happened I knew of a delightful old German Steinway located at the CBC studios in St. John's, which I discovered when I was down there doing *The Latecomers* four years before; I asked if I could have an hour with it, which they granted, and the next night, you know— sound as a baby.

I really get a feeling of autumn from your performances—with that special clear and measureless light.

Good. Then my life has not been in vain [laughing]. . . . You know, back in my touring days, whenever I had to head into the

American South or into the European South—I never have been below the equator so I can't talk about the South American experience at all—I was profoundly depressed, and not just because of the papier-mâché quality of places like Miami Beach or most of Los Angeles. It really had something to do with the quality of the light, with the sudden fadeouts at night, for example. I got very depressed, and that depression usually rubbed off on my playing. Whereas, on the contrary, the best month of my life—in many ways the most important precisely because it was the most solitary—was spent in Hamburg, where I was ill . . . though I must admit in rather luxurious surroundings. I'd managed to get myself booked into a hotel called the Vier Jahreszeiten, which translates as the Four Seasons and which looks out on one of the most splendid views of Hamburg, which city at that time was in the process of rebuilding.

And I had come down with something called focal nephritis, which is a mild variant of a very dangerous kidney disease, but in this case just viral-induced and something that takes about a month to cure. Anyway, I had to stay, in a semiquarantined state, in the Vier Jahreszeiten, and knowing nobody in Hamburg turned out to be the greatest blessing in the world. I guess this was my Hans Castorp period; it was really marvelous.

There is a sense of exaltation—I'm careful about using that word, but it's the only word that really applies to that particular kind of aloneness. It's an experience that most people don't permit themselves to know. I'm convinced of that; certainly, from time to time, most of us, because of the pressures of work or whatever, lose contact with it. But there has to be a way of redressing that balance and reestablishing that ratio that I talked about earlier. And sooner or later I'm going to spend a winter in the dark; I'm convinced of that, too.

You once wrote an article about Petula Clark which appeared in High Fidelity *magazine, and in it you compared her favorably with the Beatles. In fact, you even put the Beatles down. And I seem to remember that you identified Petula Clark with yourself in some way.*

Well [laughing], there was a little leg-pulling in that article. However, I *would* compare her favorably with the Beatles, that wouldn't take much doing.

How do you explain such a sacrilege?

Well, first of all let me tell you about the article itself and then about the sacrilege. That article was something I put more work into than anything of its length I've ever written before—in fact, I think six months separated its last word from its first. It had a very interesting formal plan—it was a sort of *Spiegelbild*, as the Germans would say; it was a mirror image. As a matter of fact, if you want a musical parallel, think of the Webern *Variations for Piano*, first movement.

You mean that your Petula Clark essay was a kind of homage to Anton Webern?

Well, it had more 32nd notes, so to speak, and a much denser texture than Webern would allow. But reduced to its skeleton, as you might say, there is a structural relationship between my article on Petula and Webern's Opus 27. And after all, if Thomas Mann could be persuaded to write *Tonio Kröger* through the study of Haydn's sonata-allegros—why not?

The mirror was inserted in the middle of the third scene—there were five scenes in the piece. Numbers one and five were set along Highway 17 in northern Ontario and dealt with a drive I took to and away from the town of Marathon; Petula isn't even mentioned until the closing lines of scene one. Scenes two, three and four, however, deal directly *with* her—two with the first Tony Hatch songs ("Downtown" and "My Love") which made her famous; there were many songs that Tony "hatched" (bad pun) for her, but those were her big hits of the early sixties. Scene four, on the other hand, deals primarily with "Who Am I?" which came along a couple of years later. But the climax of the scenes that deal with Petula—the mirror—was inserted in the center of scene three, and dealt with the comparison that you referred to between Petula and the Beatles.

And then, I suppose, all the images went into retrograde inversion, or something like that?

Something *very* like that. I should add, though, that the highway trip was not exclusively metaphorical. I actually did become aware of her early hits while driving that road—*that* much was true; it didn't actually take place in Marathon as I suggested, but I used that town because I know it rather well and because it led me to an irresistible bit of symbolism.

Marathon is the sort of town that would have delighted Franz Kafka—I think I described that at great length in the piece—because the bureaucratic structure and stratification of the town is emphasized by the kind of houses you find on various streets as you ascend from the harbor. In any event, I really did discover Petula on the highway, and not too many miles from where I said it happened.

But you did discover her on the radio.

Oh, yes, sure, sure—I'd never bought a pop record in my life. But after that I picked up every record she'd ever made. . . . We're getting now to the point where I leave the metaphor aside—no, no, let me say one more thing about that. The upbeat songs that I dealt with in scene two—"Downtown" and "My Love"—were related to the fact that, in Marathon, when you drive up the banks of the fjord on which the town is set, beyond the last and most distinguished row of houses, you reach a gate leading to the lumber run at the top of Marathon Point, with a sign saying PROCEED NO FURTHER. And, at this point, my article on Petula had reached "My Love" and "Downtown," both of which were songs of outgoingness; they were songs of burgeoning maturity, supposedly. Subsequently, I remember discovering with great delight, with an almost Milton Babbitt-ish delight, that "Who Am I?" employed the inverse motive of "Downtown." It was a song of total despair, and became, of course, the prime topic of scene four. Anyway, the downcast songs, the songs of disillusionment, of maturity by-passed—like "Who Am I?"—contrasted with my setting off from Marathon in search of another kind of town that was laid out in a different kind of way. And that was the metaphor I was trying to pursue.

Why did you criticize the Beatles?

I have to say that I was appalled then, as I am now, by what the Beatles did to pop music. I recall that Ned Rorem once said that they were the best tune-writers since Schubert, or something of the sort. It was very *au courant* to say that kind of thing at the time I wrote my article, and I really was so outraged by this point of view, which I could not and cannot understand, that I felt somebody had to debate this Roremesque theory, however indirectly.

You know, there's a marvelous description of Mussorgsky in some biography or other in which he gets very drunk one night at a musicale, which was by no means unusual behavior for him, and takes off at Mendelssohn, who of course was several decades dead at that point. Mendelssohn, according to Mussorgsky, had ruined European music in the nineteenth century. And, to Mussorgsky's mind, that which Mendelssohn had sinned against was the sense of fantasy. I'm paraphrasing like mad, of course, that was not the exact quote, it was much more colorful than that. But the whole sort of deeply-into-your-cups, fantasy-struck madness that the Romantic movement spawned in the nineteenth century, and particularly with isolated types like Mussorgsky—isolated from the Central Western European tradition—was opposed to what Mendelssohn stood for. And that is very odd when you think of it, because Mussorgsky's successors were people like Shostakovich, who, for one reason or another, have been compelled to take note of Marxist doctrine, which holds that art is there to purify the masses, and of course there cannot be a more purifying, i.e., read, *law-abiding*, experience than the Mendelssohnian structure. But this, of course, was precisely what Mussorgsky objected to. And the point of my Shostakovich comparison is that the Russians obviously have had to confront, somehow incorporate, and yet at the same time demythologize, the Mendelssohnian legacy. But in any event, Mussorgsky didn't understand Mendelssohn, and I suspect for much the same reason that the Beatles would find it hard to understand Petula Clark.

I disagree with you about your musical criticism, but what about the Beatles' lyrics, which seem to me really special?

Well, of course, I was appalled by two aspects—one relates purely to the music, but the other involves the general production level that was encouraged by the Beatles at that time, though, to be fair, not spawned by them. There was, as you know, a tendency throughout all of the pop business in the sixties, particularly in areas that involved rock—acid or otherwise—to keep *that* pot or *those* pots which controlled the conveyers of the word, *down*—down, that is, in relation to the instrumental tracks, which were always *up*.

Now, I think that this tendency is much less prevalent today, but to those of us who grew up with the notion that pop music had something to do with big band sound—and at the risk of dating myself, that's my period—this is an appalling notion; indeed, I would have to say abstractly that it's an appalling recording notion at any time. Certainly, there's no particular reason why a certain effect should not be enhanced by lowering the primary track. But to *always* have it down, to make everybody grope for the lyrics, seems to me very foolish. I think, perhaps, I *do* understand the psychological reason, but I don't agree with it.

In any event, having said that, I have to tell you that avoiding the Beatles as best I could in the sixties—which was no mean feat—I really don't know the lyrics, I know a few fragments from them, I know the titles, but I couldn't recite more than half a dozen lines in all. So I really was speaking primarily on the musical level. The lyrics that do come through with the pot up tend to be the late ones and the early ones—the ones in between that made them a cause célèbre, do not—at least not to my ear. I mean, "I Want to Hold Your Hand"—you can understand that; "Let It Be"—you can understand that. And almost everything in between is sort of way down there, buried under piles of garbage, of instrumental garbage.

So I really can talk with some authority only about the music, and, as I've said, I find it appalling. You see, I think Mussorgsky was accurate in his observation and wrong in his concept: I think his observation that Mendelssohn was a strait-laced man who liked nice, tidy sixteen-bar paragraphs was quite correct. What he forgot to notice was that Mendelssohn was inventive on another level altogether. In order to comprehend his invention, one has to first accept that *placidity* that is the most abundant feature of his music. Having accepted that, Mendelssohn can then surprise you by the gentlest movement; he needs only the tiniest change, as they say in the jazz field, to make his effect felt. Whereas in the case of Mussorgsky, he has to hit you over the head with a forte-piano contrast, or a quasi-modal moment or something—I happen to like Mussorgsky, by the way, I really do. He wasn't very competent technically, of course, but then neither were the Beatles. However, I think that the point was indicative of a misunderstanding—and this wouldn't apply just to composers—that has always muddied the waters for artists who assume that invention has something to do with the noise you make while breaking rules. Needless to say, I don't think it does. I think it has to do with the subtlety with which you adhere to premises some-what different from those that may be expected of you. I cannot bear assaults of any kind, and it seems to me that the Beatles essentially were out to affront and to assault.

It's strange that a lot of your recordings have the kind of effect on certain persons that you say the Beatles' recordings have on you.

[Laughing] Well, I cannot top that, sir, and I don't think I should even try. In my view, my recordings have the same effect that Petula Clark's should have had, but why don't we leave that judgment to posterity.

But, you know, about ten years ago, I used to hear some very well-meaning people say that they tended to listen to classical music only when it had a beat, as it did in my playing, because they were jazz-oriented. Now, I could at least identify with that comment to some degree. I wasn't interested in the jazz scene either, but in my teens, I went through a period when it was very "in" to see profundi-ties in Lennie Tristano, and I tried, so help me, I tried, but I never succeeded.

I was once playing a friend a recording of Renaissance music performed by England's Musica Reservata, a wonderful group which emphasizes close-miked sound, clear textures, rhythmic precision, vibratoless voices, and a soprano who sings with a nasal quality simi-lar in timbre and force to that of certain gypsy vocalists. And this friend said: "This group's the Glenn Gould of Renaissance music!"

Well, that really is very flattering, but it occurs to me that the kind of clarity that you're talking about is not, never could be, the exclusive preserve of one individual or orchestra or group or chorus: it relates to a state of mind, obviously. In fact, I even wonder whether it relates exclusively, or primarily, to music which involves a continuo-like rhythmic pulse. I would think, just to play the devil's advocate for a moment, that if the music can be conducted—mentally, that is, and always assuming a ready supply of subdivided beats on behalf of the listener—the battle is already half won.

I would have to argue, for example, that, at her best, and given her best material, Barbra Streisand, whose fan I happen to be, is probably the greatest singing-actress since Maria Callas—and I hyphenate very carefully, in the sense of "singing-actress." For instance, if you take a rubato-filled song like "He Touched Me"—at least it's full of rubato in Streisand's rendition, and it's a magnificent structure harmonically, by the way; I mean, it's as good as anything Fauré ever wrote, it really is—you find that the sense of tempo change, the sense of key change, is all part of one structural concept, which of course reveals a sense of unity that plays no part at all in what is to my mind the ultrasimplistic notions that the Beatles were trying to pass off.

See, I think what I was trying to say about the Beatles was that after all of the pretension has been cut away and after all the faddish admiration of the Cathy Berberians of this world has been removed, what you really have left is three chords. Now, if what you want is an extended exercise in how to mangle three chords, then obviously the Beatles are for you; but, on the other hand, if you prefer to have the same three chords unmangled—just played nicely—then Tony Hatch is your man.

At the same time, I do think that what I said before about the Mendelssohn-Mussorgsky polarity is absolutely valid, that there happens to be a "quirk quotient" in the former's work which is minimal, but which is noticeable precisely because it *is* minimal. In Mussorgsky, in Janáček—let's take another example of the same strain—in Berlioz, the quirk quotient is very great, which is to say that the unexpected happens very frequently, and consequently it takes a tremendous gesture in order to really surprise you. In Mendelssohn it doesn't—just the tiniest movement, just one hair not *quite* in place.

Now it is my thesis, which at this point has to be subdivided, that (a) the Beatles themselves, those who wrote, and they're notably Lennon and McCartney, and (b) those who advised them in the production sense, the studio, did not have that kind of control, didn't really know where they were going. They seemed to want to say, "We are going to show you that it is possible to work with a minimal harmonic structure and to so becloud the issue that that's what we're doing that you're going to think it's new and it's different and whoopee!" And all of this eclectic garbage—I mean, you don't necessarily get it good by adding a sitar, that's really the point, I think.

But in classical Chinese music, for example, the pitch interest is minimal, and things like articulations and inflections "make" the music. And rock music isn't rich harmonically, but the chords are basic blues and country chords, and they're beautiful.

Very true, and I guess I have candidly to admit that I am not terribly fond of folk music. I can be charmed by the peasant wrong-headedness of it all, and if I were a film director trying to shoot a scene in the Hebrides, let's say, I would take every modal nuance the locals had to offer, and I would not want it undercut by the sort of triadic perfection that a certain generation of Roman Catholic organists were always trying to add to the chant. But, on the other hand, I'm not very hot on Bartók and Kodaly either, who did hear in folk sounds the basis for other more sophisticated structures. Now, if that's what the Beatles did, and if you argue that they did it persuasively and with great subtlety—a subtlety that means something to you—then what can I say! I can't hear it, and I'm stubborn enough at my advanced age to say that if I can't hear it, it ain't there. But in any event, we really have struck, at this point, a generational impasse.

But the point that we were making some paragraphs back was that clarity relates to a state of mind, and it doesn't have anything to do with one idiom or one individual or one group—Steve and Eydie can have clarity if they sing in tune together, as they usually do. In any case, it isn't the private preserve of the rock scene or the jazz scene, as it was thought to be in the forties and the fifties.

Maybe it would be fair to say that your taste in pop music is a bit sentimental.

My taste in popular music? I have almost none, so I don't know if it's sentimental, but let me put it this way: I grew up with the big band sound in my head. To the extent that I could listen pleasurably to pop music, it was music that related to the harmonic spectrum of *that* sound—not that sound itself, but the harmonic spectrum to which it conformed. Now, who sings it and how well is of rather less importance to me than how inoffensively it functions as a backdrop, if that's what I'm having to listen to.

I'd say that Streisand stands to the Beatles as someone like Bellini would stand to . . . well, to almost anyone rich and variegated and intense and lively . . . like Schoenberg, for example.

That's very odd, because I would think of Streisand as being a very intense individual and a very intense artist, and I would think of Schoenberg as being an ultraintense artist and individual. There is one difference, though—Schoenberg's funny moments were pretty Germanic and heavy-handed, things like *"Ach, du lieber Augustine"* in the Second Quartet, whereas Streisand, obviously, is a pretty funny lady.

Well, I think my Schoenberg analogy was off. Maybe Luciano Berio is a better example.

I was going to feed you Berio. They *sure* are, they *sure* are. And I will say no more [laughing]. You've hit on a really good parallel for the Beatles.

What's the matter with Berio? . . . Oh, well . . . I've gotten myself concerned here. I should have compared the Beatles to Anton Webern.

Listen, if you had done that, I would have trotted out all my alter egos, and enlisted all my exotic *Doppelgängers*, and barraged *Rolling Stone* with a Letters-to-the-Editor campaign for the next ten years. I think I'd send my letters off to Vienna, perhaps, or to London . . . Sverdlovsk, maybe, or, for the benefit of Teddy Slotz, Brooklyn Heights. I'd get them postmarked accordingly, and they'd be coming at you indefinitely. And of course they'd all contain the same message: "This idiot Cott has done it again."

STÉPHANE GRAPPELLI

The Prince
of
Violins

My grandmother used to tell me that once when I was three years old and on an outing with her to a toy store, I grabbed and tried to make off with a pretty, stuffed violin-playing monkey—much like the storybook chimpanzee that throws itself on ladies' hats decorated with artificial fruit. In fact, it wasn't the monkey I wanted, but rather that irresistible violin which I tried, unsuccessfully, to wrench from the prehensile grasp and chin of that obdurate and well-made creature.

Three years old is the beginning of the end. At home I pined away, comforting myself with a little 78rpm phonograph on which I incessantly played a recording of Mischa Mischakoff performing treacly standards like Dvořák's *Humoresque* and Fritz Kreisler medleys.

Six months later, however, my *Weltschmerz* vanished upon receiving from my grandmother an eleven-inch-long Mexican wooden toy violin (a relic which my mother, obviously sensing a legendary career in its formative stages, still keeps in one of her closets).

At seven, two things happened to change my life: first, I discovered Jascha Heifetz, whose electrifying recordings suggested to me, then and even now, the possibility of perfection. And second, my mother bought me a quarter-size violin, and I began taking lessons and practicing, scratchily and irritably, those miserable Ševčik exercises that are the bane of parents and next-door neighbors. And I progressed from first to fifth positions, but prodigy I was not.

I was eventually to enjoy the communal experience of performing Haydn and Schubert string quartets with my thirteen-year-old colleagues (though the arguments over who would play first violin were hardly harmonious). But aside from the Bach unaccompanied sonatas and partitas (which I attempted to struggle through later on) and the Brahms, Schoenberg, Berg, and Stravinsky violin concertos (which were always beyond my technical command), I began to lose interest in what I considered to be the mostly sentimental Romantic violin repertoire. And when at fourteen I flubbed my way through a Vivaldi concerto in front of an audience of parents and peers, I turned to "Heartbreak Hotel" and "Roll Over Beethoven" for solace. I started having fantasies about and casting furtive glances at sensual-sounding oboes and English horns, and realized that the love affair between me and the violin was over.

Or so I thought until January of 1976 when, almost by accident, I went to Carnegie Hall to hear the great jazz violinist Stéphane Grappelli performing with the Diz Disley Trio. I had earlier admired Django Reinhardt's and Grappelli's Quintet of the Hot Club of France recordings of "Mystery Pacific," "Nuages," "Ain't Misbehavin'," and "Hot Lips," among others. But I hadn't quite expected the faultless intonation, crisp upper-register sonorities, wine-dark lower-string timbres, rhapsodic phrasing, and vespertine lyricism of that shining, graceful, Pierrot-like figure—reminding me lightly of my grandmother in former times—playing the most mellifluent version of "Body and Soul" I had ever heard.

That night at Carnegie Hall brought on one of those Proustian moments of involuntary memory, taking me body and soul back to my three-year-old obsession, as I repressed the thought of dashing onstage to pry loose and run off with that beautiful violin.

In December of 1976 I was on the phone to Paris.

"Hello, is this Stéphane Grappelli?" . . .

"You're calling from New York? You want to see me in Paris? *Incroyable! Bien sûr*, you're invited, my dear, and bring Rockefeller Cen*taire* when you come!"

"Jazz violinists have always had to be unusually resilient to survive," Nat Hentoff has put the matter bluntly, "because until recent years their instrument has not been regarded as a legitimate jazz axe."

Considering the dominant position held by the piano and reed instruments, however, it is important to remember the efflorescence in the twenties and thirties of such inventive pioneer jazz violinists as Joe Venuti, Eddie South, and Stuff Smith (once described as the "palpitating Paganini"), who in turn inspired Svend Asmussen and Ray Nance, and, more recently, Michael White, Leroy Jenkins, and Jean-Luc Ponty.

Stéphane Grappelli not only partakes of this hardly superannuated tradition—a tradition he himself has shaped and developed —but, today [1977] at sixty-nine the violinist is at the height of his imaginative and technical powers. He lives in a compact, modest Upper-West-Side-looking apartment on the Rue de Dunquerque—an apartment filled with books, records, and souvenirs from his travels. It is just one of Stéphane's home bases (he has a room in Amsterdam and apartments in London and Cannes, where his daughter lives), and, in fact, he is continually traveling at a clip that would exhaust a person half his years. During the last three months of 1976, for example, Stéphane played in eight American and seven Canadian cities, then flew off for performances in Edinburgh, London, Amsterdam, Lyon, Stuttgart, and Hamburg.

"We are all gypsies, my dear," Stéphane says to me as we sit down in his study. "As a matter of fact, I don't like living in any one place. I don't like doing the same thing every day. The only thing in this life is to find people to have a little talk to . . . *that's* agreeable. I really don't envy [pronounced en-*vee*; lovely is love-*lee*, chopped liver is shopped lee-*vair*] people staying in the same place. I'm not *blasé* at all. I prefer to be an *ignorant* and be amazed when I see something that's new to me. Sometimes it helps to be an imbecile: you don't need a name, or a tax collector coming after you.

"I like New York in June (though I once got the most celebrated flu of my life there), San Francisco in the summer. But best of all I love New Orleans in the fall. I was there a few weeks ago, and it's the best thing I ever saw in my life. We played at Rosy's. Rosy is the woman who owns the club, she likes music very much and she even sang 'Summertime' with us. Summertime in a cool night."

"The French writer, jazz critic, and singer Boris Vian, who died in 1959, loved New Orleans, too," I mention to Stéphane.

"Oh, I knew him and loved his books," Grappelli says enthusiastically.

"Do you know about the Clavicocktail Machine that he describes in his novel *L'Écume des Jours* [The Froth of Days]? It reminds me of your playing."

"I read that book so long ago. It's a machine?"

"A machine that makes drinks to music," I say. "For each note there's a corresponding drink—either a wine, spirit, liqueur, or fruit juice. The loud pedal puts in egg flip, and the soft pedal adds ice. For soda you play a cadenza in F sharp. And if you feel like a dash of fresh cream, you just play a chord in G major. The quantities depend on how long a note is held, but the alcoholic content remains unchanged. So you can make a 'Weather Bird' drink or a 'Loveless Love' potion. Imagine what cocktails you could concoct with your music!"

"A marvelous contraption," says Stéphane. "You know, Boris Vian used to play the trumpet, and I was pinching myself not to laugh. But what a brain! He was a very spiritual man, and he used to compose some very light but amusing songs. In fact, I have a rare edition of *I Spit on Your Grave*, the detective novel he wrote which was banned in France. He used to come to Club St. Germain about twenty years ago almost every night when I was playing there. I'll never forget him. Near the end, he was completely white. I think he was suffering with his art [heart] a long time before. It was not very *solide*.

"Me, I'm A-O.K. I was just checked up. I used to smoke a lot, but no more. I started when I was ten. It was during World War I, so, *alors*, when I see an American I ask him, but they didn't often give a cigarette to me because I was too small. So I smoked the leaf of the chestnut tree—*maronnier*. But I stopped cigarettes in 1970. It was easy, and now my cere*bral* is clearer.

"Do I smoke anything else? Well, I've tried like everybody, but I'm not a *dope*. One thing that helps me through when I'm playing something that I've done over and over for fifty-four years is a couple of whiskeys before I go on the stage. When I'm at Carnegie Hall, for example, I get a little nervous, it's normal. But when you must *attack* —bang!—you need a little support behind. I always arrive one hour before I'm supposed to perform, put my fingers into good order— maybe it sounds pretentious—I take a little drink, some quick conversation like that, and then I'm onstage. Maurice Chevalier once told me: "You must start very well, finish very well and in the middle it's nobody's business. But me, I try to do the business in the middle, too."

"Whiskeys or no," I say to Stéphane, "I'm amazed that you can play those same pieces and make them sound new after all these years."

"The big groups of today," he replies, "like the Rolling Stones, always do the same thing: 'I love you, I love you, I love you' . . . you see what I mean? Anytime you go to see those people they're always saying, 'I love you, baby.' I try to catch them changing, but it's *impossible*. I can't bear those screams for nothing at all without *nécessité*. If I did that on my violin, it would be in pieces! I recently heard Morgana King singing "You Are the Sunshine of My Life.' Now, I could listen to *her* say 'I love you' for one month! But she's intelligent, she doesn't say 'I love you' for one month. She says, 'You are the sunshine of my life,' which at least is a change. But I don't want to criticize too much because these people do their best to please a certain clientele.

"*Alors*, me . . . I, too, am saying 'I love you' or 'I don't love you' with my violin. It's basically the same program every night, but sometimes we start with the entrée and end up with the appetizer. And we've got the dessert as well. No dessert in the middle, though—that would be a bad menu. And when the public is nice, we add a little salt, pepper, and a better bottle of wine. *Voilà!*

"I prefer performing for young people than for the people who ask for mustard when I'm playing 'Nuages.' That's why I like performing at the Bottom Line in New York or at the Great American Music Hall in San Francisco. A lot of atmosphere and no soup.

"I like my programs to have something *soft*, something *energetic*, something *slow*, something *blue*, something *red*, something *burning*. And it's quite difficult to do that with just two guitars, string bass, and violin. We are a bit victimized by the new aspects of electric music. We're playing like classical people except that we're doing jazz music. Segovia or Ike Isaacs—one of the guitarists I play with—is to me the same sound. I don't dare to say I'm playing like Heifetz. I play my own style—I bought it myself from my body—but I'm trying to get that sound. Those classical guys go very fast, but I go fast, too, in my music. Why not? It keeps you alive."

Stéphane has some errands to do and asks if I'd mind joining him on a little walk around the neighborhood. When we get outside— a chilly December day—he mentions that we're just a couple of minutes away from the first apartment he ever lived in as a child.

"My childhood was like a Dickens novel," Stéphane says as we start walking. "I lose my mother, who was French, in 1911 when I was three. And my father had no choice but to put me in a very poor *catholique* orphanage. My father, who was Italian, was a very strange and interesting person. He was the first heepie I ever met, a Latinist and a teacher of philosophy. He did translations from Virgil and Italian into French, and he spend most of his time in the Bibliothèque Nationale. Occasionally he worked as an instructor in a place like Berlitz, but he was incapable of making a penny. We were very good friends. But I'm the opposite of him. I'm very practical, he was *théorique,* always reading and writing. He thought he could get well by reading a book instead of going to a doctor, but he died in 1939. You know, my father got remarried, but I didn't get on with my stepmother. It's probably the reason I never got married.

"My first impression of live music was when I was six. My father wanted to take me out of that orphanage, and since he knew Isadora Duncan, who had a school then, he asked her if she wanted another student. 'Bring me the child,' she said. Of course, in those days, I was not looking like what I look like today. So she said, 'Oh, yes, I like him!' But I wasn't very successful as a dancer. I played an angel, but when you're not an angel it's *difficile.* I did, however, hear some grand music there. Musicians used to play in her garden, and I remember hearing Debussy's *Afternoon of a Faun* and the music made me *feel* the faun.

After Isadora Duncan I had to go to another orphanage because the war was breaking out. We slept on the floor and I suffered from undernutrition. That's why I like desserts now. I never ate much of anything there, and I wasn't very sunny. So I escaped that damned place and wandered in the streets. Finally I move back with my father. And because of him I become a musician. Every Sunday he used to take me to hear orchestras, and that's when I first become acquainted with a lot of Debussy and Ravel. I wanted to play something. And my father wanted to distract me and keep me a bit quiet. So he took me into a store on Rue Rochechouart and bought me a three-quarter violin. All the way home I hugged it so hard I almost broke it. In fact, I still have that violin in my desk at home—there are no cracks in it and it is one of the only things of mine that wasn't destroyed during World War II. I'll show it to you when we go back. It's my only fetish.

"There was no money for lessons, so my father takes out a book from the Bibliothèque, and we learn solfeggio together. I never had a teacher, so I learn good position and posture from sheer luck. The technique came along slowly. When I needed some more notes I had to wait. I can't play the notes with the correct classical fingering. On the other hand, a classical musician can't play jazz easily either. It's a different way. Maybe if I practiced I could succeed in playing the Beethoven concerto from beginning to end, but I'd never play like Isaac Stern or Menuhin because my hand is deformed, my brain is deformed. I love bluegrass fiddling, but maybe I could catch it if I lived down South for six months. Because learning to play music is like a language—you've got to learn it on the spot. But you can't catch anything on the street except a cold.

"At fourteen I got job in a pit band in a cinema. That's where I really learned to play and to read music—three hours during the day, three in the evening. I played in tune, and that's why they kept me."

We reach Stéphane's dentist's office, and he goes upstairs to give the dentist—"a nice guy"—two of his albums (*Stéphane Grappelli Plays Cole Porter* and *Stéphane Grappelli Plays George Gershwin*). When he comes smiling back down the stairs, I suddenly realize how much his bearing and music remind me of Charlie Chaplin and Buster Keaton.

"Did you ever play music for Chaplin films?" I asked Stéphane.

"Oh, yes, my dear, I was dying of laughter from his films. I used to laugh so deeply that sometimes I was sick. But I can't laugh like that today. Rarely do I have what we call *fou rire*. But, you know, the only kind of movie I don't like is those family affair films in which they dispute and go back with everybody kissing at the end. I can't bear that.

"It's interesting that just about this time I heard my first jazz. I don't want to sound stupid or pretentious, but I think I'm more near the black beat than the white. I was first attracted to black musical interpretation and atmosphere by chance. I remember hearing a tune called 'Stumbling' on a record performed by a group called Mitchell's Jazz Kings. It drive me insane. Soon after that I listen through the door of a night club to a pianist, saxophone, and drums playing 'Hot Lips,' and that drive me mad, too. Practically just two notes and the chords change all the time. So when Charlee Chaplin comes on the screen in that cinema, I start playing 'Stumbling' with the other musicians.

"Then one day I went out and saw musicians playing in a

courtyard and decided I wanted to earn some pocket money for some pastry, so why don't I try it? I remember concierges chasing me out with their brooms, but one or two accepted me, and I got a little money. I did this two years—though I never tell my father—and I earn more than I make from playing in silent-movie cinemas.

"In the courtyards I play little classical tunes—*Berceuses* by Fauré, melodies from *Thaïs*, and the *Serenade* by Toselli, which was a great success. It was the 'You Are the Sunshine of My Life' at the time, and if you wanted to make money you had to play that. So I begin to make some money, and my father and I move into a bigger apartment. About this time I hear Louis Armstrong and Bix Beiderbecke and teach myself the piano. I like its *harmonique* aspect and discover that I can make money playing it at private parties."

Stéphane and I have now arrived at the local optometrist, who chats with Stéphane as he loosens the violinist's glasses ("I'm very farsighted"), and out we go again.

"When did you meet Django Reinhardt?" I ask.

"Oooh, more questions about Zhango! Information about him is *everywhere*. In the subways even! One day I may sit down and write things no one knows about him. He was a very secret person. In the early thirties, I had been playing piano at the Ambassadeurs in Paris—where I hear Paul Whiteman, Bing Crosby, Oscar Levant, and George Gershwin perform—and then with Gregor and his Gregorians in Nice. Gregor got me playing the violin again. And then one day, back in Paris, I meet Zhango at a club in Montparnasse. He was looking for a violinist to 'play hot.' But I lose touch with him. Then at Hotel Claridge in Paris in 1933 we both met up again in the same hotel orchestra. One day when the tango orchestra was on we find each other backstage. I had broken a string and was tuning up, and all of a sudden we start fooling around playing 'Dinah' together— pretending we are Eddie Lang and Joe Venuti."

Stéphane is tired of telling Django stories, so I fill in the rest. Django, his brother, his cousin, and bassist Louis Vola formed the legendary Quintet of the Hot Club of France which, as Ralph Gleason once wrote, was the first and only European group of that time "accorded major-league status in jazz by musicians and fans alike."

Reinhardt was a gypsy whose third and fourth fingers on his fretting hand were left withered and paralyzed by a fire in his caravan, forcing the guitarist to develop a unique "cross-fingering" technique with which he created a dazzling musical style. A man who told

time by the sun, Django, more often than not, was off playing billiards, fishing, or painting when he was supposed to be onstage.

In fascinating interviews with Whitney Balliett in *The New
Yorker* and with Dan Forte in *Guitar Player*, Stéphane remembers
Django as "a great artist but a difficult man. His chords were always
there, but he was not there himself." Stéphane was constantly trying
to get Django to gigs on time. "But when he was annoyed with me,"
Stéphane recalls, "he would give me some funny chords."

They were in London together just about the time the Germans invaded France. "I used to get up very late," Stéphane told Dan
Forte, "six o'clock in the afternoon. Django, as a gypsy, would always
get up early. Anytime, he'd get up. Three o'clock in the morning, he'd
go be listening to a bird somewhere. He'd hear a bird and say, 'Oh,
it's the spring.' The spring was my worst enemy, because when the
new leaves came on the trees, no Django. . . . During the war we were
in London, but the first siren Django heard, he said, 'We must go, we
must go!' He was in the street when he called me, and I said, 'Fuck
off, I'm not going to get up. We'll see you later on.' But when I got
up, it was too late. And that was good for me, because at least I was
not with the Germans."

During the war, Stéphane played in London with pianist
George Shearing. "I played with George for the troops. And the
bombs dropped quite often. I remember one time we finished up
playing in a club in Golders Green. The sirens started, so we flew out
of there to get to the deepest underground station nearby, which was
Hampstead Heath. We started walking fast down the street, and
George said: 'There's no need to run, we're underground.' He didn't
know where we were because he was blind.

"One Friday night when we were performing, there was a
terrible bombing. I didn't want to disturb George, who was playing
his solo, so I ask the manager of the club if we should stop. 'Keep
blowing forever!' he shouted. And I didn't dare go because he had our
check! Another time I remember a singer we were accompanying who
was singing 'As Time Goes By' as the bombs came down. You should
have heard the tremor—'Ti-iy-i-me go-oo-oo-es bi-yi.' It was awful!
We laugh now, but those damn V-2s could drop anywhere. Always
that bloody blitz started when *we* started. It was a signal."

After the war Stéphane rejoined Reinhardt in Paris, but they
played less and less frequently together. In 1953, Reinhardt died of a
cerebral hemorrhage while playing billiards. Stéphane kept a low

profile for a while, performing at night clubs, then for five years at the Paris Hilton, and later at Ronnie Scott's Jazz Club in London. During the past ten years he has performed all over the world and recorded prolifically, releasing at least five albums a year with musicians as diverse as Duke Ellington, Jean-Luc Ponty, Gary Burton, Bill Coleman, Paul Simon, Stuff Smith, Baden Powell, Barney Kessel, George Shearing, and Yehudi Menuhin. With Menuhin he has collaborated on two scintillating albums of music of the thirties (*Jalousie* and *Fascinating Rhythm*), eliciting the following comments from his classical friend: "Stéphane Grappelli is a colleague whom I admire and would love to emulate. Although his repertoire is entirely different from mine and he plays the violin in a different style, he brings to it an imagination, a perfection of technique, and a spontaneous expression of feeling which would be the envy of every violinist."

"Where will you be playing next?" I ask Stéphane as we continue our walk.

"A trip to Tunisia and then in March I'll be performing at the Hong Kong festival; back to the States in April. I do get about. By being hectic I keep young. But here we are at Anvers Square—it's the highlight of our little stroll. I wanted to show you this square because I used to play here as a child. It's changed a lot since then: there's an underground parking lot now, and the statues have been torn down. I used to hang around here and do little things to earn some money, like opening doors of taxis, helping people with luggage, working in a laundry nearby, and delivering hats. One day I delivered a hat to a prostitute at her home. Her boyfriend and a friend of his were there playing banjos, and that woman had a violin around, so the three of us had a wonderful concert that afternoon."

Back in Stéphane's study, I notice on the wall a framed photograph of a beautiful woman.

"She was a close friend of mine," Stéphane says, "a hostess in one of the clubs I played at in London during the war. One night a bomb dropped and killed her. I lost another friend—an ice-skating champion—at that time, but in a different way. I was the Prince of Violins, but one day she met the King of Sardines, and I couldn't compete. He was an American colonel and he took her to America after the war, but a year later I received an announcement from her saying that she was marrying *another* guy. By that time I forget.

"In 1975 I was confined in New Zealand and Australia, the

most faraway places in the world. And for some reason I had a desire to read something, anything—it could have been the telephone directory. I was feeling homesick and worried about my daughter and grandsons. And by chance I found a copy of *Madame Bovary*, which I read as a child. But in New Zealand I came across two lines in the book which told me exactly what I was feeling: 'How to describe that elusive sickness whose aspects change like clouds in the sky and which whirl around like the wind.' When you feel something like that, it's an impalpable disease. It's a dreadful feeling. But it wasn't too bad and I soon forget. One gets fed up with the same thing.

"Unlike Zhango, I like a classical life. I like everything classical. I don't like that abstract business. I like Louis Quatorze, the music of Couperin and Rameau. But I always come back to jazz music. Not so much to other jazz violinists, but rather to pianist Art Tatum. For me, my god is Art Tatum [pronounced Tay-*toom*]. Tatum's melodic line is influenced by Ravel and Debussy, you know, and by orchestral work. Art Tatum *is* an orchestra. I've played with Count Basie, Joe Turner, John Lewis, Duke Ellington, Oscar Peterson, Errol Garner, Fats Waller—but never Art Tatum. My greatest ambition is to be the Art Tatum of the violin. That's why I want to keep good health and try to go on."

It was time for me to leave. Stéphane, too, had an appointment across town, so we walked to the Métro station together, and he treated me to a ticket for the first-class section.

"It's our type of *chic*," he said smiling, as we got into the train and sat down.

I noticed the red French Legion of Honor stripe in the lapel of his jacket.

"I wear it, my dear, so that I don't have to carry identification papers on me."

For some reason I also noticed what large ears Stéphane has.

"Did you know, Stéphane, that Stravinsky once said that musicians have bigger ears than most other people?"

"A donkey as well," he replied, giving me a warm bear hug as the train pulled into the station and he got up to say goodbye—beaming the way my grandmother used to, the way Stéphane always does when he plays his beautiful violin.

"When I'm playing I'm blissful, I'm happy, I improvise."

WERNER HERZOG

Signs
of
Life

R abbi Nachman of Bratzlav, the eighteenth-century Hasidic master, once told the following story: A king one day summoned his counselor. "I have read in the stars," he said, "that all who eat of the next harvest will be driven mad. What shall we do?" To which the counselor advised that he and the king should eat the previous year's dwindling reserves and let the populace eat the tainted food. "I don't wish to remain lucid in the midst of a people gone mad," replied the king, "so we shall all enter madness together. When the world is in a state of delirium it is senseless to watch from the outside: the mad will think that we, too, are mad." Yet the king also desired to keep alive the memory of his decision and of his former state. Putting his arm around his friend's shoulder, he said: "You and I shall therefore mark each other's forehead with a seal, and every time we look at one another, we shall know that we are mad."

"Make my tales into prayers," was one of Rabbi Nachman's last wishes. And perhaps no contemporary film maker has so devotedly and rapturously made these kinds of tales into movies than the thirty-four-year-old German director Werner Herzog, whose cinematic depictions of the autistic, the deaf, the dumb, the blind, ski jumpers, dwarfs and midgets, and inspired and deranged prophets remind us of the deeply longed for and remembered state of cosmic sanity and unity betokened and embodied by those who, living on the brink of experience, reveal to us the seals of our own madness.

Throughout Europe, Herzog's films are considered to be visionary masterpieces (*Aguirre, The Wrath of God* played in Paris for eighteen months). But in the United States his movies—in spite of the support of a director like Francis Ford Coppola, an actor like Jack Nicholson, film critics like Amos Vogel, Manny Farber, and Jack Kroll, and admirers like the New York Film Festival's Richard Roud and Tom Luddy of the Pacific Film Archive in Berkeley—either show up infrequently or else open and close almost as quickly as it takes moviegoers to wait in line for the latest addled Hollywood flummery.* (San Francisco is the one city in this country where it appears that *Kaspar Hauser* has developed a considerable theatrical following.)

Herzog, of course, is not the only young German film maker whose works remain relatively unknown in this country. And it is interesting to point out that after a creative void in German cinema for thirty years, the most vital and innovative areas of contemporary moviemaking are currently being explored and developed by a remarkable group of directors including Wim Wenders, Volker Schlondorff, Werner Schroeter, Jean-Marie Straub, and Rainer Werner Fassbinder who, along with Herzog, is one of the most fascinating film makers in the world today. But just as the techniques, styles, and concerns of older German masters such as Pabst, Murnau, and Lang differed from each other, so too those of the practitioners of the new German cinema.

Unlike the other important members of this multifaceted group, Werner Herzog shares less of an affinity with the political aesthetics of Bertolt Brecht and the German New Left than with the mystical tradition of Master Eckhart and Jakob Boehme, as well as of the *Märchen*, or supernatural fairy tale, tradition of the German Romantic poet Novalis. Like Herzog, Novalis was especially interested in the idea of the artist as magical synthesizer whose "eye stirs with the desire to become a true eye, a creative instrument," and whose ultimate aim—like the Gnostic-influenced Boehme—is that of perceiving and reaching out for our true home. As Herzog's Kaspar Hauser

* The following companies distribute Werner Herzog's films in the United States: New Line Cinema (*Even Dwarfs Started Small, Fata Morgana*), Cinema V (*Kaspar Hauser*), New Yorker Films (*Signs of Life; Land of Silence and Darkness; The Great Ecstasy of the Sculptor Steiner; Aguirre, The Wrath of God; Heart of Glass; Stroszek*. It also distributes four shorts: *Last Words; Precautions against Fanatics; How Much Wood Would a Woodchuck Chuck*; and *La Soufrière*.

says: "It seems to me that my coming into this world was a terrible fall."

Signs of Life, Herzog's first feature, made when he was twenty-four, is about a wounded German officer, stationed on Crete during World War II, who goes mad in a valley of windmills; *Fata Morgana,* the director's most abstract film, was shot almost entirely in the Sahara Desert and is divided into three sections ("The Creation," "Paradise," "The Golden Age"), presenting a few isolated human beings surrounded by sand and sky and the mirages created by their union; *Even Dwarfs Started Small* features a cast of both midgets and dwarfs (Herzog uses the word "dwarf" to include both midgets and dwarfs) in an isolated Borstal-type prison at Lanzarote, one of the volcanic Canary Islands, who riot and run amok as if out of a Wilhelm Busch cartoon book: starting cockfights, burning a palm tree, pouring gasoline into flowerpots and setting them aflame ("When we're well behaved, nobody cares; but when we're trouble, nobody forgets"); *Land of Silence and Darkness* is a magnificent documentary about the deaf, dumb, and blind, smelling and feeling flowers and trees, "hearing" poems through the hand signals of others, feeling the vibrations of radios through their chests, describing the imagined "real" world as if it were paradise; *Aguirre, The Wrath of God,* filmed mostly in the Peruvian Amazon, opens with indescribably beautiful shots of insurrectionary conquistadors and Indian slaves coming down a mist-enshrouded mountain, follows the adventures of the deranged Aguirre's small band of followers floating down the river in search of the lost city of Eldorado and ends with what seems to be hundreds of chattering monkeys dancing wildly over dead bodies and the remains of the drunken raft; *The Great Ecstasy of the Sculptor Steiner* is a documentary about Walter Steiner, whom Herzog considers the world's greatest ski jumper ("ski flyer" is what the director calls him), whose glorious trajectories, seen in a succession of slow-motion zooms, reveal the impassioned relationship between camera and flyer; *Kaspar Hauser* (the original title is *Every Man for Himself and God Against All*), Herzog's best-known film in America, is the director's romantic and meditative adaptation and interpretation of the famous story of the young man who, brought up chained in a dungeon without ever seeing a human being, was discovered in 1828 standing in the Nuremberg town square holding an anonymous note. Knowing only one sentence

("I want to be a gallant rider like my father before me"), Kaspar Hauser is taught to speak, is exhibited as an example of "natural" man, and is then mysteriously murdered.

"Mother, I am far away from everything," are Kaspar's first, halting words when a woman places her baby in his awkward arms. Like almost all of Herzog's characters, Kaspar Hauser is only the most recent of the director's extraterritorial creatures. Far away from their origins, these creatures' seeming inarticulateness is in fact the mark which reveals their childlike nature and their sense of homelessness. All of Herzog's characters are spiritual infants. Significantly, the derivation of the word "infancy" comes from the idea of the "inability to speak," and the obsession with language itself is at the heart of Herzog's work, for it is here that one discovers the line where communication, being, imagination, and perception touch, define, and color each other.

In June of 1976, Herzog flew to the United States in order to film a forty-five-minute television documentary about the world championship of livestock auctioneers in New Holland, Pennsylvania. "Theirs is like a new language, it's like the last poetry, the last incantations," the director told me a few days after the auction. "To me it's somehow the ultimate of human communication, showing us how far our capitalist system has taken us. It's very frightening and very beautiful at the same time. One of the auctioneers told me that as a child he would drive in a car and at each telephone pole he'd sell livestock to the poles as they passed by very quickly. Another one trained by reciting tongue twisters: 'If it takes a hen and a half a day and a half to lay an egg and a half, how long does it take a broken wooden-legged cockroach to kick a hole in a dill pickle?' "

In *Signs of Life* a young Greek boy, a little bird in his hand, suddenly says to the hero: "Now that I can talk, what shall I say?" And in *Kaspar Hauser*, the delineation of the boy's education simply acknowledges the ineradicable power of preoperational infant thinking and speaking. As an apple rolls down a path, Kaspar says: "The apples are tired, they would like to sleep." When he has a dream, he tells us: "It dreamed to me." When he listens to the piano, he says: "The music feels strong in the heart." And, finally: "Nothing lives in me except my life."

"Kaspar was between fourteen and seventeen when he was discovered," Herzog explains. "Bruno S., who plays him in my film, is forty-three. I don't care at all." Herzog chose Bruno for the part after

seeing a documentary made about his life. His prostitute mother had
deposited him in an institution for the retarded when he was three
years old. Although not retarded, Bruno lived in the hospital until the
age of nine, by which time he was psychically maimed for life.
Herzog found him living like a bum in a shack, occasionally playing
an accordion in backyards. His performance as Kaspar Hauser comes
close in intensity to Falconetti's portrayal of St. Joan in Carl Dreyer's
The Passion of Joan of Arc. To perform the scene in which he learns
to walk, Bruno knelt for three hours with a stick behind his knees
until his legs were too numb to stand. Exhausted after filming each
shot, he fell immediately asleep.

Herzog's concern with the extremities of experience is meant to
bring to light what Master Eckhart called the *scintilla animae*—the
spark of the soul. The director wants to reveal this light in and by
means of his denounced and renounced characters, and at the same
time to bring us to an understanding of the birth of the word in the
soul that is the light itself. By means of an uncanny admixture of
montage, mise-en-scène, music, silence, and language (with its hesita-
tions, gaps, and distortions), Werner Herzog has fashioned a spiritual
and aesthetic program similar to the great magus Giordano Bruno:
that of opening the "black diamond doors" within the psyche and of
returning the intellect to unity through the organization of significant
images.

Herzog made his first short films when he was nineteen
years old. "I never had any choice about becoming a director," he
says. "It was always clear, ever since I was fourteen years old. I
converted to Catholicism at fourteen—my father was a militant
atheist, and it was an enormous battle against my father. It was at
that time, too, that I wanted to go to Albania, which was completely
closed off to the rest of the world. So I walked along the Albanian-
Yugoslavian border. I can't tell you why I wanted to do this, but
Albania was *the* mysterious country in Europe. . . . I wrote scripts at
school and submitted them, but there was a long chain of humiliations
and failures, so I decided to work at a steel factory at night to make
money to produce my first short films."

His sense of resolution and determination has become legendary. At the end of 1974, Herzog walked six hundred miles from
Munich to Paris—it took him three weeks—as a tribute to the great

German film historian Lotte Eisner, to whom he dedicated *Kaspar Hauser*. "She was in a hospital in Paris, and I was afraid she was going to die," Herzog explains. "And somehow, out of protest, I started to walk, thinking that when I arrived in Paris she would be out of the hospital. And she was. It was just some crazy thought in the back of my mind.

"I'm a friend of hers. But she's important not only to me personally but to the whole of German film making. You know, she was chased out of Germany in 1934 during the years of barbarism, and she remained the historical and cultural link to the great and legitimate German cinema of the twenties and thirties. Film makers like myself started from zero—we didn't have the cultural continuity of France or the United States. And Lotte Eisner witnesses for us that we are legitimate again. She is the only person alive who knows film history in person from Lumière and Méliès to Eisenstein and Pudovkin and the early Chaplin. She's like the last surviving mammoth. And when she dies, something unique will be gone forever. It will be the tragic hour of my life."

Herzog's films share certain visual and thematic concerns with the work of Luis Bunuel, Tod Browning, Georges Franju, Ruy Guerra, but, most especially, with the films of F. W. Murnau. "*Nosferatu* in particular," the director agrees. "It's the most incredible film ever made in Germany. Once I make a film on that level, I'll be able to step back and be satisfied with my work. But I don't feel any continuity of culture with Murnau—he could have been from Japan or anywhere else, it's his way of seeing things, his narration, that I feel close to. I just see something at the horizon and try to articulate it."

Of all the major directors, Werner Herzog is perhaps the first to use music in such a way that the visual integument of his films at moments seems almost to become transparent as the exorcistic, floating, and numinous sounds of chorales, chants, and motets lead us inward to the mysterious foundations of being. (Herzog's choice of Johnny Cash and Leonard Cohen songs to accompany and transfigure the shimmering desert horizons of *Fata Morgana* seems, on hindsight, to have been an aesthetic gaffe, occasioned, one might surmise, by the director's overestimation of the mystical glamour of those songs and voices.)

The night before I went to interview Herzog, I made a little cassette tape of pieces by Landini (the blind fourteenth-century organist and composer) and Gesualdo (the mad sixteenth-century composer-prince), both of them musically and emotionally akin to Herzog's own work and obsessions. The interview began with my playing this tape for him (this was, in a sense, the real interview), and it turned out that both composers were among Herzog's favorites. ("Some people have written that I'm a figure out of the nineteenth century," the director says in the following interview, "but the appropriate time for me would be the late Middle Ages.")

As the tape neared the end, on came a minute-and-a-half lullaby sung by a little Balinese girl (I'd forgotten I'd recorded it), whose tiny, disembodied voice ravished us completely. Suddenly, Herzog said: "I hear a rooster in the background!" and there it was, crowing somewhere in the Balinese countryside.

"It's strange," I said to him, "I've noticed that there are lots of chickens and roosters in your films, and in fact I was planning on telling you a Rabbi Nachman story about a prince who became a rooster."

"Please, I must hear it," Herzog insisted.

"In a distant land, a prince lost his mind and imagined himself a rooster. He took refuge under the dining-room table, stripped naked, and refused to eat anything but grain. The king called in magicians and doctors to cure his son, but to no avail. One day an unknown sage arrived, took off his clothes and joined the prince under the table, saying that he, too, was a rooster. Eventually, the sage convinced the prince to get dressed and finally to sit down to eat with the others. 'Don't ever think,' the sage told the prince, 'that by eating like man, with man, at his table, a rooster ceases to be what he is. You mustn't ever believe that it is enough for a rooster to behave like a man to become human; you can do anything with man, in his world and even for him, and yet remain the rooster that you are.'"

Werner Herzog made me promise to include this story here, along with our conversations that began in September 1975 and concluded in June 1976.

In your films you always show chickens and roosters as malevolent, scavengerlike creatures. You seem to be obsessed with them.

I've been searching all over the United States for the most gigantic rooster I could find, and recently I heard about a guy in

Petaluma, California, who had raised a rooster named Weirdo. Weirdo weighed thirty pounds. Weirdo had died, but his offspring were alive and as big as he. So I went out to see Ralph, a thirty-one-pound rooster, and then found a horse that stood only twenty-two inches high. I wanted to film them—the rooster chasing the horse with a midget rider on it (the horse and midget rider together were shorter than Ralph)—but the guy who owned the horse refused to allow it to be taken to a sequoia tree forest, about a hundred fifty miles away.

I *am* obsessed with chickens. Take a close and very long look into the eye of a chicken, and you'll see the most frightful kind of stupidity. Stupidity is always frightful. It's the devil: stupidity is the devil. Look in the eye of a chicken and then you'll know. It's the most horrifying, cannibalistic, and nightmarish creature in this world.

Once I had a dream. I dreamt that one of my girlfriends got married—I had wanted to marry her myself—and I was standing in the rear aisle of the church, while she was being interrogated by the priest, who held a big book and asked stereotyped questions like: "Do you reject all the powers of the demons?" and she replied: "Yes, I reject all the powers of the demons," after which he intoned: "Do you reject all the tricky devices of the devil?" and so on. And all of a sudden I walked up the aisle, closed the book, and said: "There is no devil, there's only stupidity." They chased me out of the church, I fled with the bride, and at the corner of a street I took a left turn and went up the hill, and she took the right turn, and after twenty steps I realized that she was gone. So I ran back down this hill and just at the corner a mule came galloping by and hit me so hard that I woke up. . . . That's the dream.

In your films, I always get a sense of secret correspondences between animals and states of mind. The kneeling camel, for example, is another ubiquitous creature in your movies—in Kaspar Hauser, *and most powerfully, as the presiding presence over the final scenes of madness in* Even Dwarfs Started Small.

We tried out about sixty camels until we found one that was obedient enough to freeze in a position halfway between sitting and standing up. When a camel sits down it falls to its front knees and then sits down completely. And we had one camel whose owner would say, "Sit down," and before it sat down he'd then say, "Get up,"

"Sit down," "Get up"—and finally the camel was so confused that it froze halfway in this awkward position. The smallest dwarf begins his horrible laughing fit, and the director of the institution goes berserk and points with his finger at a branch, demanding the branch to lower its arm while he himself raises his arm and says: "I will hold my arm out longer than you and I will stand longer than you." It seems as if this will go on for weeks and weeks, and that when you return three weeks later they will still be there, the camel kneeling. It's so pathetic, it really moves me. And I only know the camel has to be there. Without the camel the film is nothing.

Animals are so important in my films. But I have no abstract concept that a particular kind of animal signifies this or that, just a clear knowledge that they have an enormous weight in the movies.

Giordano Bruno wrote: "The forms of deformed animals are beautiful in heaven." A number of persons have wondered why you seem fascinated with "deformed" people in your movies.

That's a great statement, but there are no deformed people in my films. The dwarfs, for example, are well proportioned. What *is* deformed are the very normal, average things: counsmer goods, magazines, a chair, a doorknob—and the religious behavior, table manners, educational system . . . *these* are the monstrosities, not the dwarfs.

But there's another aspect to the way you present animals in your films. Sometimes—as with the turtle in Fata Morgana, *the swan in* Kaspar Hauser—*they appear as creatures whose presence conveys a sense of liberation suggested in one of the most famous passages from Whitman's* Song of Myself:

> *I think I could turn and live with*
> *   animals, they are so placid and*
> *   self-contain'd,*
> *I stand and look at them long and*
> *   long.*
> *They do not sweat and whine about*
> *   their condition,*
> *They do not lie awake in the dark*
> *   and weep for their sins,*
> *They do not make me sick discussing*
> *   their duty to God,*

> *Not one is dissatisfied, not one is*
>   *demented with the mania of owning*
> *things. . . .*

Yes, Whitman can say it in words, I can't. I can show it only. But it comes very close to what my animals are about. . . . But not the chickens: they're vicious, neurotic, the Real Danger.

Chickens are birds, but birds that can't fly. Perhaps that's one reason you dislike them so much.

Yes, maybe it has some significance, because I myself can't fly. I used to love ski jumping, but I had to give it up. I was so deeply shocked by an accident that happened to my best friend, who almost died.

I have to tell you the story that's in my film *The Great Ecstasy of the Sculptor Steiner.* Steiner—who's a woodcarver, and in my opinion, the world's greatest ski jumper—had a photo album which I happened to leaf through, and there were pictures in it of when he was a kid, and one strange shot of a raven. So I asked him about the raven, I kept bothering him about it, and finally he told me the story.

When he was twelve, his only friend was a raven which he raised and fed. And both the raven and Steiner were embarrassed by their friendship, so the raven would wait for him far away from the schoolhouse, and when all the other kids were gone it flew onto his shoulder, and together they'd walk through the forest. Finally the raven lost its feathers and the other ravens started to pick on him and hack him. The raven wanted to flee, it fell down from the tree because it couldn't fly any more, and Walter Steiner shot his own raven because he couldn't stand the cruelty any longer.

At this point in the film there's a cut, and you see Steiner flying in slow motion for more than a minute. On skis he flies. An incredible man, he flies in complete ecstasy, as if into a ravine, as if he were going into the darkest abyss that is imaginable. He flies into it, and he flies and flies and then lands, he is all alone on that slope, and you see him in a blurred, very strange way. Then a text appears, a written text based on words by Robert Walser, over the image. And it says: "I should be all alone in this world, I, Steiner, and no other living being. No sun, no culture, I naked on a high rock, no storm, no snow, no streets, no banks, no money, no time, and no breath. Then I wouldn't be afraid any more."

In Goethe's Elective Affinities, *one of the characters says: "We may imagine ourselves in any situation we like, but we always think of ourselves as* seeing. *I believe that the reason man dreams is because he should not stop seeing. Some day perhaps the inner light will shine forth from us, and then we shall need no other light." I quote this because it seems to me that the mystery of your films lies in the way you reveal this special inner light emanating from the autistic, the deaf, the dumb, and the blind.*

Yes, I always try to go to the innermost light that is burning inside of us. In *Kaspar Hauser*, Kasper is writing his name with weeds in the grass, and his face reveals this light. Or when Kaspar says: "I dreamt of the Caucasus"—you see it then, too.

I hardly ever dream in my life, I have a dream maybe once in a year. But when I walk, for example, I live whole novels. Or when I drive for a long time in the car I see whole films, and I get afraid. And one time I almost had an accident in my car because there were hundreds of butterflies in the car and they wouldn't get out. I knew they weren't real so I stopped the car and let them out. I opened the door, but still they wouldn't go. I was on the Autobahn in the country, but it was as if I were on a big street in Vienna, with old-fashioned houses and hundreds of people leaning out, staring at me, and I was frightened, and I was driving and there were these butterflies around my head . . . and whole stories developed out of it.

There's also an extraordinary dreamlike quality to your directing and editing. In the beginning of Even Dwarfs Started Small, *for example, you show Hombre, the smallest midget, sitting between the windows as he's being interrogated, and when he says: "My ears are ringing. Someone is thinking of me," the camera . . .*

Yes, that's the only time the camera moves, the camera starts to move toward the window and looks out of the window because Hombre looks at the window and says: "Someone is thinking of me," and then you see that barren place as the camera moves away in a half circle.

At that moment you hear on the sound track that otherworldly malaguena melody sung by a young Spanish girl, and then you see the landscape again, but this time from a distance and almost in a mist, as if the landscape were now being seen by a different and higher consciousness.

Yes, I direct animals and I also claim that you can even direct a landscape.

In Fata Morgana, *the narrator says: "In paradise you cross the sand without seeing your shadow. There is landscape even without deeper meaning."*

It's even stated twice. . . . There is something visionary about these landscapes, the way they're shown. Most of my films have their origins in locations and landscapes, and then they start to build up around those locations.

I'm looking for new images in film. I'm sick of the images in magazines, I'm sick of post cards, I'm sick of walking into a travel agency and seeing a Pan Am poster of the Grand Canyon: it's a waste of worn-out images. And somehow I have the positive knowledge of new images, like a far-distant strip of land on the horizon; I see new images and try to articulate them. I've tried to do this in *Fata Morgana* and in the dream sequences in *Kaspar Hauser*. I'm trying to discover our innermost conditioning; it's a very deep-down brooding knowledge.

We were listening before to some music of the thirteenth and fourteenth centuries: *that's* my time. Every person can be identified with a certain type of landscape or season. A man like De Gaulle—his landscape is Lorraine, and to me he's a November person. And perhaps a certain epoch of time would apply as well.

Some people have written that I'm a figure out of the nineteenth century, but they're wrong. The appropriate time for me would be the late Middle Ages. I feel close to the music and painting of that time. It would also fit the concept of my work. I don't feel like an artist, I feel like a craftsman. All the sculptors and painters of that period didn't regard themselves as artists, but rather as craftsmen, and they did professional work as craftsmen. That is exactly how I feel about my work as a film maker—as if I were anonymous, I couldn't even care.

I knew, for instance, that *Fata Morgana* was very frail, that the film itself was like a cobweb and very sensitive. I said to my friends: I've made a film now, but it has to be untouched. There shouldn't be any brutality. It shall be untouched, anonymous, I will keep it and show it only to my very best friend before I die. And this friend has to keep it, and before he dies must show it and hand it over to his best friend, and it should go on like that for a few generations . . . and only then might it be released. I kept the film for almost two years without showing it, and then I was somehow pushed into it, tricked into it. It makes sense that it's being shown, but I did have that idea of never releasing it. And in fact I have a short film that I've not shown to anyone for twelve years—it's called *Game in the Sand*. A rooster is the leading character in the film, by the way; it's about four children and a rooster.

There's one scene in Kaspar Hauser *showing a carnival in which we see Kaspar hired out as a freak-show oddity; Hombre, who appeared in* Even Dwarfs Started Small; *and the young Mozart in a trance, peering into the deep holes of the earth, "his mind engrossed in his own twilight." It's interesting that this little scene by itself seems to contain in microcosm most of the thematic cells and motifs of all your films.*

It was in fact the idea for an entire movie that I was thinking of making. Kaspar Hauser literally comes out of darkness, dwarfs come out when night is at its darkest, and many of my figures come from the very deep night. It is the dark night that's in my films.

I couldn't help feeling that Kaspar Hauser's impassioned and craggily imperfect piano performance of the Mozart sonata suggested that the spirit of Mozart was somehow entrapped in the sonata-allegro form itself.

Exactly, I feel so much compassion when I hear how Bruno played the piece. That's exactly right. People used to laugh at his performances because they'd say, "Oh, this is ridiculous and dilettantish," and I'd say, "No, this is the great cultural event of the year, it's not Bernstein or von Karajan: this agitation, this sheer agitation of the mind is culture. This is the true culture, that's what culture is; and therefore he's a great man, he is really great." People don't understand it, but they will.

There are two other wonderful scenes in Kaspar Hauser: *the desert dream sequence, for one, in which Kaspar is told that the mountains are just his imagination . . .*

The blindness of that old leader of the caravan . . . that's his virtue because he cannot be misled. He tastes the sand as if it were food and leads the people out of the desert because he's blind. This is his virtue . . .

And then the scene on the lake with the swan gliding . . .

And the boat. The boat drifts into it, but they don't row, they stopped rowing just outside the frame, and it just drifts into the frame. . . . For five consecutive nights the crew went to the lake at 3 A.M., and we waited until four, and each time there was something wrong; we wanted it a little foggy and there was no fog. That swan rests calmly at one point, and all of a sudden it starts to move, and the music . . . by Albinoni . . . we organized the music to the movement of the swan. Just look at how the animal starts to swim away and how the music pulls with it.

The most beautiful and privileged moments in your films either occur in silence ("Can't you hear that terrible screaming all around us that men call silence?" are the words that appear at the beginning of Kaspar Hauser) *or are accompanied by a music that seems to represent a kind of audible silence.*

Silence is very important in *Aguirre*, for example. We spent weeks recording birds' voices, and I composed the sound track out of eight tapes, and there isn't one single voice of a bird that isn't properly placed as if in a big choir. All of a sudden there is silence. And when there's silence, someone is going to die on the raft because it means that Indians must be hiding in the trees, and all the birds stop singing. Everybody's so afraid that they start to scream and shout and to fire their rifles in order not to hear the silence.

I also remember the eerie, noisy silence when the soldier goes mad in Signs of Life, *walking in that field filled with what looks like thousands of whirring windmills—I think that's one of the most haunting moments I've ever experienced in films.*

Yes, it starts with silence and then there's a very strange sound. I took a recording of the applause of about 1500 people after a concert and distorted this applause electronically in such a way that it sounds like the clacking of wood. Have you ever placed your ear against a telephone pole when there was a lot of wind? As children we used to call it the "angels singing." And that kind of sound goes over it. There were 10,000 windmills. People ask me what kind of trick I used, but it was nothing but a normal camera that looked across this field with 10,000 windmills. This is exactly what I was referring to before with regard to the new images I'm after: something that is even beyond what one can dream, something beyond our dreams.

I also remember one powerful scene in Even Dwarfs Started Small *in which you see scavenger chickens, then a willowlike tree with leaves in mist, then goggle-helmeted dwarfs with their sticks, sitting like little boys pretending to be kings in the stone garden . . .*

I really like that scene. You can't describe it and there are no words to explain the strength of those images. I'm glad you've seen these things.

And then there's that first image in Land of Silence and Darkness—*a ski jumper flying through the air and the innocent, wavering voice of a deaf and blind woman saying: "When I'm touched I jump."*

I asked the woman to say this line—she'd never seen a ski jumper—and I said: "This is going to be important for the film; maybe you don't understand, but please say this text for me as if you'd seen the ski jumper." I'm not a cinéma vérité person, I hate cinéma vérité, by the way. There is such a thing as the plain truth, but there are also different dimensions in truth—and in film there are more dimensions beyond the cinéma vérité truth. That's where it starts to become exciting.

In your films, these new forms of truth often occur when language disintegrates. There's that scene in Signs of Life *when the soldiers meet this young autistic girl . . .*

The two soldiers are on this reconnaissance, and they meet a shepherd who gives them water to drink. And there's that little girl, and he says: "This girl, my daughter, can hardly speak at all because it's so lonely up here. I'm out at night with the sheep and my wife is away during the day and we don't talk, so, even though she is seven years old, she can hardly talk at all. Sometimes she picks up a few words down in the town when she sees her aunt." And then all of a sudden, the father wants to demonstrate that his daughter is really all right, and he asks her: "Please, won't you say the words of a song for these gentlemen." And the girl starts to recite the text of a song, but all of a sudden she gets stuck, she loses her speech, and she starts to twist her skirt in despair, she's so upset. It's a poem I wrote myself about sheep, ninety-eight sheep in Lasithi Mountain (it's a mountain range in Crete), and one of them got lost. The text goes: "Hurry, ye shepherds, hurry. For over the range, there are circling the vultures." And she doesn't remember the word "vultures," so she hesitates on that word.

It's important that she loses her speech only minutes before the soldier goes insane. The same thing almost occurred to me when I climbed up that mountain and looked down into that valley with the 10,000 windmills. I sat down and it was at that very moment when I was sure I was insane. And I had a very hard time getting out of that place. . . . I claim that I'm not insane. I think the *others* are, or most of the others are. I think I make sense to some extent. But that was a moment when I felt I must be insane: it can't be true, it can't be real.

In all of my films, in moments of utmost despair, there's silence and an exchange of signals—people exchange some kind of signals. You don't see the soldier any more as a private person, as a psychological figure. You see him from a distance of four hundred yards away, like an ant, as little as that. And he gives signals or signs—the same kind of signs of violence and despair that he himself had received all the time. He wants to destroy the whole town with toy rockets. It's humiliating for him. It's such a humiliation that he only scorches a chair and he only manages to kill a donkey. And that's all, and then he's captured by his own people.

He lacks the divine madness of Kaspar Hauser, doesn't he?

But they are close to each other, too, because both try to articulate themselves and their loneliness.

The overwhelming intensity of your films makes some people feel that you lack a sense of irony.

I don't understand irony. I recently received a national film award, which gave me a lot of money for my next film. So two days after I had received a letter from the minister of the interior, the phone rang and I picked it up and a voice said: "This is the minister of the interior." And I said, "Well, sir. . . ." And that guy started to stutter: "I'm so sorry. We've made such a mistake that I personally had to call you up. We sent you a letter saying that you've received a big award, but it's a mistake. And I had to tell you." So I said: "Sir, how could this have happened? I mean, there are three signatures on this letter. It must have passed through three departments. It's all right, I accept this, but how can this have happened? How can this occur?" Then, after ten minutes of talking, this guy started to scream with laughter. And then I found out it was a friend of mine who was just pulling a trick on me. It's a habit to kid each other in the United States. But I'm just like a fool, I'm sitting around like a fool because I take it all literally. There are things in language that are common to many people, or to almost all, but they are lost on me. I have some defects of communication in the form of language.

I was very silent as a child, and violent. I was very choleric and really dangerous to other kids because I didn't speak for days, and they kept singing around me and just pulling on me, and all of a sudden there was an outburst of rage and violence and despair.

I read that after you finished making Even Dwarfs Started Small, *you jumped into a giant, seven-foot cactus.*

There were always catastrophes. During the shooting of that film, I was so shocked by the fact that one of the dwarfs caught fire—you know, they take gasoline to water the flowers and they set a flowerpot aflame, and all of a sudden one of those guys was just burning like a tree. And all of the rest of the crew looked at him as if this guy were a Christmas tree, with open eyes and giving them a beautiful stare. So I was the first one to react. I jumped over that little guy, buried him under me, and extinguished the flames—his face was only a little scorched. And then two days later the same guy was hit by the car that was circling around him. The guy fell and the empty car went right over him. That man just stood up and walked away, but when that occurred I couldn't continue and had to stop shooting.

There was a big field of cactuses, each with long spines as long as my finger. And I said to them, "If all of you survive this shooting, if all of you get out of it unhurt, I will do the big cactus leap, and you can have the camera." And so, the last day of shooting, when it was all over, they took the super-8-millimeter camera, I put on big goggles to protect my eyes, and I really took a big jump. Today there are still some spines in my knee sinews from the jump. The bad thing wasn't the leap itself but the getting out of it . . . that's painful. I suffered for half a year. I didn't imagine beforehand how painful it would be.

There were many catastrophes during the shooting of *Fata Morgana*, too. In the Cameroons we wanted to cross the country to get to an eastern Congolese province for some locations there. Unfortunately there was an aborted coup d'état a few weeks before we arrived. Some mercenaries had been involved in the whole thing, one of them was condemned to death in absentia, and unfortunately, the cameraman had almost an identical name to one of the mercenaries. So we were captured at night and dragged into prison, I had malaria and a very bad parasitic disease. We were hardly able to hold the camera still because we were shaking with fever and we were locked into a room that was maybe 15′ × 18′, but there were more than seventy people cramped together in that room. There was no light, no water, and two people were tortured to death. And we were very badly mistreated there. It went on like that, too. There was a warrant out for us all over the country. And either on purpose or out of slovenliness the officials forgot to destroy that warrant. So every time we passed through a town, we were arrested.

Just before the shooting of *Signs of Life*, the military coup d'état occurred in Greece, and everything was forbidden to us. I was forbidden to have fireworks in my film. I told the army major: "It's so essential, it's the main motif in the film. This film is more important than your private life and my private life. And you're just scared because you might do something wrong when you allow this. I will do it, even though it's forbidden." And he said: "Then we'll arrest you." And I said to him: "Go on and arrest me. But I won't be without a firearm tomorrow. Keep in mind that the very first man who touches me, who lays a hand on me to arrest me, will drop down dead with me." And I was not unarmed next morning. There were fifty policemen and soldiers who watched us, and 3000 people of the town who wanted to see the fireworks; they all watched us and nobody dared to touch me.

It seems to me that Aguirre *is about a man who takes his imagination to be reality and that* Kaspar Hauser *is about a person who takes reality to be his imagination.*

That's a good formula. And my new film is in between *Aguirre* and *Kaspar Hauser*—both stylistically, in terms of the images and action, and thematically, in terms of the idea of the striving for something . . . not for Eldorado this time but for a special ruby glass.

The film is called *Heart of Glass* and it's about a legendary prophet in Bavarian folklore—a shepherd with prophetic gifts and visions. The story is mine and tells of a disaster at a glass factory. The prophet is called in because the secret required for the mixture of this very valuable glass has been lost. Everyone becomes halfway insane and the prophet foresees that the factory is going to burn down. At the end, the factory owner performs a ritual murder of a fifteen-year-old servant girl, thinking that virgin blood in the mixture will create rubies. He burns his own place down, as foreseen, but the prophet is blamed for it and is imprisoned. Here he has a vision of a place so remote from the inhabited world that the few people living there haven't learned that the world is round. And the prophet has a vision of a man standing on the cliff and staring for years over the ocean. And years later a second person joins him, then another, until four men stand over the ocean which, for them, ends in an abyss. And after many years of hypnotic staring, they decide to take a rowboat and find the end of the world. . . . Most of the film was shot in a glass factory and in a forest in northern Bavaria. And the prophet's vision was shot fifteen miles off the west Irish coast on a little island where monks built a settlement 1400 years ago.

I've heard that you hypnotized the members of your cast for this film.

I have to say that I was interested in hypnosis mainly for the way it could be used as a means of stylization. We tested out about 450 people; we needed persons who could be hypnotized under very difficult circumstances—standing around with reflectors shining on them and with a lot of activity going on. And they had to be hypnotized so deeply that they could open their eyes without waking up. However, we rehearsed the basic movements and lines of the dialogue without hypnosis.

During the tryouts, I wanted to find out about the poetic quality of the cast, so I hypnotized them and said: "You are in a beautiful and exotic land which no person from our country has ever set foot on. Look in front of you—there is an enormous cliff, but on looking at it more closely you'll find that it's actually one solid piece of emerald." And I continued: "In this country, a couple of hundred years ago, a holy monk lived here and he was a poet and he spent his entire life engraving just one inscription into this emerald cliff." And I said: "Open your eyes, you can read this inscription."

And one of the men there who tends to the horses in the police stable—he took a look, opened his eyes, and read: *"Why can't we drink the moon? Why is there no vessel to hold it?"* And the guy next to him was a law student. He took a look and started to read: *"Dear Mother, I am doing fine, I just don't know where we're going, but I think everything is all right. Hugs and kisses, Your Son."*

WALTER LOWENFELS

The Poet
in the
Flying Suit

May 10, 1897–July 7, 1976

To think of roses and gardens inside is bad,
to think of seas and mountains is good.
Read and write without stopping to rest,
and I also advise weaving,
and also making mirrors.
I mean it's not that you can't pass
    ten or fifteen years inside,
       and more even—
   you can,
   as long as the jewel
   in the left side of your chest doesn't lose its luster!

      —Nazim Hikmet: "Some Advice to Those Who
        Will Serve Time in Prison"
        (trans. by Randy Blasing and Mutlu Konuk)

I't's always better to call than not to call. And it was none too soon when, in late May of 1975, I decided to phone the then seventy-eight-year-old poet, anthologist, and political activist Walter Lowenfels in Peekskill, New York.

"Hello, is Mr. Lowenfels there?"

"Mr. Lowenfels?" replied the sparkling, fake-gruff voice. "Call me Walter . . . as in Walther von der Vogelweide."

"Walter," I said, "I've read a few of your wonderful poems in the past, and I've just chanced upon a little volume of yours entitled *The Revolution Is to Be Human*. I opened the book and came across the following words: 'I suppose the last poem we can see ahead now is the rhythm of producing and distributing—from the grass on the fields to the milk from the cow to the human bloodstream—all synchronized in a living dance where action and belief are one and people are reunited to natural things, but on a different hypotenuse. . . . *When the tragedy of the world market no longer dominates our existence, unexpected gradations of being in love with being here will emerge.*' Passages like these took my breath away, and I'd really like to meet and find out about you."

"Of course," said Walter, "but you'd better do it soon. The doctors don't think I'm going to live forever."

"When I was trying to find out where you lived," I mentioned, "someone told me that one of your ambitions was to outlive the Two-Party System."

"Well," Walter considered, "I thought I'd make it to my nineties. But just in case I don't, why not come up to Manna's graduation party on June 7. We'll say hello there."

Manna Lowenfels Perpelitt is one of Walter's four vital daughters—a talented poet and teacher, the mother of three kids, the executor of her father's literary estate, and a person who, in her conversation and letters, reminds you of the intensity and magnanimity of Walter Lowenfels himself. Like her twin sister Judy (who was given the name Dew when she was born), Manna lives a short car ride's distance from Walter's house on the outskirts of Peekskill, a fairly depressed, small industrial city about forty miles north of New York—the scene, in 1949, of a notorious American Legion–inspired race riot, occasioned by the appearance at a local concert of Paul Robeson.

Manna, who had gone back to college (State University of New York at New Paltz), was hosting a party in honor of her graduation, and her guests that night—writers, musicians, boarders, and friends—included Earl Robinson (composer of *Ballad for Americans* and "Joe Hill"), folk singer Barbara Dane, and Miriam and Walter Schneir (authors of *Invitation to an Inquest: Reopening the Rosenberg "Atom Spy" Case*). The food was delicious, the communal music jam lively, and the spirit of the guests was a testament to the fact that not all left-wing humanists have felt it necessary to turn themselves into sour and crabbed right-wing apostates—smugly judging and betraying, on hindsight, the dreams of their youth.

Everyone knew that Walter had cancer and was terminally ill, but no one was moping or feeling solicitous. After all, Walter himself had once written: "When you participate in the future and help transform life, you also transform death." And when he arrived in lively spirits—the proud guest of honor—wearing a tiger-decorated yellow dashiki and dark beret, I thought of some other characteristic Lowenfels maxims: "I am saying that it is through participation in singing, dancing, the creativity of poems, of any art form—all of them part of the business of remaking the world—that we enter into the mysteries of what's really going on. . . . In a word, my point of view might be summed up as follows: The goal of life isn't socialism; the goal of socialism is to live. . . . If you have to grow old, please do it in a worthy cause, and don't get a heart attack or arthritis in your 60's because you roamed the fields not with Corydon or Chloe but with tiny invisible Profit and Loss."

After greeting all of his friends, Walter took me aside, chatted with me, and autographed a copy of his latest published little book, *Reality Prime: Pages from a Journal*, which I took to a quiet room, opened, and read:

> You can say this 3,000 times and it won't be solved: We are the sad songs of a lost race.
>
> I salute the new dinosaurs.
>
> Tomorrow is a jet wing.
>
> The main point is to have no regrets for anything unsaid.
>
> I mean—there comes a time when you can no longer say it all.
>
> Is it my fault this is a dress rehearsal for the real performance?
>
> We are alive on the bias, on an angle to the possibilities. Who catches up with Mozart at the age of 15? Or Lenin at the age of 45?
>
> What we hear is the obvious—songs of marriage, love, sex, joy, death screams, feeding, little peeps from new-born chicks and grunts from older ones who stub their toes.
>
> What Coltrane heard was the blaze of Andromeda chasing its spiral tail.

My next meeting with Walter occurred a week later at the Unitarian Meeting House, Croton-on-Hudson—the scene of a memorial service for Walter's wife and literary collaborator of some forty years, Lillian, who had died on May 9.

If I had called a couple of months earlier, I would have met this remarkable woman. Lillian Apotheker's father was a Yiddish scholar and writer, a humorist whose pen name was Hinke Dinke Schlemazel ("Limping Ne'er-do-Well") and who had died when Lillian was a child—a legendary character who liked to tell about his having escaped from Czarist Russia in a sauerkraut barrel. "There were prodigious aunts, uncles, sisters," Walter recalls. "Lillian came complete, not only with youth and a college degree, but also with family." Walter met her in New York in 1924, and they were married in Paris two years later following a stormy courtship, after which they honeymooned for the rest of their lives—celebrating two wedding dates: June 19, when they made up old quarrels, and September 28, when the ceremony actually took place.

In 1958, Lillian suffered a stroke, which has been attributed to a high blood-pressure condition, aggravated by her being called up

before the House Un-American Activities Committee four years earlier, because of which she was fired from her teaching job in Philadelphia. The day she was hospitalized, Walter went to the hospital
and worked at her bedside on the translation of a twenty-three-page
poem by Paul Eluard, *Poésie Ininterrompue*—or, as Walter called it
in English, *The Poem That Can't Be Stopped*—a translation which he
had undertaken with Lillian's help and which concludes:

> As for spring it's just waking up
> Your mouth tastes of the morning sun
> Your eyes live forever
>   Putting everthing in the right place
>
> The two of us you naked
> I everything that I have become
>
> You the root of our seed
> I with hands open
>   Like my eyes
>
> The two of us we live only to be
> Faithful to being alive

A hemiplegic for the last seventeen years of her life, Lillian
was cared for almost entirely by her husband. And when, in 1965, she
went for several months to a rehabilitation clinic in Budapest in one
final and unsuccessful attempt to regain movement in her left side,
Walter wrote:

It's easier to communicate with the nebula known as The
Crab, from which we get radio noises that don't say a thing to
us (except that it's very hot, like three billion degrees) than to
wig-wag across the semaphore of being one-armed in a two-
armed world. But if you look at it the other way, the handi-
capped are We who never can feel what *they* live; and to think
we do and can tell them what to do is the real insanity, a parallel
in our "peaceful way" of the marines thinking they can tell the
Vietnamese via napalm and B-52 Bombers how to live (as the
President says) "in peace."

But there is no peace in the world for the one-legs and
one-arms. It's just lesser and greater degrees of torment and
curses at why should it have been Me? What did I do? A million
Jobs cursing God, but there is no God, so even your hemiplegic
curses roll back on you with the thunder of the inevitable—the
laws of chance that rule this world of statistics so that you, for

no reason at all, have one ear instead of two and Marianthe has almost none.

I look around the streets and rooms for people who are minus something or are in wheel chairs or crutches. When I see a man with a seeing-eye dog—my heart jumps and I cry "Comrade!"—only softly, so as not to embarrass him.

At the memorial service for Lillian on June 15, I met the oldest and youngest of the Lowenfels daughters—Michal and Angela, who live in Pottstown, Pennsylvania, and Chicago respectively—and most of Walter's and Lillian's twelve grandchildren. Writers Clarence Major, Nancy Willard, and Millard Brand read tributes, and Pete Seeger sang several songs. But most of all I remember someone getting up to read Walter's "For Lillian"—a poem about how showering becomes a form of devotion and adoration:

Let's get a bulldozer
plough up every street we ever lived,
    begin all over from scratch
as if it were the first day
    we met and you were lame
but I never noticed
    because you were so much you
and did everything your own way
    anyhow.
Believe me it's not all gloomy
    like when you're half-paralyzed
and showering is an agony
    on a hard chair,
we can always rely
    on doing it together—
    you hold the shower rail
and I hold you
    and what love
        can be purer or cleaner
than going into the shower
    hugging each other?
        Just to stand up
and get soaped
    clean to the end,
so happy you don't have to
    wash alone in that cold
hospital chair.
    So, as I said,
        it's not all gloomy—

just a question of balance.
I love you
even though all I say is
"please pass the soap."

Two weeks later, Manna met me at the Peekskill train station and drove me to Walter's unpretentious, unabashedly messy, two-bedroom house. ("You will never be remembered for your cleanliness," was one of his mottoes.) The study was a veritable gallimaufry —manuscripts scattered about, files bulging open, little magazines on the floor. Nailed up on the walls or on any surface that would accept a tack were little pieces of paper containing short, typed statements and proclamations: "Your strength is the only roof that can shelter my dying"—Trien Vu, Vietnamese poet to the children; "To be cultured is to be free"—José Martí; "There are millions of suns left"—Whitman; "It is only the young who possess the world"—Sean O'Casey.

Walter's dining room—"wall-to-wall disorganization" is the way Manna described it—also served as a library overflowing with books by Marx and Lenin, Artaud and Miller (Henry), histories of the American labor movement and civil rights struggles, and a special bookcase devoted to Walter's own, mostly out-of-print works. A copy of *Thou Shalt Not Overkill: Walter Lowenfels' Peace Poems* was on the dining-room table, while on a shelf above it—leaning against a wall—was a sign: CAUTION . . . YOU ARE NOW ENTERING A RADIATION AREA.

Manna had told me that Walter was feeling tired because of his ongoing cobalt therapy, but he greeted me as if his wife had never died, as if he were going to live forever, and we went outside to the garden.

"I've tried talking to my tumor in order to reduce it," Walter said to me, laughing. "But I've been getting mumbo-jumbo results, so I'm thinking of taping it and sending the tape to a linguist who will probably tell me that *tumorese* is a lost language."

"Well, Walter," I say, "I'm here to find out about you."

"Then you should ask me about butter," he obliged. "When I was young, you know, I was in my family's butter business. In my autobiography I wrote: 'For me, butter was a huge, independent world, as self-contained as a spiral nebula. It was the galaxy of business.'

"You see, I got into the business—Frederick Lowenfels and

Sons, which later became Hotel Bar Butter—because I had problems as a kid. I spent a year at De Witt Clinton High School in the Bronx, but I was always cutting classes in order to see vaudeville shows at the Colonial Theater—Nora Bayes, Eva Tanguay, and Bert Williams were some of my favorite stars.

"So then my father enrolled me in the Horace Mann school. I went there for six months but didn't do too well. I was sent to two other schools, the second of which was on West End Avenue. There were three or four students in a class—mostly problem kids—and we were primed for College Entrance Exams. Well, I got some of the lowest marks ever recorded in those exams. I learned something about Shakespeare, though: I remember we had to do things like write additional stage directions for *Macbeth*.

"Next, I went to work as an office boy at an insurance agency, and then came butter jobbing . . . tub butter. . . . My brother transformed it into a wholesale business, and I went out to the Midwest—Illinois, Iowa, Minnesota—as an egg-and-butter buyer. I hired a horse and wagon and drove to the country stores.

"Nineteen seventeen came around, and everyone I knew was in the Army. I wanted to join the Canadian Air Force, but my parents wouldn't give me permission. When I volunteered for the U. S. Army Air Corps, I was asked what I knew about engines. I flunked. So I went to Pratt Institute to learn about mechanics.

"Six months later I got into the Army. Now, during that time, all the good people, like Eugene Debs, were fighting against the war, but I had no sense of that at all. It wasn't that I was illiterate just about war and peace and politics in those days . . . I was completely square about contemporary culture. Rimsky-Korsakov's *Scheherazade* was my favorite piece then, and while Ives and Schoenberg were tearing out their hearts writing unheard masterpieces, I was at the opera standing up for Wagner or clapping wildly for Kreisler playing his nineteenth-century divertimentos.

"So I was a cadet with a uniform and a white thing around my hat, and I sold Liberty Bonds. Finally, the orders came for me to go to Texas for preliminary training. Awful, awful. Marching in the sun, parading, maneuvering. Then back up to M.I.T. for six months to learn how to take airplanes apart and how to use the Morse code. But soon they announced that there weren't enough airplanes, and I was dropped.

"I next was sent to a base on Long Island, where I became

head K.P. of the Officers' Mess—a sinecure. I had four or five guys working for me, peeling potatoes. And then came the saddest day of my life—the Armistice. I went to New York, saw my girlfriend, Gabrielle, and everyone was celebrating. But it was the false armistice . . . then the real one.

"I'm a veteran of World War I.

"From 1919 until 1926 I began to get very good in butter. We had big shippers in Omaha, Toledo—everywhere. Now, during this time my father retired, and I started to write. I used to go to concerts a lot, and one night I was sitting next to a friend of mine named Aaron. He was squirming in his seat, and when I wondered why, he told me that he was trying to write a poem to a girl. I asked him to let me look. The lines read: 'I come to you with flowers in my hand, but you can't see the flowers in my heart'—something like that. He couldn't make it rhyme, so I said that I'd see what I could do. I bought a book that taught you how to write sonnets, ballades, rondels, and as I began to learn these forms, I began to have things to say.

"I used to take a pencil to bed in case I got an inspiration during the night. Well, my first poem was published in F.P.A.'s column in the *Daily Mail*—it was a ballade for Edna St. Vincent Millay. But the first of my poems that amounted to anything was "Epistle to C.S. on Mine Burial in Illinois." It was a poem about the Herrin miners killed in a strike in Illinois, who hadn't been buried properly. I read about it in the *Evening Sun*, and this theme—death without burial—continued to obsess me for a long time. Carl Sandburg, to whom the poem was dedicated, wrote me a letter about it that was better than the poem itself: 'I know the ashes and tears of all its lines. It is a document and a chant.'

"So I published a few more poems in various magazines, and then a book entitled *Episodes and Epistles* (1925), which Lillian helped me put together. The only poem that stands out is one called "From an Exposition of Power and Industrial Machinery"—it's made up of industrial words, and begins:

Open float inspirator and injector
super simplex pulverizer
gyrating cruster
armature spider
quick-change chuck and collet
clipper-belt lacer

expanding lathe mandrel
non-return vertical indicator
multiwhirl baffle . . .

"I decided then that I'd have to do better, and that I'd rather die as a poet than as a butter man. So I told my father I was going to quit his business. He just couldn't believe it, and he said: I want you to get checked up physically. I said O.K., so he told me to go to a doctor, who asked me to bring my book of poems and a urine specimen. When I got into the office, this doctor told me to lie down. (It turned out that he was a psychiatrist!) I told him: Look, I'm going to Europe. My father is the man who's sick, try to take care of *him*. So my father sent me to another psychiatrist who told my father that I should see Dr. Freud. My father said he'd pay for it, but I never went. I took a slow boat to Spain and never got to Vienna."

Walter has described his life in Paris in the first of a four-part autobiography entitled *My Many Lives*. And this still-unpublished first volume, *Paris Chapters*, is one of the most entertaining and informative glimpses of expatriate literary, cultural, and political life yet written.

To support themselves and their enlarging family, Lillian worked as a fashion correspondent and editor, while Walter typed manuscripts, worked as a ghost writer, and finally became a real estate agent. His friend Michael Fraenkel—an encyclopedia salesman who made enough money to come to Paris to write several now-forgotten works—taught him how to rent apartments to arty, rich Americans by placing ads in the Paris edition of the *Herald Tribune* that read: "Bullet-proof windows . . . hanging balconies . . . indoor garden . . . no pianist need apply . . . don't bother to knock . . . key under mat." (Walter's tenants included Tristan Tzara, Marc Chagall, Archibald MacLeish, and John Peale Bishop.)

With Fraenkel, Lowenfels launched the Anonymous movement, which advanced the notion of total anonymity in the arts. "Anonymous," they wrote with idealistic enthusiasm, "establishes the art as an ideal, not the ego. In an age when morale is collapsing, Anonymous is a discipline for disciplined artists. By remaining anonymous, the artist dedicates to all creation what is most important—his own creative efforts. He merges his individual creative consciousness in the total creative consciousness of the world. All art becomes the joint manifestation of every individual artist. The poet is merged with poetry; the musician with music; the playwright, actor, painter, director, with the theatre."

As Walter wrote later: "Wonderful ideal—realized once upon a time in primitive societies. Consider, for example, the anonymous masks and other great sculptures of African and Oceanic peoples; the wall paintings of the Cro-Magnons; Mayan and Aztec temples; totem poles and crystal skulls of other Amerindians. That era of anonymity passed away with primitive communism; we did not bring it back to life in 1930 with a 32-page pamphlet."

Between the rise and fall of Anonymous, its publishing arm, Carrefour Press, printed a novel by Fraenkel, an Anonymous Manifesto, and Walter's play *U.S.A. with Music.** Because they lacked the money, Lowenfels and Fraenkel had to pass up publishing anonymous books by F. Scott Fitzgerald (about his father), Michael Arlen, and Samuel Beckett. As Walter recalls the meeting with Beckett: "I talked myself dry explaining our theory of anonymity in the arts and its relation to the desolate condition of society. Beckett nodded and said nothing. Finally I burst out, 'You sit there saying nothing while the world is going to pieces. What do you want? What do you want to do?' Beckett crossed his long legs and drawled: 'Walter, all I want to do is sit on my ass and fart and think of Dante.' "

In the late twenties and early thirties, Paris was still the crown of the avant-garde causeway.† Little magazines and small presses were springing up everywhere. Mina Loy spoke of the "crisis of consciousness," Eugene Jolas of the "revolution of the word," Gertrude Stein of the "actual present," and Ezra Pound of "making it new."

Harry Crosby was using found forms and concrete poetry—all

* Based on the Herrin miners' strike that had inspired Walter's earlier poem to Carl Sandburg, the play was considered too dangerous politically to be given a first performance in Berlin—with music to be written by George Antheil and Kurt Weill. Lowenfels launched an unsuccessful plagiarism suit against *Of Thee I Sing*—claiming the authors had stolen scenes and dialogue from his play—but in so doing he had to come out of anonymity and thereby rang Anonymous' death knell.

† Three excellent books that deal with this period, as well as with Walter Lowenfels particularly and with American avant-garde poetry and publishing generally, are: Kenneth Rexroth's *American Poetry in the Twentieth Century*, Jerome Rothenberg's *Revolution of the Word*, and Hugh Ford's *Published in Paris*—the last of which, along with a special issue of *Small Press Review* (No. 23), contains the only extensive material about Lowenfels to date.

related to sun mythology and imagery. Bob Brown experimented with "optical" poetry and a tachistoscope-like reading machine. Abraham Lincoln Gillespie wrote "soundpieces" in a bizarre notation that anticipated the work of Jackson MacLow and John Cage. And the painter De Hirsch Margulies sat on the quays of the Seine and painted pictures in the dark. In fact, the first exhibition of these paintings, which could be seen only in a darkened room, took place in Walter's Paris apartment.

Poets were deranging their syntax and their senses, and many committed suicide during this period: Crane, Crosby, Mayakovsky, Rigaud, Essenine. "Death is the moral force of the world," Walter had stated in 1929. "We had the idea that the world was dead and that the only thing you could do was to write poems about it." And between 1929 and 1934, Lowenfels composed his *Some Deaths* series—experimental, yet stately, long modernist reveries (which he called "philosophical elegies") on the deaths of Apollinaire, D. H. Lawrence, and Hart Crane. The last and perhaps the best of these—echoing lightly both Whitman and even Swinburne—was called *The Suicide*, and concludes (in its revised version):

> Forgive him, sea-petals,
>   remember him not
>   (as you will not)
> lipped by the wave,
>   sea-moulded among the conches.
>
> His straw was in the wind
>   running like an idiot,
>   with moss in the ears—
> devising plans for killing rats,
>   for evading stenches—
> stabbing at the heart
>   to sustain himself
> among the walkers and the riders
>   and the heaven-borne.
>
> Creep into the sockets,
>   old man of the sea,
> come down into the skull.
> Only his song
>   pounds the Atlantic Highlands,
>   looking, America, for you.

Under the aegis of Fraenkel, Lowenfels and Henry Miller formed the unofficial "death school" of poetry (see Lowenfels' and

Howard McCord's *The Life of Fraenkel's Death: A Biographical Inquest*), and this triumvirate whiled away many evenings together in "death talk." Walter, of course, was the model for the magniloquent and manic Jabberwhorl Cronstadt in Henry Miller's *Black Spring*. And in a letter to Anaïs Nin, Miller described his friend Lowenfels after what must have been a particularly memorable conversation one night in 1934:

> Something snapped in me last night. I saw the drunken poet, the goat in the man, the veils sundering, the cosmic pulse shaking his leg, illustrating his technique, exorcising his abstractions. I saw what Dostoevski permits us to see when he dives into that plasmic soul stuff in which only the divine is recognizable. I saw all the poets of creation and I wanted to shout out: Mother, mother, my heart's on fire! I saw the pictures of Picasso chanting the doxology of reason, saw the steel frame of our world sagging, the whole gaseous vertebrate of life reeling in dissolution. I see Lowenfels as probably *the* poet of the age, a fine relaxed image of a man with his Janus-faced door greeting all and sundry, his hearth full of cigarettes, his gizzards whiting with Pernod, his lust for life animating all the biological processes, down to the amoeba. Saw life in its scission and fission, saw life glad, glairy and glabrous, and *healthy and wealthy* and gladrous. Saw myself writing poems over the walls, over my frescoes, over my palaces of entrails, saw my pineal eye winking and blinking, throwing off the cover of the middle brain; I saw the personification of all poetry, the man rooted in earth and blood, the dumdum bullets of his brain splashing against the ceiling of the sky, encrusting the oysters with pearls, sewing the cosmos with gem-studded ideas dripping flesh and gore; I heard the weasels of his poems running through all the cellars of music, the scratching of their paws on mica eyes, the screech of his voice in isolation, the wild hysteria of his longing. He opened the accordion of his mind and it collapsed with a bang. He ran a dagger through his heart and it burned away. He opened his blood vessels and music poured from his veins. He is the man I have been looking for and I found him with my pineal eye. He is the man I have created in my loneliness and his image is heartening.

Reading Lowenfels' autobiography, one gets the impression that he knew every writer in, or passing through, Paris. He lunched with a cranky Ezra Pound (in 1959, Walter wrote a public letter supporting the campaign to release Pound from jail, saying, "There are enough crazy people in our Capitol without adding Pound to the list"), collaborated with Ford Madox Ford in an article for *Harper's* on the Stavisky riots, became close friends with Nancy Cunard and Norman Douglas, befriended and lent money to Gurdjieff ("Gurdjieff elevated charlatanism into a world principle. The miracle about this man is that he had a sense of the uncertainties and the immediacies of being alive that he transmitted to others, but nobody seems to have sensed that he was a great comedian in the tradition of Gogol and Aristophanes"), and had tea with T. S. Eliot:

> As we sipped tea I told Eliot how startled I had been when he had proclaimed his general point of view as "classical in literature, royalist in politics, and Anglo-Catholic in religion."
> "What are your interests, Mr. Lowenfels, aside from poetry?"
> "I used to be interested in butter."
> "So you have told us—'my brother rests among the butter,'" Eliot said, reading from a copy of my *Elegy for D. H. Lawrence* he had on his desk.
> "Now I'm studying Marx and Engels. I'm afraid the proletariat is the only way out—'to renew and rebuild civilization and save the world from suicide.'"
> Eliot smiled, recognizing I, in turn, was quoting from his "Thoughts after Lambeth."
> "The proletariat may be your solution, but you don't seem to be very happy about it." He opened my Lawrence elegy and read a passage: "We are the human image of the thing/past the eventide of being/cast in fossils in the flesh...".
> "That was written before I found out that human history is just beginning. Also, I don't propose that poems will cure the world. In fact, my next book is called *The Suicide*. But whether or not it pleases me, I'm convinced the world's suicidal trend will be cured only when a different class of people take over from our present rulers. That will take place independent of any individual will. There is no other way out."
> "I think there is." Eliot smiled. "More tea?"

The three-cornered friendship of Fraenkel, Miller, and Lowenfels eventually came apart. Miller and Fraenkel began work on their *Hamlet* correspondence—a series of letters to each other (eventually collected in a two-volume book) about the death of the world—which, they hoped, would be the "longest funeral sermon in history." But already in 1932, Walter had started to read the works of Karl Marx seriously, and in that year he wrote to both Fraenkel and Miller: "The insoluble contradictions arising in the social structure are reflected in the personality of the poet. We go to pieces inwardly and, as we sing, toss up brittle pieces of ourselves. And what is it that we have reflected? Nothing more than that Mellon owns all the aluminum in the world and it's killing us."

In 1934, Walter and his family returned to the United States. And except for a small volume entitled *Steel, 1937*—poems about the Spanish Civil War and the CIO drive to organize Little Steel—he ceased writing verse until the early fifties. From 1938 to 1954 he worked as a reporter for, and later as the editor of, the Pennsylvania edition of the *Daily Worker*.

In a letter of reminiscence to his sister-in-law, Nan Braymer, in 1964, Walter explained and connected his many lives:

I never gave up my belief in death. Perhaps that's the essential continuity between my years as a poet in Paris, then as a reporter and editor of the *Daily Worker*, and thereafter my return to poems. There was a change, but the essential difference was in locating the source of the putrefaction and the life growing out of it. My integration to the working class and a Marxist outlook wasn't based on any temporary or fluctuating emotion or situation—such as unemployment, hunger, discrimination. I knew from my beginnings as a poet that we were surrounded in the United States by death. Later I found it was a world-wide disease, and cureable. No matter how the ups and downs of the struggle shook me, I was able to survive all the betrayals, disasters, defeats, because I had already taken as an irreducible fact the old world's disintegration, and I knew there was only one way out—a totally new social realignment. . . .

It's not only that you can't step into the same waters twice, as Herakleitos told us, but you can't die in the same way twice, because death too is always changing. That is what I started to document over 30 years ago when I started *Some Deaths* in Paris and even asked for a Guggenheim grant after the work was under way to research the change in burial customs—which struck me as one way of documenting the changing attitudes about death, the soul, graves. I went overboard on it and wrote "death is the moral force of the world," and that's the way I finally arrived at life—through death. My researches finally led me to Hegel and thence to Marx and the discovery that it wasn't "the world" *en tout* that was death to the creative process to which I was dedicated, but that layer of the world that dominates the northwestern hemisphere.

I began attending rallies at the Salle Bullier on the Boulevard St. Michel . . . turning toward the "real world" unconsciously and instinctively like a heliotropic plant. Remembering now the poster I saw in front of the hall of a rally to be held for the Scottsboro Boys, with a picture of one of the Scottsboro mothers, Mrs. Wright, I went to the meeting, stood in the back of the crowded hall and saw for the first time posters with slogans on them—"Free Ernest Thaelman" . . . "Free the Scottsboro Boys" . . . "For Peace and Socialism," . . . and heard dimly the speakers, not only Mrs. Wright but the French Communists of the day, whose names I forget and whose words I forget, but it stirred some curiosity in me in relation to the dead world of burials I was documenting. . . .

So I reached the end of that death in Paris through a combination of research, frustration, and the fertility of death as subject; reading Marx about two classes, which I saw as the living and dead, "class war" carrying on the fertility rites of Dionysus I had been studying in the Bibliothèque Nationale . . . the death of winter, the birth of spring. . . . And afterward the workers and the national liberation movements were not to me just a *Ding an sich*—they were the "moral force of the world" without which death would rule forever and there was no fertility left except suicide. . . .

So if you wonder how it is I remained a socialist all my life thereafter, with all the geological pressure to which we all have been subjected, you can see that there is something to what Harold Rosenberg says, "O Walter, he belongs to a party all his own." Of course, the party of spring eternal and life everlasting against the long winter of the old God we are burying—not in the way we should, but in the only way we can.

The fact that Walter Lowenfels was a visionary humanist writer should not disguise the fact that, like millions of people around the world, he was a loyal, unvacillating, dedicated Communist. In no way did he ever become a fink or betray his beliefs or party. Even after the revelations of the Stalin era, Walter never lost his faith, writing: "We are saying good-bye to our childhood. It is not easy at my age, 59, to grow up. What lies beyond the horizon for us all, I believe, is the real contour of human beings—not their make-believe, but what they really are. . . . I don't care how terrible the truth is, as long as we know it and live it. Otherwise, one lives unborn, wrapped in the dreamy cocoon of the never-was."

And shortly after his wife's death, Walter wrote: "The last night before Lillian died I attended my local meeting of the Communist Party. Lillian stayed home. At the meeting I paid our dues. Lillian's dues were 50 cents. I was given a stamp to paste in her Party book. When I returned home I showed her her stamp and pasted it in her book. So Lillian died a dues-paying member. I keep thinking of that because it gives her a continuity. She carries on among the hundreds of millions of Communists who carry on her beliefs here and throughout the world. We who are Communists all share this continuity and are part of the ever-growing youth of the world."

On July 23, 1953, FBI agents raided Walter's New Jersey home at two A.M.—"eight men pointing revolvers converged on my typewriter as if it were a machine-gun emplacement"—and arrested him for trial under the Smith Act for "conspiring to teach and advocate the overthrow of the government by force and violence." Held on $100,000 bail, he spent several weeks in jail before bail was lowered to $10,000. During his six-month trial Walter composed sonnets, translated poems by Dante and Baudelaire, and wrote: "A large part of my adult life has been spent trying to overthrow not only the government but the universe. I thought I had the ideal weapon—the word. That's the way it all began, according to a respected source. In any just society a criminal like me would be judged on the efficacy of his weapons—in my case, poems. Instead, I and my fellow defendants were tried for somebody else's words—and not words in poems, either. The words used against us at our trial were prose passages from Karl Marx and his descendants. The prosecution, fortunately, didn't quote the poems Marx wrote in his youth. They didn't even cite Lenin's observations about a period in the 1880's when, he said, all poets were socialists and all socialists were poets; they chose, rather, passages from *State and Revolution*, as interpreted by FBI Marxists."

Walter's case was eventually thrown out on appeal for lack of evidence.

The American Communist Party has not been known for its hospitality to or tolerance for poets. "I'm the only American poet who was able to survive in the Party," Walter told me. And it's a bit difficult to understand how he did survive, since his idea of a "singing Communist movement" and his belief that "the crime is to live out of yesterday's illusions" must have made him a bureaucrat's nightmare.

"Maybe it's a mistake to have a poem read at the Communist Party Convention?" Walter wrote Communist leader Ben Davis in 1957. "O.K.! Let's make that kind of mistake. It will be a mistake in the real USA tradition—of being dreamers, of having that fool notion that there is going to be heaven on earth where we—all humanity—will be the masters of machines not their victims and so, masters of all human destiny. One of our native Indian nations has a name for it—they call themselves 'the Earth People.' That is what we are becoming and have to become in order to survive. . . . Let us show that we are for the kind of socialism in the USA that doesn't make robots of people but brings out all the creative forces locked in each human cylinder. . . . One danger we face is that we will pass a resolution to be more human."

And in an extraordinary Open Letter to Nikita Khrushchev, first published in the *New World Review*, Walter attacked Zhdanov-type criticisms of modern art:

In downgrading jazz, for example, perhaps you were referring to third-rate stuff that can be heard in Warsaw, Berlin, Moscow, as well as Paris, London, New York. At its best, jazz is one of the outstanding contributions to world culture that Africa and Afro-Americans have made. (Lumumba stressed that in his final poem.)

The contemporary world is inconceivable without Florence Mills, Scott Joplin, W. C. Handy, and their contemporary successors, John Coltrane, Charles Mingus, and dozens of other great creative artists. The struggle for the rightful place of jazz in world culture is not purely an aesthetic problem. It can't be dissociated from the struggle of Negroes to walk, or go to church, or school, or work, in Alabama, Johannesburg, or anywhere else. . . .

In the USA, most artists and most audiences don't know they have a new problem to face, because most of them don't have a socialist perspective. Therefore, they live in yesterday's world, in yesterday's art. That may be all right for them, and each may get something out of it, but when you have a socialist perspective you have a great responsibility to keep on time. . . .

Humanity will find its way ahead via inexorable laws. We are heading toward a humanity who will take those laws for granted, and will be asking: "What else, what's the whole story about? What did you see in that kiss or that rose or that barricade you stormed that nobody else saw?"

We want the inaudible now. Nothing less will do.

When I see masks made by "primitives," Eskimos, American Indians, Africans—I see mirror images of some of our experiences and some of our poems where we used the magic of the world to exorcise the evil, the terror, that surround us.

By our horrors and our survival we shall be known.

"By continual suicide/I escaped being similar to myself," Walter had written in one of his Paris elegies. And at an age when many poets have become either repetitive or superannuated, Walter Lowenfels—in his late fifties—began writing his most important and characteristic works.

"Did I recover my youth?" Walter asked himself. "On the contrary, I became reinfected with its symptoms, realized there was nothing my kind of poem could achieve except to bite it off on the typewriter. I reached once more the discipline where I didn't have to care that I was saying nothing that would alter the immediate outcome—just trying to spell it out."

And he added: "All a poet has to do is to keep pace in his vocabulary with the latest orbit of the latest space ship, and his song falls into place alongside the new creators of the moon Keats never saw. . . . 'Would I were steadfast as thou art!' What a joke that would make today, when the moon is being loved with accurate thrusts by every major power with an ICBM arsenal. That's the essence of my campaign against nostalgia: not to mope for the words of yesteryear."

With a vocabulary derived from astronomy, geology, and microbiology, Walter developed a style—influenced in part by William Carlos Williams—which he called "scientific surrealism." Abandoning the slightly formalist structure of his Paris verse, he used the new verbal resources—with cadences occasionally and oddly reminiscent of both T.S. Eliot and Allen Ginsberg—to compose poems of political commitment and eschatological passion—among them the seven-part "My Spectrum Analysis":

1

We are the should-be's of collapsed
    supernovae
doomed to winter it among galactic halos
    in the cool universe of undisturbed suns.
There is no pain
        only
a swift wind of hydrogen
    sweeps us
through centuries of magnetic storms
    to an immolation we do not know.
We are the diffuse gas of electronic
    degeneracy
cast in cosmic particles in the flesh
    and in the low density of your make-believe

we kiss your mirror image
goodbye, so long, it's been good to
    know you
in the full spectrum of celestial radiation. . . .

4

For the first three billion years of inter-
    galactic dog eat dog
not a spiral nebula laughed. Followed an
    additional three billion years of cosmic alienation.
Not one microwave in the Crab Nebula
    cracked a smile.
Finally one bright green morning a mutation
    called Archimedes
joked about changing the world with a lever.
    And a one-minute routine
of scientific vaudeville began called The
    World as Good Fun.
But the real gasses came the next minute
    when some Pentagonian computer
thought it was the spiral nebula in
    Andromeda attacking us.
And the last smile of the last child went
    into orbit and cried silently forever after. . . .

7

At the last moment
    I learned to believe in failure
but only on a galactic scale
    of burned-out supernovae.
        Elsewhere,
among the carbon compounds
    where our love affair goes on,
the sweet kiss of dialectics
        keeps whispering:

What's really happening
    is terribly superior
to any history
    any story, any divinity
any super-reality
    and even the spectrum analysis
is moving toward the red.

Everything that influenced Walter got into his work: Aztec sun
dials and the *New York Times*; African masks and scrolls from the
Torah; visions from the Koran and ads from the *Scientific American*;

passages from Einstein and Charles Ives; speeches by Mother Jones, Eugene Debs, Rosa Luxemburg, Engels, Sojourner Truth, and Chief Joseph; the "American Voices" of letters-to-the-editor correspondents. And he defined his aesthetics in two small volumes of incandescent aphoristic sayings—*The Revolution Is to Be Human* (International Publishers) and *Reality Prime* (Cycle Press)—perhaps the two most inspiring statements on the divine concreteness of life and on visionary poetics since Whitman's *An American Primer*, Mayakovsky's *How Are Verses Made?* and Ruth Murray Underhill's *Singing for Power: The Song Magic of the Papago Indians*.

In the midst of the Cold War and the McCarthy era, Lowenfels was rediscovering and broadening the generally neglected Whitmanian tradition of populists like Vachel Lindsay, socialists like Carl Sandburg, anarchists like Arturo Giovannitti, and Communists like Mike Gold. The fifties, of course, saw the emergence of the Beats, the Black Mountain poets, and the New York school . . . and writers such as Patchen, Rexroth, Zukofsky, Ignatow, and Oppen were being rediscovered. But certainly Lowenfels was one of the first and most adamant opponents of what Kenneth Rexroth once called the "corn belt metaphysical" tradition of postwar American poetry. By-passing this stale and provincial establishment tradition, Walter focused attention on and reassigned importance to the international poetic and political sensibility exemplified by Neruda, Eluard, Vallejo, Guillen, Brecht, and especially Nazim Hikmet—the little-known, great Turkish Communist poet who spent almost twenty years in jail, and whose astonishing poems are close, both in tone and style, to much of Lowenfels' later work. (See Randy Blasing's and Mutlu Konuk's beautiful translations of Hikmet's selected poems in *Things I Didn't Know I Loved*.) Thinking of poets such as these, Walter once wrote: "Humanity is on the way to producing complete human beings who just can't be split up—on one hand, their politics; on the other, their poetry. . . . When you're Brecht your politics are like the bars on a page of music to Mozart—nobody hears the bars—just the music."

In his sixties and seventies, Walter—having moved from Mays Landing, New Jersey, to Peekskill—edited two excellent Walt Whitman collections (*Walt Whitman's Civil War* and *The Tenderest Lover: The Erotic Poetry of Walt Whitman*), in which he paid homage to his favorite American poet, whose works—"always aspiring to be completed in the reader"—represented Lowenfels' highest ideal of art: "The drive of the poems is toward a humanity where each will be completely alive to every experience we witness or observe. This is the essence of Whitman's many loves, each of us alive in everyone else." (Allowed to take one book to jail after his 1953 arrest, Walter chose *Leaves of Grass*.)

He also edited a number of anthologies, including *Poets of Today, Where Is Vietnam?, The Writing on the Wall, In a Time of Revolution, From the Belly of the Shark,* and *For Neruda, For Chilie* —anthologies which attempted to provide a substitute for those exclusionary, "lily-white" collections that claimed to be representative of the American literary experience, and which were among the first to introduce the writings of Black, Chicano, Indian, and Puerto Rican poets—along with the work of Bob Dylan, Tom McGrath, Gary Snyder, Denise Levertov, and many unknown young and older white poets. And in line with his idea that the Proletarian Literature movement of the thirties ignored the real "proletarian literature" that existed in folk and labor songs and stories, Walter also helped found the Almanac Singers, became a contributing editor of *Sing Out* magazine, and collaborated with folk singer Lee Hays in the composition of two famous songs: "Wasn't That a Time" and "The Lonesome Traveler."

Praised in the thirties and forties by F. Scott Fitzgerald, Ford Madox Ford, Henry Miller, Howard Fast, Diego Rivera, Rockwell Kent, and Louis Aragon; rediscovered in the fifties and sixties by writers such as Kenneth Rexroth, Jonathan Williams, Studs Terkel, Robert Gover (who has edited the best introduction to Lowenfels' writings, *The Portable Walter,* published by International Publishers), and Ishmael Reed ("Walter still wallops a wangol while the spirit of his contemporaries moves thru their fingers like chicken feed giving barnyard animals indigestion"), Walter Lowenfels is still one of the great undiscovered writers of twentieth-century American literature.

In the last ten years of his life, he completed his most important lifetime projects, most of which remain unpublished: *My Many Lives,* the four-volume autobiography, of which only the second part, *The Poetry of My Politics,* was published in 1968 and is now out of print; *Autobiography of an Empire,* a monumental history of American racism, sexism, workers' struggles, and "patriotic" wars as told through brilliantly chosen excerpts from official and unofficial documents, letters, diaries, slave testimonies, and biographies of people like Rockefeller, J. P. Morgan, Carnegie, Jane Adams, Charles Sumner,

Elizabeth Gurley Flynn, Bill Haywood, and hundreds of little-known American citizens; the *Collected Poems*, Walter's gathering of and commentary on all of the verse that he wished to preserve; and *Letters*, an enormous volume of correspondence.

"Letters," Walter has written, "became one way of life for me during my Paris days in the late twenties and thirties. They have continued that way off and on ever since. I have two lives at the machine. One, poems, the other, letters." Already in his first published volume of poems, *Episodes and Epistles* (1925), Walter made it clear that, for him, letters were a form of address, as well as of transport and prayer—documents and chants, to use Sandburg's description of one of Walter's first Epistles.

"I realize that from the Greek dramatists to Vallejo and Neruda," Walter wrote, "many poets have said it all in their poems. But I belong to the Artaud generation, gripped occasionally by our particular streak of madness or vision or whatever you want to call the verbal seizure we get, and then trying later to explore it further, explain it rationally, as Artaud and others have done in letters, to find out in prose what it is we have been trying to say in our blind stutters. Identity is the key word here. The need to be heard the way you want to be heard by the one person with whom you are sharing yourself at the moment."

In the face of nuclear suicide, Walter's letters—which are among the most moving written in this century—took on an impassioned, incantatory, and prophetic tone—as if every word might be the last. "It's not our obliteration as concrete physical substance that's my main gripe," he wrote, "it's the idea of us now—that if we go out we go out as a lie."

Almost all of Walter's prose works, in fact, are either extracts from or written in the form of letters to his friends and family—especially *My Many Lives*, his part-diary/part-reverie/part-political meditation entitled *To an Imaginary Daughter* (Horizon Press), and his last work, *Be Polite to the Grass*—stories and prose poems written for his twelve grandchildren:

> Don't cheat the linen closet
> Don't lie to the dishwasher
> Don't swear at face towels
> Always tell the hot water faucet the truth
> Remember it's simpler to begin at the end

Acknowledge that the toaster is supreme
Above all, don't poke fun at the refrigerator
Pray for the curtains that they may survive in the hereafter
And you will live happily until all the tablespoons unite.

Almost all of these works attain to Walter's goal of a "writing life where there is no difference between poem and non-poem, verse and prose, letter and elegy. . . . Native Americans (Indians) have this relation with words—the sacred breath of the fathers speaking through their mouths, the divine spirit in the breath that speaks."

And in his last years, Walter's breath spoke increasingly of two great subjects. The first was geology:

> Mary Austin wrote, years ago, that there was a connection between soil and language rhythms. That's why only the United States has produced the rhythms of our Indian poems or of Whitman, i.e., the native style. I think the soil—if seen in a geologically social way—accounts for what we are doing with language today and with forms. . . .
>
> Peace changes all relations—human and inhuman—rocks, clouds, moon, people—including the relations between words in poems. Peace has become a geological force; war, geological doom. We have put our hands into the mechanism of the universe and nothing remains the same. . . .
>
> Our only problem is being human while we mix with inhuman things like poems. This awareness has given me a new understanding of Li Po, burning his poems on the water's edge and watching them float down the river. This was not an act of despair—it was the marriage of poem-time and ocean-time. And think how happy the poem is, mixing with fire and ice; whispering to the dolphins how good it is to be back home among the shrimp. . . .
>
> I am in love with geology. The sedimentary rocks give me a thrill. I know my death (like my life) is not alone. I love the earth for our common doom—and our mutual joy. We shall go out as we came in—together—and if one of us precedes the other by a billion years or two, what's that between eternal friends? I'm just a chip off the old block, and so are you, my friend, carrying your actions and inactions with you like the old man of the sea—I mean the one who rose from the galactic waters with the earth on his back.

The second subject was the galaxy. "It's natural that my final pages are geologic and galactic," Walter wrote. "We touch the universe or we die." And for Walter, socialism had a galactic, not only a political, dimension—the precondition for our eventual communication with extraterrestrial life and for the poem of the future: "In the grand procession that leads to the star libraries in Galaxy ZI[4] we are all one poet traveling at the speed of light . . . or we don't get there at all."

Although Walter believed in "scientific socialism," he never suppressed his utopian dreams. Dreaming forward, like the philosopher Ernst Bloch, he understood that it was only with the advent of Marxism that hope could wed itself to reality. And like Feuerbach, he also believed that the "future is the empire of poetry":

What we are after is *Reality Prime*. That is where you climb up the audience ladder and throw it away. Then you arrive at a point where your poet transcends the class limits of his vision, leaps out of the lenses of his eyes and sees more than he knows. Then he is really with it—at the maximum speed of light—where Shakespeare is better than his politics, and Dante likewise—and "the angels loop the loop around the poet in the flying suit" (Apollinaire).

Perpetual revolution on every level: the starry heavens above and the political law within.

Walter Lowenfels died on July 7, 1976, three days after the American bicentennial celebrations. At the memorial service to celebrate his life—held in New York City on October 9, 1976—Ruby Dee, Ossie Davis, Pete Seeger, Earl Robinson, Olga Cabral, Nancy Willard, Barbara Dane, Herbert Aptheker, Jose-Angel Figuera, the Lowenfels family, and many others paid tribute to this inspiring human being, who was—and, I'm sure, still is—at home in the universe. As he wrote in "I Belong":

There are three billion billion billion constellations (the sky book says) but I am a patriot of the Milky Way. It gives me a thrill when I look out the telescope at *our* galaxy. I mean—I know where I belong—just like those two titmice feeding together outside my window, and right now flying off together—I, too, know I have a home, an identity established not only by national boundaries, common speech, etc., not just by our own beautiful sun, and its planets, moons, asteroids, but by our own dear galaxy. O lover in your pure feathery light, across thousands of billions of spiral nebulas, you are the best of all galaxies and I know you love me too, for out of the vast riches of your fiery interstellar sperm you have given me inalienable rights to life, liberty and the pursuit of happiness and my own little life to cool.

HENRY MILLER

Reflections
of a
Cosmic Tourist

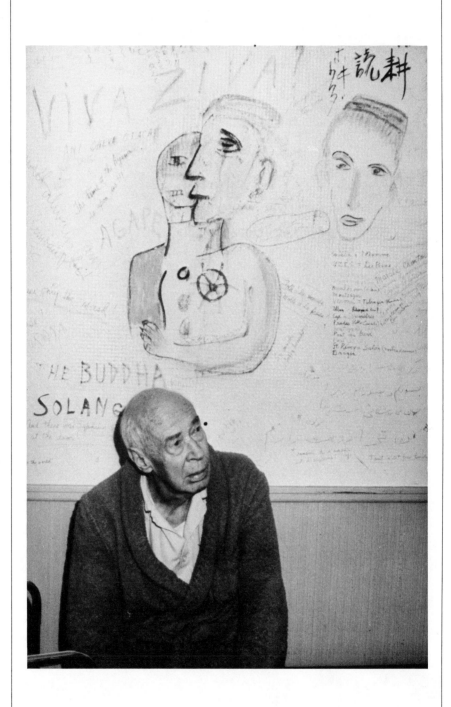

But you have so refined our sensitivity,
so heightened our awareness, so deepened our love for men and women, for
books, for nature, for a thousand and
one things in life which only one of your
own unending paragraphs could cata-
logue, that you awaken in us the desire
to turn you inside out.
　　　—Henry Miller on Blaise Cendrars,
　　　from *The Books in My Life*

H enry Miller—"confused, negli-
gent, reckless, lusty, obscene, boisterous, thoughtful, scrupulous,
lying, diabolically truthful man that I am"; author of many famous
and infamous books "filled with wisdom and nonsense, truth and
falsehood, toenails, hair, teeth, blood, and ovaries" (his words)—has
been called everything from "a counterrevolutionary sexual politician"
(Kate Millet) to "a true sexual revolutionary" (Norman Mailer); an
author who neglects "form and *mesure*" (Frank Kermode) to "the
only imaginative prose writer of the slightest value who has appeared
among the English-speaking races for some years past" (George
Orwell).

　　　Now eighty-two, and in spite of recent illnesses still painting
and writing, Miller is still accepting what he once called our Air-
Conditioned Nightmare with joyful incredulity, still continuing to find
out and tell us who he is. This year [1973] marks the fortieth anniversary of the publication of the first Paris edition of *Tropic of Cancer*—
Miller's first published book—and it is now indisputably clear that
Miller's more than forty subsequent volumes must be read simply as
one enormous evolving work—a perpetual *Bildungsroman*—manifest-
ing the always-changing, yet ever the same, awareness and celebra-
tion of the recovery of the divinity of man, as well as of the way of
truth which, Miller says, leads not to salvation but to enlightenment.
"There is no salvation, really, only infinite realms of experience providing more and more tests, demanding more and more faith. . . .
When each thing is lived through to the end, there is no death and no

regrets, neither is there a false springtime; each moment lived pushes open a greater, wider horizon from which there is no escape save living."

Gentile Dybbuck (as he once called himself), patriot of the 14th Ward (Brooklyn), American anarchist, Parisian *voyou*, cosmic tourist in Greece, sage of Big Sur, Henry Miller is today an inhabitant of an improbable-looking Georgian colonial house in Pacific Palisades, Los Angeles—a house teeming with posters, paintings, sketches, and photographs, all tokens and traces of Miller's ebullient, peripatetic life.

There are a number of his radiant "instinctive" watercolors hanging in the living room. ("If it doesn't look like a horse when I'm through, I can always turn it into a hammock," he once said of his "method" of painting in "The Angel Is My Watermark.") On one wall is a hand-inscribed poster listing the names of scores of places Miller has visited around the world—with marginal comments:

> Bruges—the Dead City (for poets)
> Imperial City, California (loss of identity)
> Pisa (talking to tower all hours)
> Cafe Boudou, Paris: Rue Fontaine
>   (Algerian whore)
> Grand Canyon (still the best)
> Corfu—Violating Temple (English girl)
> Biarritz (rain, rain, rain)

In the kitchen, posted on a cabinet, is his Consubstantial Health Menu, which announces favorite dishes: e.g., Bata Yaku! Sauerfleisch mit Kartoffelklösze, Leeks, Zucchini ad perpetuum, Calves' Liver (yum yum) . . . and a strong warning: Please! No Health Food.

Across one end of his study is a floor-to-ceiling bookshelf containing hundreds of his own works translated into scores of languages, while two other walls are completely decorated with graffiti and drawings, all contributed by visitors, friends and by Henry himself: "Kill the Buddha!" "Let's Case the Joint!" "Love, Delight and Organ Are Feminine in the Plural!" "The Last Sleeper of the Middle Ages!" "Don't Look for Miracles. You Are the Miracle!"

Most fascinating of all is the author's famous bathroom—a veritable museum which presents the iconography of the World of Henry Miller: photos of actresses on the set of the filmed version of *Tropic of Cancer*, Buddhas from four countries, a portrait of Hermann Hesse ("Most writers don't look so hot," Miller says. "They're thin blooded, alone with their thoughts"), a Jungian mandala, Taoist emblems, a Bosch reproduction, the castle of Ludwig of Bavaria, Miller's fifth wife Hoki (from whom he's now separated and about whom he wrote: "First it was a broken toe, then it was a broken brow and finally a broken heart"), the head of Gurdjieff ("of all masters the most interesting"), and, hidden away in the corner, a couple of hardcore photos "for people who expect something like that in here." (Tom Schiller's delightful film, *Henry Miller Asleep and Awake*—distributed by New Yorker Films—is shot in this very bathroom and presents the author taking the viewer around on a guided tour.)

"I really hate greeting you like this, in pajamas and in bed," Miller says as I enter his bedroom. Smiling and talking with a never-discarded bristly, crepitated Brooklyn accent and a tone of voice blending honey and retsina, he continues: "I just got out of the hospital again, you see. They had to replace an artificial artery running from my neck down to the leg. It didn't work, it developed an abscess, and so they had to take out both the artery and the abscess. I'm really in bad shape, no?" Miller says, laughing. "And this is all attributable to those damned cigarettes. I was an athlete when I was young—don't you know? I was good at track and a bicycle rider. I didn't smoke until I was twenty-five, and then it was incessant. And all my wives smoked, too. If I start again it means death. My circulation will stop, and they'll have to cut off my legs."

Again a smile and a gentle laugh. "Always Merry and Bright!" —Henry's lifelong motto.

"You'll have to speak to my left ear—the other one doesn't work. And I've lost vision in my left eye."

"Can you see me?" I ask.

"I certainly imagined you differently," Miller responds. "When I heard that someone named Jonathan was coming, I thought you'd be some tall, uptight Englishman with blond hair. But I'm glad I was wrong."

Henry, unlike his fellow expatriate novelist and namesake Henry (James)—it is impossible to think of two more wildly opposite types—is well known for his caustic Anglophobic attitudes. (Miller in a letter to Lawrence Durrell: "The most terrible, damning line in the whole of *The Black Book* is that remark of Chamberlain's: 'Look, do you think it would damage our relationship if I sucked you off?' That almost tells the whole story of England.") But strangely, it is the English Lawrence Durrell who, as a twenty-three-year-old writer and diplomat living in Corfu, wrote the then forty-three-year-old Miller an ecstatic fan letter after reading *Tropic of Cancer*, calling it "the only really man-sized piece of work this century can boast of." They have been close friends and correspondents for almost forty years, and in fact Durrell and his wife are expected this evening for dinner. (Durrell taught this past year at Cal Tech, one of the main reasons being to keep in contact with his friend.)

Hanging on the wall alongside Henry's bed is a dramatic photo of a saintly looking Chinese man, whose face bears an uncanny resemblance to Miller's own.

"That's a photo of a Chinese sage I found in a magazine thirty years ago," Henry says, noticing my interest. "I framed it and kept it ever since. I regard him as an enlightened man, even though he wasn't known."

"You yourself once characterized the French writer Blaise Cendrars as 'the Chinese rock-bottom man of my imagination,'" I mention, pulling out my little black notebook to check the quote.

"I'm sure Durrell christened me that," Henry says. "Are you sure I said that about Cendrars?"

"Absolutely, it's in my book here."

Henry looks at me bemusedly. "That's really something," he exclaims. "I should have realized this before. But with that book you really look just like that guy Columbo on television. Peter Falk plays him, and he seems a little half-witted, you know, a little stupid . . . not conniving but *cunning*. Yes, I'd like to be like that. That's my idea of a man! . . . Go right ahead with . . . what is it you want to ask me? . . . Amazing, just like that guy Columbo."

"This isn't really a question," I say, rummaging through the book, "but speaking of the Chinese, I'd like to read you a little story by Chuang-Tze, the disciple of Lao-Tze. I wrote it down to read to you because to me it suggests something very deep and basic about all of your work."

"'Just read it loudly and slowly, please," Henry says.

Chuang-Tze writes: "The sovereign of the Southern Sea is called Dissatisfaction (with things as they are); the sovereign of the Northern Sea, Revolution; the sovereign of the Center of the World, Chaos. Dissatisfaction and Revolution from time to time met together in the territory of Chaos, and Chaos treated them very hospitably. The two sovereigns planned how to repay Chaos's kindness. They said, 'Men all have seven holes to their bodies for seeing, hearing, eating, and breathing. Our friend has none of these. Let us try to bore some holes in him.' Each day they bored one hole. On the seventh day Chaos died."

"That's a fantastic story," Henry says. "And it's interesting that you see that in my work."

"I was thinking of your idea of chaos as the fluid which enveloped you, which you breathed in through the gills. And of the fertile void, the chaos which you've called the 'seat of creation itself,' whose order is beyond human comprehension. And of the 'humanizing' and destruction of the natural order. And I was thinking, too, of your statement in *Black Spring*: 'My faltering and groping, my search for any and every means of expression, is a sort of divine stuttering. *I am dazzled by the glorious collapse of the world!*' "

"Yes, that's wonderful," Henry says. "I don't even remember some of these things you say I've written. Read some more from your notebook."

"I've been thinking about your obsession in your books with the idea of China, and that photo on the wall made me realize how much you look Chinese. 'I want to become nothing more than the China I already am,' you once wrote. 'I am nothing if not Chinese,' and you've identified *Chinese* with that supernormal life such that one is unnaturally gay, unnaturally healthy, unnaturally indifferent. . . . The artist scorns the ordinary alphabet and adopts the symbol, the ideograph. *He writes* Chinese.' And in many of your works you point over and over again to the fact that our verb 'to be,' intransitive in English, is transitive in Chinese."

"Yes, yes, that's become my credo. To be gay is the sign of health and intelligence. First of all humor: That's what the Chinese philosophers had, and what the Germans never had. Nietzsche had some, but it was morbid and bitter. But Kant, Schopenhauer . . . you can look in vain. Chuang-Tze is a genius, his marvelous humor comes out of all his pores. And without that you can't have humor. My favorite American writer, for instance, is the Jewish immigrant I. B. Singer. He makes me laugh and weep, he tears me apart, don't you know? Most American writers hardly touch me, they're always on the surface. He's a big man in my estimation.

"But speaking of the Chinese, I have intuitive flashes that I have Mongol and Jewish blood in me—two strange mixtures, no? As far as I know, I'm German all the way through, but I disown it. I believe that blood counts very strongly—what's in your veins. I've had that feeling. Because I'm a real German, and I don't like that. Not just because of the war . . . long before that: I was raised among them in a German-American neighborhood, and they're worse than the Germans in Germany. . . . Of course, there's Goethe, Schiller, Heine, Hölderlin, the composers. . . . Naturally they're wonderful.

"You know something? I was recently reading Hermann Hesse's last book, *My Belief*. And the very end of this book has to do with Oriental writers. He mentions how his perspective on life changed when he became acquainted with Lao-Tze, Chuang-Tze, and the I Ching, of course. And I discovered these writers when I was about eighteen. I was crazy about the Chinese. I have trouble, however, with the novels like *All Men Are Brothers*—too many characters and there's no psychology—everything is on the surface."

"One of my favorite books of yours, Henry, is *Big Sur and the Oranges of Hieronymus Bosch*. Your meditations on and descriptions of your friends and life in Big Sur are so serene and lambent, like some of the great Chinese poems. I wish it had gone on and on."

"The poets who retired in old age to the country," Henry reflects. "Yes, that's right. I've tried to model myself on the Chinese sages. And they were happy, gay men. I've heard that the old men in China before the Revolution used to sit out on river boats and converse, drink tea, smoke, and just enjoy talking about philosophy or literature. They always invited girls to come and drink with them. And then they'd go and fly a kite afterwards, a real kite. I think that's admirable. . . . We flew kites in Big Sur, but there we had big winds in canyons with birds being lifted by the updrafts. The kites got torn and smashed."

"I especially remember," I mention, "that passage in *Big Sur* where you describe the morning sun rising behind you and throwing an enlarged shadow of yourself into the iridescent fog below. You wrote about it this way: 'I lift my arms as in prayer, achieving a wingspan no god ever possessed, and there in the drifting fog a nimbus floats about my head, a radiant nimbus such as the Buddha himself might proudly wear. In the Himalayas, where the same phenomenon occurs, it is said that a devout follower of the Buddha will throw himself from a peak—*into the arms of Buddha*.' "

"Yes, I remember that," Henry says. "Your shadow is in the

light and fog, overaggrandized; you're in monstrous size and you're tempted to throw yourself over."

"That reminds me of Anaïs Nin's comment," I mention, "that the figures in your books are always 'outsized . . . whether tyrant or victims, man or woman.'"

"That's true," Henry responds. "That's because I'm enthusiastic and I exaggerate, I adore and worship. I don't just *like*. I love. I go overboard. And if I hate, it's in the same way. I don't know any neutral, in-between ground."

Henry Miller's enthusiasms and exaggerations have led many persons to hold on to a distorted picture of the author as a writer only of six supposedly epigamic "sex" books (the *Tropics*, *Quiet Days in Clichy*, and *Sexus*, *Plexus*, and *Nexus*) for a reading constituency consisting primarily of GIs in Place Pigalle, existentialist wastrels, or academic "freaks" like Karl Shapiro (who called Miller the "greatest living author").

Of the above-mentioned works, *Tropic of Capricorn* is certainly one of the most original works of twentieth-century literature. And the fact that Henry Miller has been stereotyped so disparagingly is a peculiarity of American literary history, since his work is one that consistently evolves, perfectly exemplifying the ideas of rapturous change, metamorphosis, surrender, and growth.

"The angels praising the Lord are never the same," the great Hasidic Rabbi Nachman once said. "The Lord changes them every day." One of Henry Miller's favorite statements is that of the philosopher Eric Gutkind: "To overcome the world is to make it transparent." And it is as if with the transparency of angels that Miller reveals an unparalleled literary ability to disappear into the objects and persons of his attention and thereby to allow them to appear in an unmediated radiance. Miller's heightened identification with everything he notices is made even more powerful by means of an astonishing descriptive presentational immediacy and an attendant sense of magnanimity.

Consider his meditation on his friend Hans Reichel's painting, *The Stillborn Twins*:

It is an ensemble of miniature panels in which there is not only the embryonic flavor but the hieroglyphic as well. If he likes you,

Reichel will show you in one of the panels the little shirt which
the mother of the stillborn twins was probably thinking of in her
agony. He says it so simply and honestly that you feel like weeping. The little shirt embedded in a cold prenatal green is indeed
the sort of shirt which only a woman in travail could summon
up. You feel that with the freezing torture of birth, at the moment when the mind seems ready to snap, the mother's eye inwardly turning gropes frantically towards some tender, known
object which will attach her, if only for a moment, to the world
of human entities. In this quick, agonized clutch the mother
sinks back, through worlds unknown to man, to planets long
since disappeared, where perhaps there were no babies' shirts
but where there was the warmth, the tenderness, the mossy en-
velope of a love beyond love, of a love for the disparate elements
which metamorphose through the mother, through her pain,
through her death, so that life may go on. Each panel, if you read
it with the cosmological eye, is a throwback to an undecipherable
script of life. The whole cosmos is moving back and forth through
the sluice of time and the stillborn twins are embedded there in
the cold prenatal green with the shirt that was never worn.

—"The Cosmological Eye"

Or read Miller's descriptions of the Paris photographs of the French
photographer Brassai:

What strange cities—and situations stranger still! The mendi-
cant sitting on the public bench thirsting for a glimmer of sun,
the butcher standing in a pool of blood with knife upraised, the
scows and barges dreaming in the shadows of the bridges, the
pimp standing against the wall with cigarette in hand, the street
cleaner with her broom of reddish twigs, her thick, gnarled
fingers, her high stomach draped in black, a shroud over her
womb, rinsing away the vomit of the night before so that when I
pass over the cobblestones my feet will gleam with the light of
morning stars. I see the old hats, the sombreros and fedoras, the
velours and Panamas that I painted with a clutching fury; I see
the corners of walls eroded by time and weather which I passed
in the night and in passing felt the erosion going on in myself,
corners of my own walls crumbling away, blown down, dispersed, reintegrated elsewhere in mysterious shape and essence.
I see the old tin urinals where, standing in the dead silence of
the night, I dreamed so violently that the past sprang up like a
white horse and carried me out of the body.

—"The Eye of Paris"

Most persons seem to have forgotten (or have never known)
not only passages like these but also: the great reveries on Brooklyn,

the pissoirs in Paris and the madness of Tante Melia (all in *Black Spring*); the hymn to Saturnian effluvia and the talking-blues Dipsy Doodle passacaglia which tells the story of Louis the Armstrong and Epaminondas (*The Colossus of Maroussi*); his dreamlike discovery of the secret street in "Reunion in Brooklyn"); the letters to Alfred Perlès and Lawrence Durrell; the prose poems describing Miller's obsession with painting (*To Paint Is to Love Again, The Waters Reglitterized*); the *Hamlet* correspondence with Michel Fraenkel (long out of print); and the essays on Balzac, D. H. Lawrence, Cendrars, and H. Rider Haggard. All of these have been overlooked in the still-raging debate concerning Miller's problematic attitude toward women.

The recent Mailer/Miller/Millet literary fracas presented Kate Millet, in her book *Sexual Politics*, accusing Miller of depersonalizing women with his virulent and fear-ridden sexual attitudes, while Norman Mailer in *The Prisoner of Sex* defended him as a "sexual pioneer." There is little question, as Mailer points out, that Millet distorts Miller's escapades and determinedly overlooks the author's omnifarious, picaresque humor. But in terms of getting to the roots of Miller's sexual attitudes, neither Millet nor Mailer comes close to the perspicacious criticism of Miller's friend of more than forty years, Anaïs Nin, nor to Miller's own comments on these matters in his correspondence with various friends.

In her diaries Anaïs Nin often mentions the paradox between what she sees as her friend's gentle and violent writing, his veering from sentimentality to callousness, tenderness to ridicule, gentleness to anger. And she suggests that because of what she saw as Miller's "utter subjection" to his wife June (Mona, Mara, Alraune in his novels), Miller used his books to take revenge upon her.

Miller himself has written: "Perhaps one reason why I have stressed so much the immoral, the wicked, the ugly, the cruel in my work is because I wanted others to know how valuable these are, how equally if not more important than the good things. . . . I was getting the poison out of my system. Curiously enough, this poison had a tonic effect for others. It was as if I had given them some kind of immunity."

Sometimes, in his letters, we find Miller protecting himself, describing himself as "a little boy going down into the street to play, having no fixed purpose, no particular direction, no especial friend to seek out, but just divinely content to be going down into the street to see whatever might come. As if I did not love them! Only I also loved others, too . . . not in the way they meant, but in a natural, wholesome, easy way. Like one loves garlic, honey, wild strawberries."

But he is unsparing of himself as well: "The coward in me always concealed himself in that thick armor of dull passivity. I only grew truly sensitive again when I had attained a certain measure of liberation. . . . To live out one's desires and, in so doing, subtly alter their nature is the aim of every individual who aspires to evolve."

The idea of self-liberation—what psychologists today like to call "self-actualization" or "individuation"—has always been Miller's great concern in all of his books, which progress from the *via purgativa* to the *via unitiva*. And even as his novels work counterclockwise (*Tropic of Cancer* tells of Miller's life in thirties Paris, *Tropic of Capricorn* and *The Rosy Crucifixion* of his earlier life in New York City), Miller gives, as he tells us, in "each separate fragment, each work, the feeling of the whole as I go on, because I am digging deeper and deeper into life, digging deeper and deeper into past and future. . . . The writer lives between the upper and lower worlds: He takes the path in order eventually to become that path himself."

This path is often filled with the "strong odor of sex" which, to Miller, is "really the aroma of birth; it is disagreeable only to those who fail to recognize its significance." And it is a path which leads to his rebirth at the tomb of Agamemnon—described in *The Colossus of Maroussi* as "the great peace which comes of surrender"—and to his rebirth at the conclusion of *Tropic of Capricorn*: "I take you as a star and a trap, as a stone to tip the scales, as a judge that is blindfolded, as a hole to fall into, as a path to walk, as a cross and an arrow. Up to the present I traveled the opposite way of the sun; henceforth I travel two ways, as sun and as moon. Henceforth I take on two sexes, two hemispheres, two skies, two sets of everything. Henceforth I shall be doublejointed and double sexed. Everything that happens will happen twice. I shall be as a visitor to this earth, partaking of its blessings and carrying off its gifts. I shall neither serve nor be served. I shall seek the end in myself."

And this amazing passage suggests—if not that Henry is a prototype of Norman O. Brown—at least something quite different from what Millet and Mailer are arguing about.

Henry Miller is hardly an enthusiastic supporter of psychological criticism. "This seeking for meaning in everything!" he once exclaimed. "So Germanic! This urge to make everything profound. What nonsense! If only they could also make everything unimportant at the same time." But I decided to ask him about the woman question anyway.

"Henry," I say, "Anaïs Nin wrote in her diaries that in *Tropic of Cancer* you created a book in which you have a sex and a stomach. In *Tropic of Capricorn* and *Black Spring*, she says, you have eyes, ears, and a mouth. And eventually, Anaïs Nin suggests, you will finally create a full man, at which point you'll be able to write about a woman for real."

"I don't remember her writing that," Henry responds. "That should have stuck in my head. That's quite wonderful. But it's interesting, isn't it? It's like that Chuang-Tze story you read me, about the drilling of the holes into Chaos, don't you know?" Henry smiles. "But if you saw Anaïs today I think she'd give you the feeling that I *am* a whole man today.

"Tom Schiller told me that there was a bomb scare in Copenhagen when they were going to show his film about me [*Henry Miller Asleep and Awake*]. A woman's lib group called up the theater to stop the film from being shown—they showed it anyway—but I want so badly to write a letter to the women who are against me. The woman I could write it to would be Germaine Greer. I adore her—the others I don't know—and I'd like to say: 'My dear Germaine Greer, isn't it obvious from my work that I love women? Is the fact that I also fuck them without asking their names the great sin? I never took them as sex objects. . . . Well, maybe I did at times, but it wasn't done with evil thought or with the intention of putting the woman down. It just so happened that there were chance encounters—you meet and pass, and that's how it sometimes occurred. There never was any woman problem in my mind.' "

"You've been criticized, perhaps validly," I say, "for portraying women either as phantasmagoric angels disappearing into the clouds or as down-to-earth whores. Or do you think I'm distorting the picture?"

"I don't think that's true. I really don't," he replies. "To talk jokingly about it: they're all layable, even the angels. And the whores can be worshiped, too. Naturally. That's what Jesus did. The famous religious leaders always spoke well of whores."

"Again, Henry," I say, "Anaïs Nin has said that in *Tropic of*

Cancer you seemed to be fighting off the idea of Woman because there was a woman inside of you whom you couldn't accept."

"It was my mother," Henry replies without hesitation, "whom I couldn't accept. I was always the enemy of my mother and she of me. We never got along—never. Not till her dying day. And even then we were still enemies. Even then she was berating me and treating me like a child. And I couldn't stand it. And I grabbed her and pushed her back on the pillow. And then I realized the brutality of it—I didn't hurt her—but the very thought of doing this to such a woman! And then I went out to the hall and sobbed and wept."

"I saw a photo of your mother recently," I mention, "and she looked like a strong, handsome woman."

"You really think so? Is that so?" Henry says with interest. "I always think of her as a cold woman. . . . But sometimes I think Anaïs analyzes everything too much. She believes so much that she's had such great help from psychoanalysts, and I'm always saying: fuck the analyst, that's the last man to see, he's a faker. Now, he isn't a faker, he's honest, and there are wonderful men. I read Jung and I know that Hermann Hesse said he was indebted to Jung and Freud. I can't read Freud today, but when I was nineteen or twenty I fought a battle for him. Today I don't think it was worth wasting time on, but that's a prejudice again, and I don't deny that. I don't see why we haven't got a right to be prejudiced."

"But psychologically there are so many interesting things in your books, Henry," I say. "The conclusion to *Tropic of Capricorn*, for example, where you say that from then on you'd be both male and female—everything that happened would occur twice. Or the earlier, even more amazing 'Land of Fuck' interlude, which is a reverie about the purity and infancy of sexual desire, in which you seem to become the sexual process itself in an out-of-body journey."

"Yes," Henry agrees, "you're lifted out of the body of the narrative, you're floating somewhere and sex is something like x, y, z —you can't name it. You see, that was a windfall. Every so often you get a gift from above, it comes to you, you have nothing to do with it, you're being dictated to. I don't take credit for that interlude. . . . And the last part of *Capricorn* . . . yes, that was a wonderful passage. Sometimes I don't know what these things mean. They come out of the unconscious. It's interesting, these questions. No one picks these things out."

In order to lighten things up, I innocuously ask Henry about rock and roll—something I assume he likes.

"I detest rock and roll," he retorts passionately. "To me it's noise, I miss the beautiful melodies. But I suppose it's an omission. What rock and roll musicians do you like?"

"I like Bob Dylan for one," I say, "and I was thinking that some of your work must have influenced someone like Dylan. Like that passage in 'Into the Night Life' from *Black Spring*."

"Do you have it there in your book?" Henry asks. "How does it go?"

I read:

The melting snow melts deeper, the iron rusts, the leaves flower. On the corner, under the elevated, stands a man with a plug hat, in blue serge and linen spats, his white mustache chopped fine. The switch opens and out rolls all the tobacco juice, the golden lemons, the elephant tusks, the candelabras. Moishe Pippik, the lemon dealer, fowled with pigeons, breeding purple eggs in his vest pocket and purple ties and watermelons and spinach with short stems, stringy, marred with tar. The whistle of the acorns loudly stirring, flurry of floozies bandaged in Lysol, ammonia and camphor patches, little mica huts, peanut shells triangled and corrugated, all marching triumphantly with the morning breeze. The morning light comes in creases, the window panes are streaked, the covers are torn, the oilcloth is faded. Walks a man with hair on end, not running, not breathing, a man with a weathervane that turns the corners sharply and then bolts. A man who thinks not how or why but just to walk in lusterless night with all stars to port and loaded whiskers trimmed. Gowselling in the grummels he wakes the plaintiff night with pitfalls turning left to right, high noon on the wintry ocean, high noon all sides aboard and aloft to starboard. The weathervane again with deep oars coming through the portholes and all sounds muffled. Noiseless the night on all fours, like the hurricane. Noiseless with loaded caramels and nickel dice. Sister Monica playing the guitar with shirt open and laces down, broad flanges in either ear. Sister Monica streaked with lime, gum wash, her eyes mildewed, craped, crapped, crenelated.

"What a passage!" I exclaim. "That's certainly rock and roll to me."

"I'm glad you liked that," Henry says, "but I have no way of knowing whether Bob Dylan was influenced by me. You know, Bob

Dylan came to my house ten years ago. Joan Baez and her sister brought him and some friends to see me. But Dylan was snooty and arrogant. He was a kid then, of course. And he didn't like me. He thought I was talking down to him, which I wasn't. I was trying to be sociable. But we just couldn't get together. But I know that he is a character, probably a genius, and I really should listen to his work. I'm full of prejudices like everybody else. My kids love him and the Beatles and all the rest."

At this point, Robert Snyder walks into the room. Snyder is the director of an excellent two-hour film entitled *The Henry Miller Odyssey* (distributed by Grove Press Films, which also handles Snyder's films on Buckminster Fuller and Anaïs Nin)—a film in which Miller is shown in his swimming pool reminiscing about his childhood, playing Ping-Pong, bicycling around Pacific Palisades, revisiting old friends in Paris, and conversing with Durrell, Anaïs Nin, and other friends.

Henry has been a film buff ever since his days in Paris, and his essays on *Ecstasy*, Bunuel's *L'Age d'Or*, and the French actor Raimu are marvelous pieces of film criticism.

"Do you still see a lot of movies?" I ask.

"Well, as you can guess, I'm a little behind. Bob brought over a film to show here recently—a film that made me sob and weep: Fellini's *Nights of Cabiria*. I could see it again and cry again. And I just saw the original *Frankenstein* again. And of course, the original story ends at the North Pole where everything is ice, and that's the only proper ending for that monstrous story. It's really a work of art."

"There are films that you detest, Henry, aren't there?" Snyder asks.

"*Bonnie and Clyde!*" Henry exclaims. "Did I hate that! I was clapping to myself when they machine-gunned him to death at the end. Dynamite them! Blow them to smithereens! It was so vulgar, that film. I love obscenity but I hate vulgarity. I can't see how people can enjoy killing for fun. Also, there was a perverse streak there. There was a suggestion that the hero was impotent. I don't like that, I like healthy sex. I don't like impotence and perversion."

"What's perversion?" I ask.

"Well . . . what is it?" Henry laughs, confused. "You got me stumped for a moment. Perversion. Now you've got me stumped. Now I'm moralizing. Well, to get out of it nicely, I'd say it's what isn't healthy. I think you know what I mean, don't you?"

"Not exactly."

"Have you become so broad-minded—I'm not being sarcastic —that to you there's no such thing as perversion?"

"I have my preferences, but I wouldn't make a definite judgment."

"I once asked someone what he'd rather be: ignorant or stupid," Henry explains. "I'd rather be ignorant, but I've done stupid things every day of my life. I think we all do, don't you? Every day we're wrong about something. But I have no remorse, no regrets. That's what I call being healthy."

"Just to take you back for a minute, Henry," I say, "someone told me that you knew Gurdjieff when you were living in Paris. Is that true?"

"I wish I *had* met him," Henry replies, "because I think he's one of the greatest figures in modern times, and a very mysterious one, too. I don't think that anyone has ever come to grips with him yet. I was going to make a tour of France with one of my wives, and she didn't know how to ride a bike. So we went out to the park in Fontainebleau—and we drove around Gurdjieff's place, never knowing he was there. What a misfortune!"

"You often write about how it's possible to become aware and awake in the flash of a moment. This concern with being 'awake' was also important to Gurdjieff."

"I think there are two valid attitudes to this," Henry comments. "Because even in the Zen movement in Japan there are those who think you have to work at it, meditate, study hard, be ascetic. And then there's another group, whose attitude is exemplified by the story of the Master of Fuck. It was written by a famous American living in Japan, and it's about a young man whose parents sent him to become a Zen monk. He's a good student, disciplined, but after ten years he's not getting anywhere—he's not enlightened. After fifteen years he feels he'll never make it and so he decides to live the worldly life, leaves the monastery and runs into a prostitute who looks wonderful. And in the middle of the fuck he attains satori. . . . I never thought of such a thing and naturally he didn't either, and that's why it happened. Do you know the quote from the Buddha: 'I never gained the least thing from unexcelled complete awakening, and for that very reason it is called that.' "

"Once you're awake, how do you keep awake?"

"I can't answer that question really. But: Do you believe in conversion and that it's sincere? Well, I do, I've seen it in people, and they don't have to struggle every day to hold on to it. It remains with you. I don't know if it ever really happened to me. But I think perhaps it did in Paris in 1934, when I moved into the Villa Seurat and was reading the books of Mme. Blavatsky. And one day after I had looked at a photograph of her face—she had the face of a pig, almost, but fascinating—I was hypnotized by her eyes and I had a complete vision of her as if she were in the room.

"Now, I don't know if that had anything to do with what happened next, but I had a flash, I came to the realization that I was responsible for my whole life, whatever had happened. I used to blame my family, society, my wife . . . and that day I saw so clearly that I had nobody to blame but myself. I put everything on my own shoulders and I felt so relieved: Now I'm free, no one else is responsible. And that was a kind of awakening, in a way. I remember the story of how one day the Buddha was walking along and a man came up to him and said: 'Who are you, what are you?' and the Buddha promptly answered: 'I am a man who is awake.' We're asleep, don't you know, we're sleepwalkers."

Henry is showing Robert Snyder some photographs. "Some fan of mine wanted to cheer me up," Henry says, "and so he sent me these post-card photos showing the house in Brooklyn where I lived from the age of one to nine. I spent the happiest times at that age, but these photos are horrible, they're like insanity. The whole street I grew up on has become like a jaw with the teeth falling out. Houses uprooted . . . it looks so horrible."

"What was your first memory of Brooklyn?" I ask.

"A dead cat frozen in the gutter. That was when I was four. I remember birds singing in the cage and I was in the highchair and I recited poems in German—I knew German before I knew English.

"I had three great periods in my life. Age one to nine was Paradise. Then 1930–1940 in Paris and Greece. And then my years at Big Sur."

"Why are you living here, Henry?"

"L.A. is a shithole. Someone selected the house for me and told me to move in. But it doesn't bother me because I have nothing to do with it. I'm in this house, this is my kingdom, my realm. It's a nice house, I have a Ping-Pong table, and when my leg was okay I used to play every day."

"Tell Jonathan about the new book you're working on," Bob Synder interjects.

"It's called *The Book of Friends* [published in 1976 by Capra Press], and it's an homage I'm paying to close, intimate old friends. It begins when I was five years old—what happened seventy-five years ago is so fresh and vivid to me!—and it starts off with childhood friends. I always made friends easily—all my life, even now. And in this book I'm repeating myself often, overlapping, covering ground I've already written about, but from a different angle. It goes up to Joe Gray—an ex-pugilist, a stuntman, and stand-in for Dean Martin. An uncultured guy but a great reader. After reading my books, he started to read everything else. He died two years ago, and he was a great friend. With each friend, you know, I was different."

"The last thing I wanted to ask you about, Henry," I say, leafing through my little book, "was the initiation ordeal imposed by the Brotherhood of Fools and Simpletons—an ordeal you've humorously written about in *Big Sur*."

"The Brotherhood of Fools and Simpletons?" Henry wonders. "I've completely forgotten what that was all about."

"Well, the Brotherhood asks three questions of the initiates. The first is: 'How would you order the world if you were given the powers of the creator?' The second: 'What is it you desire that you do not already possess?' And the third: 'Say something which will truly astonish us!' . . . How would you answer these questions?"

"Ah ha!" Henry exclaims. "That third question I borrowed from Cocteau and Diaghilev. They met in the dead of night and Diaghilev went up to Cocteau and said: 'Étonne-moi! Astonish me!' The second question was a rhetorical question because there isn't any such thing. And the first question about ordering the world: I would be paralyzed. I wouldn't know how to lift a finger to change the world or make it over. I wouldn't know what to do."

Lawrence Durrell and his wife have arrived for dinner and are now chatting in the living room with Henry's daughter Val and his son Tony and Tony's wife. Henry appears in his bathrobe and speaks to Durrell with the generosity and gentleness that one might imagine a younger son would feel toward an adored older brother. And I am reminded of that beautiful letter Henry wrote to his younger friend in 1959:

> Ah, Larry, it isn't that life is so short, it's that it's everlasting. Often, talking with you under the tent—especially over a vieux marc—I waned to say, "Stop talking . . . let's *talk!*" For 20 years I waited to see you again. For 20 years your voice rang in my ears. And your laughter. And there, at the Mazet, time running out (never the vieux marc), I had an almost frantic desire to pin you down, to have it out, to get to the bottom. (*What is the stars?* Remember?) And there we were on the poop deck, so to speak, the stars drenching us with light, and what are we saying? Truth is, you said so many marvelous things I never did know what we were talking about. I listened to the Master's Voice, just like that puppy on the old Victor gramophone. Whether you were expounding, describing, depicting, deflowering, or delineating, it was all one to me. I heard you writing aloud. I said to myself—"He's arrived. He made it. He knows how to say it. Say it! Continue!" *Oui, c'est toi, le cher maître.* You have the vocabulary, the armature, the Vulcanic fire in your bowels. You've even found "the place and the formula." Give us a new world! Give us grace and fortitude!
> —*A Private Correspondence:*
> *Lawrence Durrell and Henry Miller*

As they sit down at the table, Henry says to Durrell: "This guy here mentioned three terrific questions asked by my Brotherhood of Fools and Simpletons. I'd really forgotten them."

"What were they, Henry?"

"What were they, Jonathan?"

I repeat them.

"I bet I know how you'd answer the first," Durrell says, "about how you'd order the world."

"What would you think?"

"Like a Gnostic," Durrell says, "you'd wipe it out."

"I said that I wouldn't know what I'd do, I'd be paralyzed," Henry replies. "But sometimes I do think the world is a cosmic error of a false god. I don't really believe things like that but I like the idea. Life is great and beautiful—there's nothing *but* life—but we have made of the world a horrible place. Man has never handled the gift of life properly. And it is a crazy world, everything about it is absurd and wrong, and it deserves to be wiped out. I don't think it's going to last forever. I think there is such a thing as the end of the world or the end of this species of man. It could very well be that another type of man will come into being.

"You know," Henry turns to me, "Larry recently gave me a book to read called *The Gnostics*. It's written by a young Jesuit, of all people. And you know something . . . you were asking me before about rock and roll and the happenings with young people in the sixties. Well, when all that was happening, I wasn't aware that it was a revolution. Now they look back and they call it that. But the hippies are like toilet paper compared with the Gnostics. They *really* turned the world upside down. They did fantastic things. They were deliberately amoral, unmoral, immoral, contra the government and establishment. They did everything possible to increase the insanity."

A toast is proposed to insanity.

Even in his early days in Brooklyn, Henry Miller saw through the Social Lie as easily as through Saran Wrap, embodying the alienating Lie as the Cosmodemonic Telegraph Company in *Tropic of Capricorn*. While gainsaying Ezra Pound's dimwitted social-credit economics in a famous essay filled with sublime truisms ("Money and How It Gets That Way"), Miller rejected any and all "political" paths (for which he has been often criticized), preferring instead to lambaste every irruption of corporate mentality in any number of pasquinades—one of his most delightful being his attack on American bread:

Accept any loaf that is offered you without question even if it is not wrapped in cellophane, even if it contains no kelp. Throw it in the back of the car with the oil can and the grease rags; if possible, bury it under a sack of coal, *bituminous* coal. As you climb up the road to your home, drop it in the mud a few times and dig your heels into it. When you get to the house, and after you have prepared the other dishes, take a huge carving knife and rip the loaf from stem to stern. Then take one whole onion, peeled or unpeeled, one carrot, one stalk of celery, one huge piece of garlic, one sliced apple, a herring, a handful of anchovies, a sprig of parsley and an old toothbrush, and shove them in the disemboweled guts of the bread. Over these pour a thimbleful of kerosene, a dash of Lavoris, and just a wee bit of Clorox. . . .
—*Remember to Remember*

And in *The Colossus of Maroussi*, he writes: "At Eleusis one realizes, if never before, that there is no salvation in becoming adapted to a world which is crazy. At Eleusis one becomes adapted to the cosmos. Outwardly Eleusis may seem broken, disintegrated with the crumbled past; actually Eleusis is still intact and it is we who are broken, dispersed, crumbling to dust. Eleusis lives, lives eternally in the midst of a dying world."

Miller has always chosen reality over realism, action over activity, intuition over instinct, mystery over the mysterious, being over healing, surrender over attachment, conversion over wishing, lighthouses over lifeboats, enlightenment over salvation, and the world-as-womb over the world-as-tomb. Strangely, cosmologists have recently given credibility to the intuition that we probably all exist within a universe composed of space and time created by the original, erupting, fecundating "big bang"—all of us and all of our worlds trapped inside the gravitational radius of a universe from which no light can escape.

In the forties George Orwell criticized Miller's idea of passive acceptance as it was revealed in the image of the man in the belly of the whale (the world-as-womb)—an image which Miller first presented in his impassioned introduction to and defense of Anaïs Nin's then unpublished diaries. Miller wrote:

We who imagined that we were sitting in the belly of the whale and doomed to nothingness suddenly discover that the whale was a projection of our own insufficiency. The whale remains, but the whale becomes the whole wide world, with stars and seasons, with banquets and festivals, with everything that is wonderful to see and touch, and being that it is no longer a whale but something nameless because something that is inside as well as outside us. We may, if we like, devour the whale too—piecemeal, throughout eternity. No matter how much is ingested there will always remain more whale than man; because what man appropriates of the whale returns to the whale again in one form or another. The whale is constantly being transformed as man himself becomes transformed. . . . One lives within the spirit of transformation and not in the act. The legend of the whale thus becomes the celebrated book of transformations destined to cure the ills of the world.

"Un Être Étoilique"

"The stars gather direction in the same way that the foetus moves toward birth," Miller has said. And his own books of transformations are remarkably in tune with the new cosmological perspectives of the universe. Rather than regressing to agoraphobic passivity, his books continually open themselves up to include and become a perpetually metamorphosing personality which itself becomes a "creation." "You have expanded the womb feeling until it includes the whole universe," Miller wrote Durrell after reading *The Black Book* for the first time—generously praising a fellow author, yet also accurately describing the direction of his own work.

Henry Miller has continued to foster his "cosmic accent" and his mantic gift, but like the Greek poet Seferiades whom he praises in *The Colossus of Maroussi*, his "native flexibility" has equally responded to "the cosmic laws of curvature and finitude. He had ceased going out in all directions: His lines were making the encircling movement of embrace."

As the world falls rapidly on its measured ellipse, Henry Miller is writing, painting, and dreaming his life away in Pacific Palisades: "Some will say they do not wish to *dream* their lives away," he writes in *Big Sur*. "As if life itself were not a dream, a very real dream from which there is no awakening! We pass from one state of dream to another: from the dream of sleep to the dream of waking, from the dream of life to the dream of death. Whoever has enjoyed a good dream never complains of having wasted his time. On the contrary, he is delighted to have partaken of a reality which serves to heighten and enhance the reality of everyday."

HARRY PARTCH

Sound-Magic
and
Passionate Speech

June 24, 1901–September 3, 1974

I n 1930, the then twenty-nine-year-old composer Harry Partch was living in a small room on Charles Street in New Orleans. Somewhere earlier or later, sleeping in one of the many California arbors where he picked grapes and prunes as a hobo during the Depression, Partch woke up one morning and realized that he and Western European music were through.

In that luminescent hour, it seemed as if the concert hall ("where inhibited strangers sit stiffly in flank, before and after"), the restricting twelve-note scale with its faithful and obsequious servant (the piano), and the entire corpus of symphonic "classics" were a claustrophobic cultural mirage receding into the Western night.

"Out of such abysses," Nietzsche once wrote—as if to describe the moment—"also out of the abyss of great suspicion, one returns newborn, having shed one's skin, more ticklish and sarcastic, with a more delicate taste for joy, with a more tender tongue for all good things, with gayer senses, with a second dangerous innocence in joy, more childlike and yet a hundred times more subtle than one has ever seen before."

"*Pure* music, *pure* drama, *pure* telephone poles in the virgin grazz," Partch later wrote, nose-thumbing the cultural establishment; "*pure* black-and-white tails, *pure* orchids on a *pure* bosom (*I love music!*)," as he pulled away the veils covering the traditional notions of what music should be: "Whistle softly, and as each loving muscle snuggles under, and each tiny cilia wiggles free, you will *see*—

shimmering before you—the curves of x million perceptible changes in pitch, at least 127 varieties of female giggles, and no less than 17 kinds of falsetto wails in each cubic foot of free vibrating air."

Back in that room in New Orleans, cilia struggling to wiggle free, Harry Partch gathered up sixteen years' worth of his youthful compositions, placed them in a potbellied stove and burned them all in what must have been a ravishing *auto-da-fé*. "*Not* free *from* what, but free *for* what" might have been Partch's motto for the next four decades, during which the now-seventy-three-year-old composer revealed himself to be one of the great "originals" in the history of American music. Jacques Barzun has called Partch's work "the most original and powerful contribution to dramatic music on this continent." And his admirers have included composers as diverse in style as Howard Hanson, Otto Luening, Douglas Moore, and Lou Harrison —as well as jazz musicians like Scott LaFaro, Chet Baker, Gerry Mulligan, Gil Evans, and Bob Brookmeyer.

But because Partch's instruments are one-of-a-kind, requiring specially trained musicians to perform them and master the composer's forty-three-tones-to-the-octave scale, and because works like *The Bewitched* are enormous ritualistic music dramas demanding at least six months of rehearsals, there have been few opportunities to experience directly Partch's extraordinary art.*

"The work that I have been doing these many years," Partch has said, "parallels much in the attitudes and actions of primitive man. He found sound-magic in the common materials around him. He then proceeded to make the vehicle, the instrument, as visually beautiful as he could. Finally, he involved the sound-magic and the visual beauty in his everyday words and experiences, his ritual and drama,

* A number of persons have known about the composer's works through his privately distributed Gate 5 Records series (almost all of which are now out of print) and the five films Madeline Tourtelot has made about the composer, preserving certain performances, or in which she counterpointed his music with her images (*Music Studio, Rotate the Body, Windsong, U.S. Highball, Delusion of the Fury*—these films are distributed by Grove Press). But it is only within the past ten years that Partch's music has been made commercially available on five excellent and invaluable recordings: *The Music of Harry Partch, And on the Seventh Day Petals Fell in Petaluma,* and *The Bewitched* (Composers Recordings CRI 193, 213, and S-304E respectively) and *The World of Harry Partch* and *Delusion of the Fury* (Columbia MQ 31227 and M2 30576). Also, the best introductory film on Partch—a half-hour portrait entitled *The Dreamer That Remains* (distributed by Tantalus Films, L.A.)—was released in 1973.

in order to lend greater meaning to his life. This is my trinity: sound-magic, visual beauty, experience-ritual."

In order to realize his new conceptions of sound-magic, Partch, over a period of forty years, has designed and built close to thirty beautiful-looking and -sounding instruments. These include:

The Zymo-Xyl, an "exercise in hither and thither aesthesia" constructed out of hubcaps and a kettletop, oak blocks placed above a triangular resonator, and wine and liquor bottles turned upside down in two banks—starting with Old Heaven Hill and gently lurching up a scale consisting of Vat 69 and Gordon's Gin (among others), finally ending up with Harvey's Bristol Sherry.

The Gourd Tree And Cone Gong, an instrument made up of twelve temple bells attached "like exotic fruit" to a bar of eucalyptus —each bell bolted to a gourd resonator—and two nose-cone gongs salvaged from a reject Douglas aircraft bomber.

The Mazda Marimba, an instrument named after Ahura Mazda—the Persian god of light—consisting of banks of tuned light bulbs, severed at the sockets and with their entrails removed, and sounding like "the percolations of a coffee pot."

The Spoils of War, an instrument made of seven artillery shell casings, Pyrex chemical solution jars, a woodblock and marimba bar, a gourd *guiro*, and spring steel flexitones (known as Whang Guns): "How much better to have them here than shredding young boys' skin in the battlefield," Partch once remarked.

The Cloud-Chamber Bowls, an instrument created out of the tops and bottoms of Pyrex chemical-solution jars (Partch found them in the glass shop of the University of California radiation lab) which are suspended on a rack and hit on their sides and tops with soft mallets.

"I am not an instrument builder," Partch once said of his musical and sculptural wonders, "only a philosophic music man seduced into carpentry." The result of "an acoustical ardor and a conceptual fervor," Partch's instruments are specifically designed to perform his forty-three-tones-to-the-octave music. Early in his life, the composer decided that the twelve-note scale represented an unacceptable structural rigidity and conceptual imprecision. Certainly, Partch was hardly the first person to turn to the principles of *just intonation*—a system of tuning in which all the musical intervals are derived from the perfect fifth and perfect third and their multiples. (Our twelve-tone scale is acoustically "distorted" for the sake of modulatory simplicity. Play an F sharp and G flat on a guitar or violin and compare these results with the one note on our equal-tempered—or, as Partch likes to say, "ill-tempered"—piano. Or listen to a perfectly sung blues seventh note and contrast it with the piano equivalent.)

The twelve-tone scale, in other words, is not a God-given construct. A fifty-three-tone system was proposed by both the Chinese Ching Fang in the first century B.C. and the seventeenth-century Danish mathematician Nicolas Mercator. Chinese, Indian, and Arab systems of tuning, of course, are based on microtonal proportions. Scores of musicians and theorists used these intervals during the Renaissance as well. In 1555, for example, the Italian composer Vicentino made a harpsichord in which the octave was divided into thirty intervals spread over six manuals, each being tuned to one of the six Greek modes. And in this century, composers like Ives, Haba, Bloch, Bartók, Lou Harrison, Alan Hovhaness, and John Cage, among others, have employed microtonal elements in their work. (It goes without saying that jazz musicians have been the most natural practitioners in this area.)

But Harry Partch is undoubtedly the only Western composer to use successfully a specific just-intonational scale as the basis for all his music. With this scale—forty-three-tones-to-the-octave, whose basic tone is 392 cycles per second, our tempered G—Partch dispenses with key harmony and conventional modulations, thereby allowing for an "expanded" harmony and overtone enrichment and offering what the composer claims to be twenty-eight possible tonalities. As the critic Peter Yates has described it, this scale creates "a continuous field of melodic and harmonic relationship among the degrees of spoken, intoned, chanted, sung, melismatic, and shouted vocal utterance—a tonal spectrum filling in the gap between the vocal coloration of opera and the spoken drama. Spoken melody may be taken over by the instruments and translated back again to chant and song."

As performed on his predominantly plectral-percussive instruments, Partch's works certainly reveal affinities with Indonesian, Polynesian, Japanese, and African musical practices (as well as with Yaqui, Zuni, and Cahuilla American Indian chants which, in fact, Partch uses in several of his works)—existing in that region where, as James Joyce once wrote, "that earopean end meets Ind." But rather than suggesting and languishing in an easily imitated and modish kind of atmospheric musical chinoiserie, Partch's compositions instinctively reflect and operate as counterparts to the specific structural and expressive qualities—timbral, articulative, vibratory, and rhythmic—of much non-Western music.

It is interesting, too, to recall a statement that Arnold Schoenberg once made, and one which he never really applied seriously in his own music: "I cannot unreservedly agree," Schoenberg wrote, "with the distinction between color and pitch. I find that a note is perceived by its color, one of whose dimensions is pitch. Color, then, is the great realm, pitch one of its provinces. . . . If the ear could discriminate between differences of color, it might be feasible to invent melodies that are built of colors. But who dares to develop such theories?" And it is exactly this theory (though he dislikes "theory") that Partch put into practice in his shimmering, vibrant music—exhibiting an enormous variety of articulative shadings, fluctuating tremolos, rotating rhythmic patterns . . . with the steam engine whistles of the Chromelodeon and moaning Crychord sounding like trains passing through the New Mexico and Arizona deserts that Partch remembers from his youth.

Concomitant with Partch's discovery of the world of music within himself came his insight that "spontaneity of execution is the essence of music, vitally connected to the human body through the mouth, the ears, and the emotions. . . . This thing began with truth, and truth *does* exist. For some hundreds of years, the truth of just intonation has been hidden—one could say *maliciously*, because truth always threatens the ruling hierarchy . . . or they so *think*. Nor does the spiritual-corporeal nature of man fare any better. We are reduced to specialties—a theater of dialogue without music, for example, or a concert of music without drama—basic mutilations of ancient concept. My music is visual; it is corporeal, aural, *and* visual."

Partch continually talks about how his musicians "must always present pictures of athletic grace" when they're performing. He speaks of caressing, embracing, and even raping the instruments. And the instruments themselves seem to embody male and female sexual characteristics—resonating tongues in bamboo, nose cones—while their tones and timbres often cause a powerful physical excitation. About his Marimba Eroica—an instrument made of four spruce timbers and large boxlike resonators that can produce an almost inaudible twenty-two-cycles-per-second sound—Partch says: "In the right room, acoustically, the Eroica is felt through the feet against the belly, and if one sits on the floor, it ripples through his bottom. . . . I've dreamed of an Eroica with reinforced concrete resonators going down into the ground and boxes mounted above them like a stairway. One could therefore trip barefoot up the scale to bed and box down to breakfast. Or trip both ways at once to a musical apotheosis."

In 1923 Partch began to develop the two seminal ideas that would fertilize all his later work—those of the One Voice (Monophony) and the Corporeal. The composer saw in ancient Greek drama, whose spirit he thought originated in epic chant, a one-voice/one-instrument idea that has kept itself alive from Homer to the Balkan minstrels. Between 1930–1947, in fact, Partch himself performed on only one instrument—his Adapted Viola, built with an elongated neck and played between the knees—with which he accompanied himself singing Biblical passages, Li Po poems, and the hitch-hiker inscriptions that he included in his hobo epic *The Wayward* (1943), consisting of *Barstow*, *The Letter*, *San Francisco*, and *U. S. Highball*. These four works use on-the-road conversation fragments, boxcar graffiti, signs from derelict havens, newsboy cries, hitch-hiker inscriptions, names of railroad towns, and fleeting thoughts—all recited, sung, intoned and chanted against microtonal moans, instrumental imitations of railway noises, snatches of bar tunes, pentatonic shouts, and seventh- and ninth-chord guitar riffs.

Partch's criticism of the "classical" operatic and lieder tradition was that it avoided the natural spoken rhythms and tonal glides of everyday speech, insisting instead of artificial devices such as rolled r's, precise attacks and releases, the affected stylization of "refined" English, and a choral technique that gloried in the singing of meaningless syllables, short reiterated phrases, and highly dramatic but unbelievable "unison" passages. (Needless to say, Robert Johnson and Chuck Berry had pretty much the same idea. So did W. B. Yeats and William Carlos Williams, the latter of whom, when writing about Lelia Zukofsky's *Music to Shakespeare's Pericles*, talked about the "shouting and spouting, distortion and clouding of words and phrasing that is opera.")

In his book *Genesis of a Music* [first published in 1949 and revised and reissued by Da Capo Press in 1974], Partch took his notion of the necessary relationship between speech and music—a notion subscribed to by philosophers and composers from Plato to Carl Orff—and followed it through Western history in order to point out how this relationship broke down in the "word distortion of florid secular polyphony and restrictive liturgical polyphony." Partch sees the "musical phoenix rising from the ashes of ancient Rome" in some of the early operatic works of Peri, Caccini, and Monteverdi (the seventeenth-century Italian composers who brought the *word* back into importance after the musically delirious styles of Nenna and Gesualdo). To Partch, Bach and Beethoven represented an unacceptable abstractional approach to art, and he gives approval to only a small number of European compositions, among them pieces by Berlioz, Mussorgsky (a personal favorite of Partch's—"word-loving, sensitive, subtle and natural Mussorgsky," Partch says of him), Wagner (who wrote: "We have to recognize Speech itself as the indispensable basis of a perfect Artistic Expression"), Hugo Wolf, Mahler (*The Song of the Earth*), Debussy (*Pelléas and Mélisande*), Satie (*Socrate*), and Schoenberg (*Pierrot Lunaire*, and *only* that work by Schoenberg). To Partch, the works of these composers are the small lights in the abstract darkness of Western music.

The idea of a music that becomes a "language in itself" seems, to Partch, to deny the human body. But by unequivocally pressing his antagonism to such an idea, he does away with extraordinarily vital music by composers such as Machaut, Dufay, Bach, Beethoven, and Stravinsky—is this really the "Abstract" and "non-Corporeal" enemy? Partch himself in a new preface to *Genesis of a Music* admits now that "this survey was not adequate to the facts." Still, his attacks on the concert-hall, "star"-system, and the mathematical orientation of establishment musical life are at the service of a life-enhancing artistic vision: "One's beginning is a decent and honorable mistake, and long before life has run its course, one is obliged to contemplate—both dazed and undazed—the endless reaches of one's innocence. . . . Rules and standards become meaningless once the simple truth is faced. Let us give to nuts and bolts the standardization of thread that we have come to expect, but let us give to music, magic; to man, magic. . . . My peaks of wrath and nadirs of depression, through some four decades, were akin to the fulminations and despair of the Hebrew prophets, and for exactly the same reasons: the endowed priests of the temple sanctifying form without content, ritual without value. Hollow magic."

Drawing on his idea of Corporeal music and the principles of Greek and Noh drama, Japanese kabuki and Mummer's plays, Partch has created a number of music dramas containing music, dance, mime, shouting, whistling, and slapstick—in all of which the instruments are part of the stage set, their performers in costume, both singing and acting.

Revelation in the Courthouse Park (1960) presents a psychological parallel to Euripides' *The Bacchae*. Shifting between ancient Thebes and a modern park in which Dionysus becomes Dion, the Hollywood king of Ishbu Kubu, Partch's work features—in addition to the actors, musicians, and dancers—a marching brass band, acrobats, gymnasts, and a filmed fireworks display.

Water! Water! (1961) takes place in Santa Mystiana, a large American city whose inhabitants include a disc jockey, an alderman, a lady mayor, and a baseball radio commentator. The city calls on a black jazz band to invoke rain in a voodoo ritual, and when the rains fall, the baseball game is washed out, and civilization collapses. After the flood, Arthur, the jazz musician, and Wanda the Witch are sued for millions of dollars and stand trial. But at this moment, the dam begins to overflow, and the citizens accept their fate to the tune of Santa Mystiana the Beautiful. The producer drives the traveling instruments into the pit of the stage, for "the highest goodness is like water. It seeks the low place, that all men dislike" (after Lao-tzu).

Delusion of the Fury (1963–69), Partch's most recent and most powerful music-drama, is based on a Noh drama theme about a murdered man who, in death, must exorcise the moment of his dying in his past existence, as well as on an African folk tale about a deaf man, a deaf judge, a judgment, and the intercession of pagan deities. In *Delusion* and the ravishing instrumental composition *And on the Seventh Day Petals Fell in Petaluma*, which served as the "musical sinews" for *Delusion*, Partch has fully realized his idea of Corporeal music. And the composer's longstanding attraction to Noh drama gives the key to his understanding of "sound-magic, visual beauty, and experience-ritual." Early on in his career, Partch had spoken of Noh as a "drama of accomplished grace," and one is sure he meant to suggest both the idea of the highly charged "gesture" as well as of the state of immanence. In his notes for his composition *Oedipus* (1952), Partch spoke of the music as being "conceived as emotional saturation." And like the Noh drama, where subsisting tensions and longings are resolved in the form of a final dance, all of Partch's later music-dramas are at once rituals of enormous emotional charge and allegories presenting the force of the unrepressed body and spirit in its progress through the abstract world.

Partch's *The Bewitched* (1957) reveals this most clearly. A tribe of Lost Musicians, representing instinctual life, unmaliciously destroys the fake products of twentieth-century European civilization. Titles for the scenes of the drama suggest the amazing humor of the work: "Three Undergraduates Become Transfigured in a Hong Kong Music Hall"; "A Soul Tortured by Contemporary Music Finds a Humanizing Alchemy"; "Visions Fill the Eyes of a Defeated Basketball Team in the Shower Room." Partch's seven-page program notes for *The Bewitched*—filled with discussions about matriarchal society, sexual evolution, adolescent love, and recidivism, and written with his characteristic verbal brilliance—not only suggest the tone of the work but reflect the composer's larger ideas and feelings about his artistic endeavor. Here is Partch's description of the work's Prologue, entitled "The Lost Musicians Mix Magic":

"The forms of strange instruments are seen onstage. How did they get here? They came on in a dark celestial silence, doing tumbles and handsprings, and for no other purpose than to be discovered by *these* musicians in *this* theater before *this* audience.

"One of the musicians gives a low beat, and others swing in, one at a time. They are neolithic primitives in their unspoken acceptance of magic as real, unconsciously reclaiming an all-but-lost value for the exploitation of their perception in an age of scientific hierarchs—a value lost only about a minute ago in relation to that ancient time when the first single cell moved itself in such autoerotic agitation that it split in two. The first animate magic.

"In the enveloping ensemble the lost musicians have momentarily found a direction, a long-arm extension of first magic. Their direction becomes a power, and their power a vision: an ancient witch, a prehistoric seer untouched by either gossip or popular malevolence, and with that wonderful power to make others see also. The perceptive witch corresponds to the Greek oracle, while the chorus [the orchestra]—like the choruses of ancient tragedy—is a moral instrument under the power of perceptive suggestion.

"The lost musicians are quite without malice. On wings of love they demolish three undergraduate egos temporarily away from their jukeboxes. It is the kind thing to do. On wings of love they turn an incorrigibly pursuing young wooer into a retreating misogynist. It is the kind thing to do. On wings of love they catapult the cultural know-it-alls into limbo, because limbo will be so congenial. It is certainly the kind thing to do.

"The witch surveys the world and immediately becomes sad

and moody, then takes command: 'Everybody wants background music!' the witch-like sounds seem to murmur, and the conspiratorial tone is clear even in gibberish. Let us dance."

In April 1973, I wrote to Harry Partch in San Diego to ask him if I could fly over to visit him and, since I wouldn't have a car, if he could recommend a motel near his home. A week later I received this note:

Dear Jonathan Cott—
    The Alamo Motel, 4567 Texas St., San Diego. It is the closest, $10–$12 a day, kitchenette, swimming pool—$35 a week. I think I'll move there—it sounds better than this wretched place. It is close to the No. 11 bus, on Adams Ave. Take that east to Felton, then walk north. . . .
    I will be 72 in June, and I've been interviewed for over 40 years. The interviewers are generally nice guys and gals, but very frankly I am sick to death of my "career."
    However, you will be welcomed. It is an old habit.
                                                            Yours,
                                                        Harry Partch

The Alamo Motel is one of an enormous number of culturally rootless family members constituting those Southern California apartment-motel dwellings bearing names like Rampart Manor, the Telstar, Lee Tiki, Il Pompeii, and Fountain Bleu which the architect Robert Venturi has classified as "the ugly and the ordinary." By that, Venturi doesn't mean that these places lack charm or interest— Venturi's recent architecture, in fact, uses exactly this quintessential American style to construct things like a firehouse built along the lines of an expanded Lionel toy train station.
    And the Alamo is certainly a "real" cheerful place: The friendly couple who run it chat with the guests right through the day, invite you in for coffee—and when you're not watching TV, you can contemplate the tiny swimming pool stuck in the courtyard alongside a row of rubber plants, banana and kumquat trees, flag lilac, geraniums, and swamp grass. (It's the place W. C. Fields might have retired to in *It's a Gift*).
    Harry Partch lives a mile or so up the road in a small, nondescript suburban home on a street like any other, with TV aerials—five times the height of the houses—rising out of every roof. Partch, who

lived as a hobo for twelve years, has since the forties moved his lodgings every few years—from a chick hatchery in Petaluma where he composed *Petals*, to a laundromat in Venice, L.A., to several homes in the San Diego area where his devoted friend and musical associate Danlee Mitchell works with and assists the composer. (Mitchell, who has been training musicians and performing all of Partch's recent works, stores the Partch instruments in a special studio at San Diego State College where he teaches.)

The first thing that distinguishes Partch's home from any other on the block is a strange sign hanging on the door:

OCCUPANT IS A HEATHEN CHINEE
MISSIONARIES AT THIS DOOR WILL
FACE THE DOWAGER EMPRESS
AND ANOTHER BOXER REBELLION
PLEASE DO NOT DISTURB
11 AM–2 PM
MISSIONARIES NEVER

"I'm always being bothered by the Jehovah's Witnesses," Partch says as he greets me one morning, dressed in pajamas and bathrobe. He's just gotten over a minor illness, and his living room looks a bit untogether—but comfortably so: a Chinese coolie hat and a Balinese shadow puppet on the wall and a table filled with sharpened colored pencils, black pepper containers, post cards, jumbo Gem clips, a package of Tums, and several books (including *Japan's Imperial Conspiracy* and *Maximum Security: Letters from Prison*, edited by Eve Pell—both of which Partch has recently been reading avidly).

He sits down in the driftwood-supported hammock-type couch and lights up his pipe. "My parents were missionaries in China," Partch says, "and they went *through* the Boxers' Rebellion, but I don't think anyone around here has ever heard of it."

"They probably imagine it has something to do with Joe Louis," I suggest.

"Joe Louis!" Partch laughs heartily. "Probably do. . . . I'm making some chicken soup and milk. Please have some."

"I know you were born in Oakland in 1901," I say as he goes into the kitchen. "Did you know Gertrude Stein once said that in Oakland there's 'no there there'?"

A big laugh from inside. "Well, what are you going to say about L.A.?"

"There's too much there there."

"Yes, too much. . . . But I like Oakland, really. You see, we left when I was two, so I don't remember that part. But later I lived there, and in fact I wrote *Oedipus* there. Hell, man, I don't care where I am. If I were in the North Pole I'd go on writing. I don't care if I'm in euphoria or in despair—I go on producing. It doesn't make any difference. I went to Hawaii when I was twenty, and everyone said: 'You won't do a *thing* in Hawaii.' Well, I never wrote so many fugues in my life."

Partch comes back with soup and milk and tells me a bit about his life. In the 1880's, his parents received the "call" and were sent to China as missionaries. When they resigned their posts, they moved to Oakland and then homesteaded in a number of towns in southeastern Arizona, where Partch grew up.

"I remember that once when I was hitchhiking during my hobo days," Partch says, "that I happened in 1940 to be on the road near Big Sur. Well, I was picked up by this painter named Varda—who became well-known later on in Sausalito—and I told him about my music and he said: 'You *must* spend the winter with me.' Varda was living in a place called Anason Creek—fifteen dollars a month—and when the wood ran out, he used to tear down a shack. I remember he once described Arizona to me, saying how it seemed to him to be just like Christianity. '*Touch me not*, say the ants, the cactus, and the hot sand,' Varda exclaimed. 'But the purple hills say: *Come, come, come.*' "

Partch's apostate father became involved with agnosticism, secularism, and atheism, while his mother read a lot of Mary Baker Eddy and the New Thought writers. But, as Partch has written, his parents' reading materials—whether Robert Ingersoll or Mary Baker Eddy—"simply did not stack up, in excitement, beside the wild immoralities of Greek mythology, or, in adventure, with the *Anabasis* of Xenophon. In our library there were more books in Chinese, accordion-folded with ivory thongs, illustrated with gory colored lithographs of the beheading of missionaries, than there were books in English."

At one point during his childhood, Partch lived just outside a tiny Arizona railroad town called Benson, which had a population of three hundred, and eleven saloons for transient railroaders along its boardwalk. Partch began ordering instruments through the Sears,

Roebuck catalog and learned one at a time—cello, violin, harmonica, mandolin, guitar, and cornet. "I was already devouring the *idea* of music," he says.

In Albuquerque, when he was fourteen, Partch began to write music seriously, played "Hearts and Flowers" in the local movie houses, and worked part-time delivering pharmaceutical drugs on his bicycle to the red-light district. (Partch remembers one lady there offering him his first cigar, which he smoked all the way through without getting sick.)

Self-taught, the composer picked up and devoured an enormous range of nontraditional musical possibilities that obviously influenced his later work: Christian hymns like "Nearer My God to Thee," Mandarin Chinese lullabies (sung by his mother), Yaqui Indian and Congo puberty rituals, Hebrews chants for the dead (heard on Edison cylinder records played for him by a store owner in Arizona), and, later, Okie songs in California vineyards and those of the Cantonese music hall. Partch remembers experiencing these musical worlds—"certain small shafts of intense light"—with a "kind of intimate passion."

For a number of years he worked as a fruit-picker, school-teacher, and proofreader. Then in 1934 he received a Carnegie grant to study the history of intonation in England. On a trip to Ireland at that time, he took the first instrument he had designed and built—the Adapted Viola—and went to meet and play for William Butler Yeats. "I had read his prefaces—I *love* prefaces, incidentally—and Yeats had written some wonderful things about music and passionate speech."

In *Ah, Sweet Dancer*—a collection of Yeats's letters to Margot Ruddock—we find the following entry: "A Californian musician called a few days ago and is coming again tomorrow. He is working on the relation between words and music. He has made and is making other musical instruments which do not go beyond the range of the speaking voice but within that range make a music possible which employs very minute intervals. He speaks to this instrument. He only introduces melody when he sings vowels without any relation to words."

"The minute I brought out my viola and sang," Partch recalls, "Yeats just loved it. He's not one for theory. I played and sang 'By the Rivers of Babylon.' 'Marthe, Marthe!' he shouted, 'come here.' Later I met the poet Æ at a party in London and told him about my having played for Yeats. 'Yeats has a tin ear,' Æ said. I told him I disagreed, and we had a discussion. 'He can't tell one tone from another,' Æ insisted. 'That *proves* he has a good ear,' I replied, and Æ was a little taken aback by that. You see, I *contend* this: We hear so *much*, and it's hard to stick with only the twelve tones of the octave. . . .

"Anyway, I had no chance of making a living over in Europe, so I went from English salons to the San Joaquin Valley where I worked as a dishwasher and flunky and picked fruit and cotton all through the Depression. They were really terrible, terrible times. But I slept out in the fields, and the hobos were my friends. (I kept my music in my hobo bundle wherever I went.) Most of the hobos were reform-school boys or orphans. One of my most beautiful pals was farmed out at the age of five, ran away at eight, and was raped before he was twelve. He was so kindly, I loved the guy. Of course I lost him after six weeks. . . . But I don't worry about these people because any good hobo can take care of himself."

With a little help from his friends, Partch has been taking care of himself for many decades, yet it is unfortunate that, aside from the fact that he has an enthusiastic but small number of admirers, his work is generally unknown in this country.

Today, on some Middle-American street in San Diego, Harry Partch is talking about the Greek musician Timotheus (446–357 B.C.), who dared to expand the scale on the Kithara (an instrument Partch has rebuilt after 2000 years) by adding four strings to the eight approved of by Pythagoras. Partch picks up a copy of *Genesis of a Music*, and reads—as well as dramatically elaborates on—a passage he once wrote describing a scene by the comic poet Pherecrates in which the personification of Music bemoans her outrage at the hands of Timotheus' twelve strings:

"But now comes Timotheus," Partch speak-sings, "who has most shamelessly ruined and massacred me. Who is this Timotheus? asks Justice, one of the other persons in the play. A red-haired Milesian, is the answer. He has exceeded all the others in wickedness. He has introduced weird music like the crawlings of an antheap, unharmonic with most unholy high notes and pipings. He has filled me full of maggots like a cabbage. And once, when by chance, he met me walking alone, he disrobed me and tied me up in pieces with 12 strings.

"The Spartans drove away the immoral Timotheus," Partch dramatically concludes. "He was catapulted onto a Spartan hillside by a Spartan bouncer. To dream of undesirable changes is one thing, to act upon these dreams quite another."

There is a scene in an excellent new film about Partch entitled *The Dreamer That Remains* (directed by Stephen Pouliot and produced by one of Partch's devoted admirers, Betty Freeman) in which the composer recalls the words he once saw on the wall of an L. A. screening room belonging to a company specializing in children's films. Along with various appreciative, graffiti-type comments written by children was the following tiny poem: Once upon a time/There was a little boy/And he went outside.

Harry Partch himself has put it quietly and beautifully:

The small child feels that he is the center of the world, in both his joys and his disasters. It is redundant to say, *the world he knows*. There is no other. And every lonely child builds worlds of his own, both with objects and in fantasy, a dozen a year, or even a dozen a day.

Can this world
From of old
Always have been so sad,
Or did it become so for the sake
Of me alone?
—Anonymous Japanese poem,
trans. by Arthur Waley

And this quality would be unchanged if other words were substituted: *Always have been so happy for the sake of me alone.*

MAURICE SENDAK

King
of All
Wild Things

OVERTURE: LITTLE BROTHER, LITTLE SISTER

This is the way the fairy tale begins: "Brother took his little sister by the hand and said, 'Since our mother died we have not had one happy hour. Stepmother beats us every day and when we want to come to her she kicks us away with her foot. Come, we will go out into the wide world together.' All day they walked over meadows, fields, and stony paths and when it rained sister said, 'God and our hearts are weeping together.' In the evening they came into a great forest and were so tired from misery, hunger, and the long journey that they sat down in a hollow tree and went to sleep." Bewitched by the evil stepmother, Little Brother is transformed into a deer, but Little Sister promises never to leave him. Untying her garter, she ties it around his neck and leads him deeper into the forest." And when they had gone a long, long way, they came to a hut and the girl looked in and thought, here we can stay and spend our lives. And so she collected leaves and moss to make a soft bed for the deer, and every morning she went out and found roots and berries and nuts for herself, and for the deer she brought tender grasses which it ate out of her hand and it was happy and gamboled all around her. At night, when sister was tired and had said her prayers, she laid her head on the fawn's back and that was her pillow on which she fell gently asleep. And if only brother had his human form, it would have been a lovely life."

"Perhaps it is only in childhood," Graham Greene has said, "that books have any deep influence on our lives." But it is important to realize that it is exactly in those books that children have adopted as their own that our deepest wishes and fantasies are most simply expressed.

One of the most haunting of these fantasies concerns the Two Forsaken Children who, as these archetypal siblings are beautifully described by the poet H.D. in her meditative *Tribute to Freud*, form a "little group, a design, an image at the crossroads." One child, H.D. tells us, is sometimes the shadow of the other, as in Greek tragedies. Often one is lost and seeks the other, as in the ancient fairy tale of the twin brother and sister of the Nile Valley. Sometimes they are both boys, like Castor and Pollux, finding their corresponding shape in the stars. In the nineteenth century we discover them in the story written by Edmond Goncourt about two acrobats (actually foils for himself and his beloved brother Jules) who "joined their nervous systems to master an impossible trick," as well as in the unsurpassed visionary tales of George MacDonald. But they are most deeply imprinted in our minds in the Grimms' "Little Brother, Little Sister."

When Maurice Sendak was six years old, he and his eleven-year-old brother Jack collaborated on a story called *They Were Inseparable*, about a brother and sister who, Maurice says, "had a hankering for each other—it was a very naïve and funny book. We both idolized our sister, she was the eldest and by far the prettiest, and we thought she was the crown jewel of the family. So because we idolized her, we made the book about a brother and a sister. And at the very end of the story, as I recall, an accident occurs: the brother's in the hospital, they don't think he's going to recover, the sister comes rushing in, and they just grab each other—like at the conclusion of *Tosca*—and exclaim: *we are inseparable!* Everybody rushes in to separate them as they jump out the hospital window. . . . Yes, you see, we *did* know dimly that there was something wrong, we were punishing them unconsciously.

"I imagine that all siblings have such feelings," Maurice continues. "The learning process makes children become aware that there's a taboo with regard to these feelings, but before you learn that, you do what comes naturally. My parents weren't well-to-do, and we had only two beds—my brother and I slept in one, my sister Natalie in the other, and often we'd all sleep in the same bed. My parents would come in—sometimes with my uncle and aunt—and they'd say: 'Look, see how much they like each other.' I loved my brother, and I didn't know that that could be this, and this that . . . kids find that out later."

Three years ago [1973], Sendak illustrated "Little Brother, Little Sister" in *The Juniper Tree*, a collection of twenty-seven tales by the Brothers Grimm—with accompanying Dürer-like drawings by Sendak—in the brilliant, unadorned translations of Lore Segal and Randall Jarrell. "A story like 'Little Brother, Little Sister' says everything in metaphor," Maurice comments, "so that it isn't upsetting to anybody. It's something we've always known about fairy tales—they talk about incest, the Oedipus complex, about psychotic mothers, like those of Snow White and Hansel and Gretel, who throw their children out. They tell things about life which children know instinctively, and the pleasure and relief lie in finding these things expressed in language that children can live with. You can't eradicate these feelings—they exist and they're a great source of creative inspiration."

This is, of course, what the child psychologist and writer Bruno Bettelheim has pointed out in his recently acclaimed *The Uses of Enchantment*, a strong, humanistic/psychological defense against the always-continuing attempts to bowdlerize and palliate fairy tales. But Bettelheim has certainly made an about-face since the time he admonished parents not to buy Sendak's immensely popular *Where the Wild Things Are*, warning them that little Max's dreamlike foray into the world of befanged and beclawed monsters would scare children, and that Max's rebellion against adult authority was psychologically harmful.

Sendak himself has answered these and other criticisms (my favorite comes from the *Journal of Nursery Education*'s review of *Wild Things*: "We should not like to have it left about where a sensitive child might find it to pore over in the twilight") in the acceptance speech he gave upon receiving the 1964 Caldecott Medal:

"[There are] games children must conjure up to combat an awful fact of childhood: the fact of their vulnerability to fear, anger, hate, frustration—all the emotions that are an ordinary part of their lives and that they can perceive only as ungovernable and dangerous forces. To master these forces, children turn to fantasy: that imagined world where disturbing emotional situations are solved to their satisfaction. Through fantasy, Max, the hero of my book, discharges his anger against his mother, and returns to the real world sleepy, hungry, and at peace with himself.

"Certainly we want to protect our children from new and painful experiences that are beyond their emotional comprehension and that intensify anxiety; and to a point we can prevent premature exposure to such experiences. That is obvious. But what is just as obvious —and what is too often overlooked—is the fact that from their earliest years children live on familiar terms with disrupting emotions, that fear and anxiety are an intrinsic part of their everyday lives, that they continually cope with frustration as best they can. And it is through fantasy that children achieve catharsis. It is the best means they have for taming Wild Things.

"It is my involvement with this inescapable fact of childhood— the awful vulnerability of children and their struggle to make themselves King of All Wild Things—that gives my work whatever truth and passion it may have."

BROOKLYN KIDS

Here are the inescapable facts of Maurice Sendak's childhood. Born in Brooklyn in 1928, he was the youngest of three children of Philip and Sarah Sendak, both of whom came to America before World War I from Jewish *shtetls* outside Warsaw.

One of Maurice's earliest memories dates from the age of three or four. "I was convalescing after a long, serious illness. I was sitting on my grandmother's lap, and I remember the feeling of pleasant drowsiness. It was winter. We sat in front of a window, and my grandmother pulled the shade up and down to amuse me. Every time the shade went up, I was thrilled by the sudden reappearance of the backyard, the falling snow, and my brother and sister busy constructing a sooty snowman. Down came the shade—I waited. Up went the shade—the children had moved, the snowman had grown eyes. I don't remember a single sound."

Perhaps Sendak's later interest in animated toys and transformation books begins here. His love of wonder tales certainly derives from the stories his father told him as a child. Philip Sendak was apparently an inspiring improviser of stories, and would embroider and extend a tale over a period of nights. Maurice recalls one of the more memorable of these in an illuminating *New Yorker* profile written in 1966 by Nat Hentoff:

"It was about a child taking a walk with his father and mother. He becomes separated from them. Snow begins to fall, and the child shivers in the cold. He huddles under a tree, sobbing in terror. An enormous figure hovers over him and says, as he draws the boy up, 'I'm Abraham, your father.' His fear gone, the child looks up and also sees Sarah. He is no longer lost. When his parents find him, the child is dead. Those stories had something of the character of William Blake's poems. The myths in them didn't seem at all factitious. And they fused Jewish lore with my father's particular way of shaping memory and desire. That one, for instance, was based on the power of Abraham in Jewish tradition as the father who was always there—a reassuring father even when he was Death. But the story was also about how tremendously my father missed his parents. Not all his tales were somber though. My father could be very witty, even if the humor was always on the darker side of irony."

Maurice's sister Natalie gave him his first book, *The Prince and the Pauper*. "A ritual began with that book," Sendak once told Virginia Haviland, "which I recall very clearly. The first thing was to set it up on the table and stare at it for a long time. Not because I was impressed with Mark Twain; it was just such a beautiful object. Then came the smelling of it . . . it was printed on particularly fine paper, unlike the Disney books I had gotten previous to that. *The Prince and the Paper—Pauper—*smelled good and it also had a shiny laminated cover. I flipped over that. I remember trying to bite into it, which I don't imagine is what my sister intended when she bought the book for me. But the last thing I did with the book was to read it. It was all right. But I think it started then, my passion for books and bookmaking. There's so much more to a book than just the reading. I've seen children touch books, fondle books, smell books, and it's all the reason in the world why books should be beautifully produced."

Following his brother Jack's example, Maurice first began writing his own stories when he was about nine, hand-lettering and illustrating them on uniform pages, then binding them with tape and decorated covers. He combined cutout newspaper photographs and comic strips with sketches of the Sendak family. And he began to draw.

"I was miserable as a kid," Sendak recalls. "I couldn't make friends, I couldn't play stoopball terrific, I couldn't skate great. I stayed home and drew pictures. You *know* what they all thought of me: sissy Maurice Sendak. When I wanted to go out and do something, my father would say: 'You'll catch a cold.' And I did . . . I did whatever he told me.

"People imagine that I was aware of Palmer and Blake and English graphics and German fairy tales when I was a kid. That came later. All I had then were popular influences—comic books, junk books, Gold Diggers movies, monster films, *King Kong, Fantasia*. I remember a Mickey Mouse mask that came on a big box of corn-flakes. What a fantastic mask! Such a big, bright, vivid, gorgeous hunk of face! And that's what a kid in Brooklyn knew at the time."

In the Night Kitchen, one of Sendak's greatest works, shows little Mickey falling naked through the night into the Oliver Hardy bakers' dough, kneading and pounding it into a Hap Harrigan plane, flying over the city, diving into a giant milk bottle, then sliding back into his bed to sleep. It is a work that pays extraordinary homage to Sendak's early aesthetic influences—especially to Winsor McCay—to the cheap, full-color children's books of the period, as well as to the feelings about New York City he had as a little boy.

"When I was a child," he told Virginia Haviland, "there was an advertisement which I remember very clearly. It was for the Sunshine bakers, and it read: 'We Bake While You Sleep!' It seemed to me the most sadistic thing in the world, because all I wanted to do was stay up and watch . . . it seemed so absurdly cruel and arbitrary for them to do it while I slept. And also for them to think I would think that that was terrific stuff on their part, and would eat their product on top of that. It bothered me a good deal, and I remember I used to save the coupons showing the three fat little Sunshine bakers going off to this magic place at night, wherever it was, to have their fun, while I had to go to bed. This book was a sort of vendetta book to get back at them and to say that I am now old enough to stay up at night and know what's happening in the Night Kitchen!

"Another thing is: I lived in Brooklyn, and to travel to Manhattan was a big deal, even though it was so close. I couldn't go by myself, and I counted a good deal on my elder sister. She took my brother and me to Radio City Music Hall, or the Roxy, or some such place. Now, the point of going to New York was that you *ate* in New York. Somehow to me New York represented eating. And eating in a very fashionable, elegant, superlatively mysterious place like Long-champs. You got dressed up, you went uptown—it was night when you got there and there were lots of windows blinking—and you went straight to a place to eat. It was one of the most exciting things of my childhood. Cross the bridge and see the city approaching, get there and have your dinner, then go to a movie and come home. So, again,

In the Night Kitchen is a kind of homage to New York City, the city I loved so much and still love."

At fifteen, Sendak worked after school drawing backgrounds for All-American Comics, adapting Mutt and Jeff comic strips, fitting them into a page, filling in backgrounds (puffs of dust under running heels), and extending the story line when necessary.

"I began illustrating my own books during this period," Maurice recalls. "My first book was Oscar Wilde's *The Happy Prince*, which is a story I don't admire any more, but as a young person I felt was extraordinary. And I illustrated Bret Harte's *The Luck of Roaring Camp*. It was my favorite story, and what is it about? A baby that is adopted by a lot of rough men, lumberjacks—an illegitimate child abandoned after the death of its mother. I'm writing a book now about a baby—most of my books are about babies—and it seems as if I've been doing the same thing since I was six years old. I'm a few inches taller and I have a graying beard, but otherwise there's not much difference.

"People used to comment continually on the fact that the children in my books looked homely—Eastern European Jewish as opposed to the flat, oilcloth look considered normal in children's books. They were just Brooklyn kids, old-looking before their time. But a baby *does* look a hundred years old.

"I love babies' faces and I draw them all the time. They're uncanny. When my father was dying, he'd dwindled—he had the body shape of a boy—and as I held him, I noticed that his head had become bigger than the rest of him and was rolling back like an infant's. Death at that moment was like going to sleep: 'Shhhh, it will be all right.' It's what you'd say to a feverish baby, except that he was dead.

"Infants' heads are wonderful to draw because they're so big and ungainly. You know how they fall back? Babies cry when they're held badly, they always know when they think they're going to be dropped, and when some klutz holds them, they cry. They're enormous kvetches with those mean little faces—'Give me this!'—and at the same time there's a look that they get that makes them so vulnerable, poignant, and lovable."

Shortly after graduating high school, he began to work full time at Timely Service, a window-display house in lower Manhattan, where he assisted in the construction of store-window models of figures such as Snow White and the Seven Dwarfs made out of chicken wire, papier-mâché, spun glass, plaster, and paint. With his brother, he began to make animated wooden toys that performed scenes from *Little Miss Muffet* and *Old Mother Hubbard*, which led to his being hired as a window-display assistant at F.A.O. Schwarz toy store. His only formal art study took place at this time—two years of evening classes at the Art Students League. Unbeknownst to him, Frances Chrystie, the children's book buyer at Schwarz, and Richard Nell, the store's display director, arranged for Ursula Nordstrom of Harper and Row to see his work, and she immediately asked him to illustrate Marcel Aymé's *The Wonderful Farm*, which was published in 1951. "It made me an official person," Maurice says.

Since then, as a writer, illustrator, and both, Sendak has published more than seventy books here and abroad, and he has been the recipient of scores of prizes and awards. He thinks of *A Hole Is to Dig* (1952)—with his exiguous and playful illustrations accompanying the poet Ruth Krauss's assemblage of children's definitions like "A face is so you can make faces"—as "the first book that came together for me." And he is still half pleased with *Kenny's Window* (1956)—the story of a little boy who, upon waking from a dream, remembers meeting a rooster who gave him seven questions to answer ("Can you fix a broken promise?" Kenny's reply: "Yes, if it only looks broken, but really isn't"). "It's the first thing I wrote," Maurice explains. "The pictures are ghastly—I really wasn't up to illustrating my own texts then—and the story itself, to be honest, is nice but overwritten: 'Singing chimes in the city lights and the songs of the city.' Today that kind of stuff sounds like Delius combined with Bruckner!"

After the introverted Kenny, Sendak introduced us to the fussy and sulking Martin in *Very Far Away* (1957). But it was in 1960 that Sendak's most indomitable character appeared on the scene: Rosie of *The Sign on Rosie's Door*. Based on a ten-year-old girl he spotted on the streets of Brooklyn in 1948, she is the prototype of all Sendak's plucky children, and he lovingly describes her genesis and transformations in his essay-portrait, "Rosie."

Sendak's *Nutshell Library* (1962)—four tiny books, each of which can be held in the palm of one's hand—is intimately tied to *The Sign on Rosie's Door*: Alligator, Pierre, Johnny, and the nameless hero of *Chicken Soup with Rice* are modeled on the "men" in Rosie's life. In 1975, Sendak drew all these characters into a marvelous half-hour animated film entitled *Really Rosie Starring the Nutshell Kids*— a film which Sendak both wrote and directed and which features the music and singing of Carole King. (The film soundtrack, *Carole King —Really Rosie,* is available on Ode Records.)

From Kenny and Martin to Pierre, Max, and Mickey, Sendak's characters have their origins in those Brooklyn street kids he used to observe and sketch while leaning out of his parents' second-story window—all of them enlivened and connected by that amazingly animated anima-figure who could, in Sendak's words, "imagine herself into being anything she wanted to be, anywhere in or out of the world." As her discoverer and creator remarks: "A mere change of sex cannot disguise the essential Rosieness of my heroes."

THE
HUNGER
ARTIST

Although Sendak has an apartment in New York City, he works and spends most of his time in the country just outside a small Connecticut town which, ironically, is the birthplace of Samuel Griswold Goodrich (1793–1860)—perhaps the best-known and most influential figure in nineteenth-century American children's literature. Goodrich's Peter Parley books (about 116 of them) sold 7 million copies—not including the thousands of imitations and pirate copies printed and sold in the United States and England. Illustrated with wood engravings, they were generally nationalistic but occasionally tolerant utilitarian schoolbooks written in the compendious and moronic style that has served as the model for generations of first-grade primers: "Here I am! My name is Peter Parley! I am an old man. I am very gray and lame. But I have seen a great many things, and had a great many adventures, and I love to talk about them. . . . And do you know that the very place where Boston stands was once covered with woods, and that in those woods lived many Indians? Did you ever see an Indian? Here is a picture of some Indians."

Aside from the fact that—a century apart—they resided just a few miles down the road from each other, two creators of children's literature more dissimilar than Goodrich and Sendak would be hard to imagine.

At the age of twelve, Goodrich read *Moral Repository* by Hannah More (1745–1833), an evangelical English educator and writer, and was instantly bowled over. (To counter what she considered "vulgar and indecent penny books" popular among young people at the time, More produced amiable-sounding works such as *The Execu-*

tion of Wild Henry. It is frightening to remind ourselves that 2 million of her Cheap Repository Tracts—sobering and moralistic tales largely designed to keep the poor in their place—were sold in their first year of publication, and this at a time when the population of England numbered fewer than 11 million.) So, when Goodrich visited More in Bristol (he was thirty and she was seventy-eight), he was thrown into a state of ecstasy. As he recalled this meeting in his *Recollections of a Lifetime*: "It was in conversation with that amiable and gifted person that I first formed the conception of the Parley Tales—the general idea of which was to make nursery books reasonable and truthful, and thus to feed the young mind upon things wholesome and pure, instead of things monstrous, false, and pestilent."

Goodrich particularly objected to the moral obliquity of *Puss in Boots* and *Jack the Giant Killer* ("tales of horror, commonly put into the hands of youth, as if for the express purpose of reconciling them to vice and crime"), and he detested nursery rhymes, declaring that even a child could make them up. To prove his point, he produced the following nonsense on the spot: "Higglety, pigglety, pop!/ The dog has eaten the mop;/The pig's in a hurry,/The cat's in a flurry,/Higglety, pigglety, pop!"

Irony upon irony. A century later, Maurice Sendak wrote and illustrated perhaps his most mysterious and extraordinary work, *Higglety Pigglety Pop! or There Must Be More to Life* (1967), a modern fairy tale about Jennie the Sealyham terrier—modeled after one of Sendak's own dogs—who packs her bag, goes out into the world to look for something more than everything, and winds up as the leading lady of a theatrical production (costarring Miss Rhoda, Pig, Cat, and a lion) of the "Higglety, Pigglety, Pop!" nursery rhyme itself. "Hello," Jennie begins the letter to her old master that concludes the book: "As you probably noticed, I went away forever. I am very experienced now and very famous. I am even a star. Every day I eat a mop, twice on Saturday. It is made of salami and that is my favorite. I get plenty to drink too, so don't worry. I can't tell you how to get to the Castle Yonder because I don't know where it is. But if you ever come this way, look for me. . . . Jennie."

The morning I was supposed to take the train up to visit Sendak in Connecticut, I received a call from him. Visit postponed, I thought.

"My dogs aren't well," Maurice said sadly. "But I think it will cheer me up to have company. . . . It's my birthday today."

"What would you like as a present?" I asked.

"Well, if it's no trouble, some sandwiches from a deli. Any kind. Anything. It's hopeless around here."

"What about hot pastrami with coleslaw and mustard on rye?"

"Fantastic."

"And pickles?"

"Fantastic. And perhaps a really gooey chocolate layer cake for dessert?"

When Maurice picked me up at the station, he apologized for being late. "There are hundreds of children parading through town," he said incredulously. And as we began to drive slowly back to his house, I saw hordes of kids marching silently along the roads, as if they were following an invisible and inaudible Pied Piper. "What's going on?" I wondered aloud.

"I live here," Maurice grimly replied.

Sendak's house is hardly grim, surrounded as it is by beautiful ash, sugar maple, dogwood, and locust trees, and with irises, lilies, phlox, and roses growing near a little wood hut, the whole scene reminding me of a German landscape.

"Mahler went into the woods to write his symphonies in *his* little *Waldhütte*," Maurice says as he shows me his cottage. "And in the first movement of his Third Symphony, you can almost hear him in those woods, with those menacing trees and ferns that turn into fingers—like the trees that catch Snow White. You get a sense of that forest in the first movement—very ambivalent to the artist: is it going to give him something or frighten him to death? [See Sendak's cover illustration for RCA's new recording of Mahler's Third, which depicts a silhouetted Mahler in his *Waldhütte* receiving the gift of inspiration from an angel.] And Mozart, too. When he was alone in Vienna writing *The Magic Flute*, he was invited to live in a tiny summer cottage outside the theater grounds to continue his work. . . . The only way to find something is to lose oneself: that's what George Mac-Donald teaches us in his stories. And that's what this little hut, where one can be alone, means to me."

Sendak takes me back to the main house, which is filled with the most wondrous, imaginative, and variegated things. On the walls are posters by Penfield, Will Bradley, Lautrec, and Bonnard; a glorious Winsor McCay triptych showing Little Nemo and a princess walking down a resplendent garden path surrounded by daffodils with smiling faces; children's toys, a pillow in the shape of the *Night Kitchen*'s Mickey and his bottle of milk, and a bunch of stuffed Wild Things; and in almost every room, books by James, Melville, Dickens, Stifter, MacDonald, Blake, Beatrix Potter, Palmer's illustrated Milton . . . as well as art books (Dürer, Grünewald) and books on music (Mahler, Wolf, Wagner, Beethoven, and Mozart).

Birthday presents from friends are lying on the dining-room table: a Mickey Mouse mirror and Mickey Mouse music box, an eighteenth-century tin coach from Germany, miniature bottles of Dry Sack, a floral bouquet, a T-shirt inscribed "Some Swell Pup"—the title of his recently published cartoon book—and three little scissors for cutting cloth, paper, and letters. I add the sandwiches, and we begin lunch.

"Maurice, this is as good a time as any to ask you about the idea of incorporation in your work."

"While I'm eating the sandwich?"

"In *Pierre* the lion eats Pierre. In *As I Went over the Water* a sea monster ingests a boat. In *Higglety Pigglety Pop!* Jennie eats a mop. Things and people get swallowed, and out they come again. And in one of your best fantasy sketches, you show a baby eating its mother. This happens a lot in Grimms' tales and especially in Winsor McCay's early animation films about dinosaurs. What's this all about?"

"Well," Maurice says, "I'm certainly not going to disgorge this sandwich—it's delicious, and I feel better already. You know, I used to love *biting* into my first books when I was a child, so maybe it's a hangup from that time . . . but a pleasant one: things being eaten and then given out again—it's an image that constantly appeals to me, and to most children, too. It's such a primary fantasy of childhood—the pleasure of putting things in the mouth, of chewing, of swallowing, of shitting, and pissing. Before children are told it's not a nice thing—the whole toilet-training process—there's nothing nicer."

"Sometimes, though, it can be scary," I add, remembering how Maurice once described his feelings as a child when grown-ups would endearingly lean over him and say, Oh, I could eat you up! "I was very nervous," Maurice had then recalled, "because I really believed they probably could if they had a mind to. They had great big teeth, immense nostrils and very sweaty foreheads. I often remember that vision and how it frightened me. There was one particular relative who did this to me, and it was really quite terrifying. I immortalized him in *Wild Things*.

"In the fantasy sketch that shows the child devouring his mother," Maurice now adds, ". . . of course that's what children must feel: that great big luminous breast hanging over its head is sent there by God. Obviously it's there for you, why not? Until you're told differently, how are you going to know? There's something both monstrous and poignant about it: the poignancy comes from the fact that a child's going to realize soon enough that it's not so, that he's mortal, that he'll have to compete for it, but that for the second's worth that it's there it's a glorious pleasure. And all I'm saying is, what's wrong with the pleasure? Why must we assume that the knowing is the correct thing and that the pleasure is the bad thing, which is what most people do feel.

"People who objected to Mickey bathing in milk and floating naked—every part of his body having a sensuous experience . . . as if that's naughty. Why? Why are we all so screwed up, including me? But at least creatively I try to convey the memory of a time in life when it was a pleasure.

"I don't understand the destructive aspect. In my little cartoon, the baby eats the mother—on the surface, what could be more destructive? But in fact the child doesn't think of it as a destructive act, it's the most natural thing to him: if you have that much of the mother, have more!"

"Well," I interject, "someone could look at it another way: mother destroys child/child destroys mother."

"That's just mental maneuvering to me," Maurice replies. "I take from the image as much as it's necessary for me to use creatively. I'm not going to analyze it. Now, I'm not against psychology or analysis on principle. I'm sure that the things I draw—little boys flying and falling—reveal something. In one sense it seems very obviously Freudian, as if coming out of my own analysis. People fear that analysis will castrate and dry up artists, but it's just the contrary, in my opinion: it gives wonderful clues and cues as to what you're doing. I don't think of what I'm creating in strict Freudian terms, but surely it's a result of the fact that a large part of my twenties was spent on the analyst's couch. And it enriched and deepened me and

Fantasy Sketch

gave me confidence to express much that I might not have without it.

"Coming back to the fantasy sketch: the bird is in there because birds were my father's favorite fairy tale symbol. He used to tell stories of birds taking children away. And I think that they enter into a lot of my things because it's an image of his that has always appealed to my heart.

"Incidentally, I did another and earlier version of this sketch in the fifties, and in that version the baby comes out of the fish, the mother is there—furious that the baby's been lost—turns the baby over on her knee, and spanks him. And he, in his rage, this tiny baby in his little diaper, pulls away from her, pulls out a gun and shoots her dead.

"*That* sketch, shall we say, was *unsynthesized*. Whatever it was, it certainly was blatant, and I think that this later one is much better. The earlier version was done while my mother was living, and this one after she died. So, obviously, I've thought and rethought a lot about her during that interval."

"I was reading recently," I say, "that certain librarians were covering up Mickey's little penis in copies of *Night Kitchen* and that others had suggested that you draw in a little diaper on Mickey in later editions of the book. But take a look at these illustrations I brought up to show you from Jacques Stella's seventeenth-century *Games and Pastimes of Childhood*—all of them depicting naked little putti capering and frolicking."

"It's an amazing coincidence," Maurice exclaims. "I was given this book again recently because my new work is in part concerned with babies doing odd things, and I've been looking at the book for weeks. The illustrations are beautiful . . . and strange. There's a hallucinatory quality about them: they're just children playing games, but why are they all naked? Yet we often make a mistake of reading heavy, tedious, psychological overtones into things that in the seventeenth and eighteenth centuries weren't considered that way at all. I couldn't do that book today, I'd be thrown out of the country. But *that* book is a classic. Adults will take their kids to museums to see a lot of peckers in a row on Roman statues and say: That's art, dearie, and then come home and burn *In the Night Kitchen*. Where's the logic in that? Art in people's minds is desexualized, and that would make the great artists sick.

"In the illustrations I just completed for Randall Jarrell's *Fly by Night*—the last book he wrote for children before he died—I have an eight-year-old boy flying naked in a dream. I tried to draw the boy first with pajamas—he looked too much like Wee Willie Winkie. Then I tried him in underwear, and it looked like an ad for Fruit of the Loom. I tried him wrapped in sheets and blankets, but it looked too baroque. He had to be naked. But I know they're going to say it's typically me, arbitrarily making somebody nude. I had a picture showing a girl with her vagina in full view in *The Light Princess*, and nobody made a fuss about that, which makes me think that the whole world is male chauvinist—vaginas don't count."

"What's *Fly by Night* about?" I ask Maurice.

"It's a dream: the boy David dreams. Every night he dreams he floats. During the daytime he tries to remember that he can float at night, but he can't. When he wakes up he can't remember. And the entire story is about what happens to him in this one dream. He floats out of his house, over certain animals, and each of the animals has a little poem written by Jarrell—they're delicious poems—and yet they're much deeper, with a kind of funny, starved feeling in them.

"David meets the owl, floats into her nest, and she sings David and her baby a song about getting a little sister and being taken care of by a mother. For me, that's what the whole book is about—it may or may not have been for Randall. It's about being starved for a mother or for safety or protection or for some place where you can nest or land or be.

"It has a happy ending. David comes home, floats back into his bed, and when he wakes up, there's his mother who's made breakfast for him. He looks at her, she looks familiar—someone looks just like her. Of course it's the owl, he's losing all memory of his dream.

"I drew myself as a baby in it—you can see me in my mother's arms in the book's only double-spread picture. And I may have taken a very lopsided and fanciful view of the story, but what I read into it was a great hunger pain—that longing I once felt in Jarrell's *The Animal Family*—and I interpreted it as a looking-for-mama pain. . . . Maybe it's my pain.

"Come back next week," Maurice says to me, "and I'll tell you the rest."

MOZART AND THE MAN IN THE MOON

Maurice has three dogs: Agamemnon, a male shepherd; Erda, a female shepherd; and Io, a female retriever. "Zeus had a fling with Io," Maurice says, "and jealous Hera transformed her into a bull calf who was bitten by a gadfly throughout eternity. The minute I saw Io, she looked like a victim—blond and beautiful."

Aggie and Erda are immortalized in the dream sequence of Sendak's latest cartoon book, *Some Swell Pup, or Are You Sure You Want a Dog?* Written in collaboration with Matthew Margolis, director of the National Institute of Dog Training, the book is an *echt*-Sendak burlesque, telling a cautionary tale of two kids and how they learn to train and love their rambunctious new puppy—which ironically takes on the role of the stereotypical unruly child—with the guidance of a caftanned canine saint.

"I love this book," I say to Maurice the following week, having read *Some Swell Pup* in the interval. "How did it come about?"

"Matthew suggested the ideas about puppy rearing, and I found a group of scenes for them and refashioned his language. The rules had to be simplified and humorized because we wanted kids to enjoy it.

"I was looking for real crazy kids who could act out these little scenes, and so I chose the two I had first used some years back in a sequence of drawings for *Family Circle* magazine and who later appeared as the players of *King Grisly-Beard*. Matthew and I realized that these two would be perfect. She's an aggressive and hysterical yenta, and he's a passive and selfish kid. Their secret names, by the way, are Vernon and Shirley. She's really a Shirley, and he's a real *vaserdiker gornisht* type."

"It's certainly the wittiest tale about how to get gently and humanely socialized that I've ever read," I say. "Just compare it to the typical late-Georgian English stories for children whose 'message,' as the critic Gillian Avery once put it, was 'Be punctual and diligent, obedient and dutiful, do not lie or thieve or blow up your sister, beware of mad dogs and gaming, and you will live to be a successful sugar planter and give your rivals a handsome funeral.' But *Some Swell Pup* is all about true human nature and relationships and patience and acceptance and love and light and . . ."

". . . and orifices," Maurice adds.

"It's probably your most complete work."

"Jesus, I hope not," Maurice replies. "In terms of orifices it is. One reviewer said: 'There's all this fuss about whether the puppy is a girl or a boy, but we don't even see the anatomical truth.' The reviewer thought I'd gotten coy. But, I mean, how do you show a puppy's sex organ? You'd have to have a microscope to see it at that stage."

"I just saw another review, Maurice, in which the writer spends most of her time commenting on puppy poop."

"Naturally. What does she say?"

I read: " 'Sendak is up front about dog droppings, liberally sprinkling in piles and puddles and deliberately risking a flap similar to the one over frontal nudity in *Night Kitchen*.' "

"Here we go again," he sighs with resigned good humor.

Maurice invites me to drive with him to the veterinarian's to pick up Aggie. To cheer him up, I quote what I think is an appropriate little vignette that appears in Gustav Janouch's *Conversations with Kafka*. Janouch writes:

"Out of a house in the Jakobsgasse, where we had arrived in the course of our discussion, ran a small dog looking like a ball of wool, which crossed our path and disappeared round the corner of the Tempelgasse.

" 'A pretty little dog,' I said.

" 'A dog?' asked Kafka suspiciously, and slowly began to move again.

" 'A small, young dog. Didn't you see it?'

" 'I saw. But was it a dog?'

" 'It was a little poodle.'

" 'A poodle? It could be a dog, but it could also be a sign. We Jews often make tragic mistakes.' "

Maurice laughs so hard he almost has to stop driving. "*It could be a dog, but it could also be a sign.* What book *is* that?"

"Janouch was a teen-ager when he met Kafka. Kafka befriended him, and Janouch later wrote down and published their conversations, which are filled with wonderful statements such as: 'Art like prayer is a hand outstretched in the darkness, seeking for some touch of grace which will transform it into a hand that bestows gifts. Prayer means casting oneself into the miraculous rainbow that stretches between becoming and dying, to be utterly consumed in it, in order to bring its infinite radiance to bed in the frail little cradle of one's own existence. . . . Life is as infinitely great and profound as the immensity of the stars above us. One can only look at it through the narrow keyhole of one's own personal existence. But through it one perceives more than one can see. So above all one must keep the keyhole clean.' "

"That's too much," Maurice says. "It's so wonderful it's like getting drunk. Whistle-clean keyholes . . . every metaphor describes his own work. You didn't know this, but one of my fantasy projects has always been to illustrate Kafka. For years I've been thinking about it, wondering whether I was old enough to do it—just as I waited until I thought I was old enough to do *The Juniper Tree.* He's one of the few writers who could express the act of creating so beautifully. I feel so close to him. The only difference is that he's a genius."

"I've noticed," I mention to Maurice, "that a lot of the theatrical performances that take place in your books—*Higglety Pigglety Pop!* and *King Grisly-Beard* especially—share certain characteristics with the Nature Theater of Oklahoma as Kafka describes it in *Amerika.*"

"To put it mildly," Maurice responds. "Where do you think I got it from? From there and from Richard Strauss's *Ariadne auf Naxos* —characters and an impresario looking for a performance. I love opera, theater, pantomime, ballet, and I've tried to express this love and appreciation in my books."

At the vet's, Aggie seems to be feeling better, and when we arrive back at Maurice's, he happily greets Erda and Io, and off they go running around the grounds. Maurice keeps a watchful eye on them as we sit under the trees, and I ask him about the new picture book he's just started.

"This will be the last part of my trilogy that began with *Wild Things* and *Night Kitchen*. And of the three, this one will be the strangest. *Wild Things* now seems to me to be a very simple book—its simplicity is probably what made it successful, but I could never be that simple again. *Night Kitchen* I much prefer—it reverberates on double levels. But this third book will reverberate on triple levels. It's so dense already . . . I don't know what it means and I can't get beyond the first seven lines.

"But I'll get there, I feel it in me—like a woman having a baby, all that life churning on inside me. I feel it every day: it moves, stretches, yawns . . . it's getting ready to get born. It knows exactly what it is, only I don't know with my conscious mind, but every day I get a little clue: Listen, dumdum, here's a word for you, see what you can make of it. So it throws it out and I catch it: oh, a word, fantastic! And then I do without for three days, and the unconscious says, This man's too much to believe, he walks, he thinks, sits, he doesn't do anything, he's a bore, throw him another word, otherwise he'll sit there forever and have a coronary. . . . And one by one it throws me words.

"Is it the right time for a book? It's like getting pregnant when you've just gone crazy and you've found out your house has burned down. Externally I'm in turmoil, I didn't want to get pregnant now. When I write the book, it may be an abortion, but let's hope not. I'm definitely with life, as they say, sitting like a mother on a stump, thinking, Thank you, God, thank you."

"D. H. Lawrence," I interject, "used to describe the pregnant mother as feeling at one with the world."

"The *maven* on how women felt!" Maurice replies. "What does that mean? It sounds like being glued to something. I don't feel at one with the world, I never have. The only thing that's miraculous is the creative act, and I call it miraculous because I don't understand it. I don't understand, for example, how Mozart could write semitrivial but deliciously funny letters to Daddy at the very moment he was composing his sublime works. And when Daddy says: 'Look, Wolfgang, I don't want you messing around in Munich, you're there to get a job, I don't like your going out dancing every night—your mother's written to me all about it. Pull yourself together. You're not the type to do this kind of thing. Your loving father.' 'But Daddy, Daddy,' Mozart writes back, 'I just went out with Fraülein so-and-so, she's a nice girl, I had two dances, came home at eleven o'clock, I've been good, haven't been drinking wine, and on top of that I just wrote the horn concerto, two violin concertos, and the famous *Sinfonia Concertante*. Isn't that enough for this week, Daddy? I'll try and be better.'

"Now, of course I made that up, but that's the sound of it, and Mozart wrote those pieces that same week he was thinking those nothing thoughts and trying to get his boring father off his back. And while he was doing this, he was creating something that was completely beyond his father, beyond anyone's father, and beyond any of us two hundred years later. *That's* the miracle.

"I've always loved Mozart. I read Alfred Einstein's wonderful book on him, and I've read a dozen books since then, although not one of them is up to that. But best of all is Mozart's letters. I'm only up to age twenty-two, but it doesn't matter. Every letter is beautiful, no matter how trivial it is. And they're very scatological—not only Wolfgang's but sober Frau Mozart's as well: 'When you go to bed, shit well till it busts,' she writes to her husband. Now, you *know* she's not a maniac. And Wolfgang writes something like: 'My darling, my quintessential sister, I kiss you, stuff your arse in your mouth tonight and bite with all your heart. Then shit and let it bust good.' It's so strange! What does it mean? Very conceivably one might think that Mozart was an anal retentive, that he never got past the toilet-training stage. . . . But it was the eighteenth century. And there's also that very Germanic quality of every day being based on the quality of the bowel movement."

"I seem to remember," I add, "that in one of his letters he writes: 'Do we live to shit, or shit to live?' That's very advanced existential humor."

"It's that combination of gravity and grace that I love so much in Mozart," Maurice says. "He's the ideal, and God knows I'm not like him. I'm not good-humored and I don't juggle the problems of life well.

"Recently I've been reading about Beethoven and his relationship with his nephew, Karl. When Karl said he wanted to go out, Beethoven suffered terribly: the child didn't want him all the time, unlike the music that was so compliant. Beethoven could be who he was, do what he did, and then try to apply the same grandiose, creative rules of art to everyday life. The dummy just couldn't accept the fact that it wasn't possible to force a little boy to love him the way he could force the *Hammerklavier* to appear on paper. Beethoven's special kind of love—'I-hypnotize-you-into-total-love'—overlooked what did come from the child: affection, pleasure in having an extraordinary man named Beethoven as his uncle. But it wasn't enough for him.

"And yes, I do identify with Beethoven—it's like the Achilles' heel of the artist who lives on a grandiose plane, conjuring his art up, but failing in real life because his inflated ego can't be satisfied. I don't like Beethoven the man, but I have tremendous sympathy for him.

"I hope," Maurice says suddenly, "that you don't think of me as some kind of *shlump*."

"As you've been talking," I say to him, "I've been thinking of that early nineteenth-century Mother Goose illustration you praised so highly in one of your essays. It's an illustration that juxtaposes the curmudgeonly Man in the South slopping porridge over his head and the mysterious, ambiguous and graceful Man in the Moon floating through the mist and clouds. This seems to be the Beethoven-Mozart split in your being, this one image suggesting the unity of personality. You've been talking about two composers, but you really seem to be talking about reality and imagination, heaviness and lightness."

"Music," Maurice replies, "is a metaphor for everything."

THE SHAPE
OF MUSIC

It is possible to see Sendak's books as falling into either the major or the minor *key*—in the musical sense. The major works consist of the color picture and cartoon books like *Night Kitchen, Hector Protector,* or *Some Swell Pup,* which feature simple, broad, outlined drawings, often done with a Magic Marker. The minor works—his haunting illustrations for *The Juniper Tree, Higglety Pigglety Pop!, Fly by Night,* MacDonald's *The Golden Key,* and *The Light Princess* —are distinguished by their elaborate pen-and-ink crosshatched style.

Sendak continually talks about the illustrator's task in musical terms. "To conceive musically for me means to quicken the life of the illustrated book," he wrote in his essay "The Shape of Music." And he speaks of his favorite illustrators as if they were musicians.

The pictures of the Victorian artist Randolph Caldecott, Sendak writes, "abound in musical imagery; his characters are forever dancing and singing and playing instruments. More to the point is his refinement of a graphic counterpart to the musical form of theme and variations, his delightful compounding of a simple visual theme into a fantastically various interplay of images. In one of his greatest and most beautiful pictures—'And the Dish ran away with the Spoon' from *Hey Diddle Diddle*—you see a cat playing his violin for objects in the kitchen (a flask, dishes, bowls) and, in the foreground, the dish running away with the spoon. You can almost hear the music coming from the back room as you observe the couple fleeing, obviously in love."

About the illustrations for La Fontaine's fable "The Wolf and the Lamb" by the late-nineteenth-century artist M. Boutet de Monvel, Sendak writes: "The lamb performs, before meeting an unjust fate, a sequence of linear arabesques, a superb dance of death that painfully conveys and dramatically enlarges the fable's grim meaning. The eye follows from picture to picture the swift development of the story—the fatalistic 'folding up,' the quiet inevitability of the lamb's movements, ending in a dying-swan gesture of hopeless resignation. And then the limp, no longer living form hanging from the raging wolf's mouth. I think of these fine, softly colored, and economically conceived drawings as a musical accompaniment to the La Fontaine fable, harmonic inventions that color and give fresh meaning in much the same way that a Hugo Wolf setting illuminates a Goethe poem."

Sendak admires the "tremendous vitality" of Wilhelm Busch ("Mickey in *Night Kitchen* gets baked, just like Max and Moritz"), the clarity and simplicity of the French artists Felix Valloton (especially his illustrations for *Poil de Carotte*) and Bonnard ("their simple lines, strokes, washes of color—it's that Mozart quality I don't have, my things are so heavy . . . like latkes and mashed potatoes"), and, most of all, the "terse, blocked images" of the English artist Arthur Hughes—"so graphically precise and unearthly. Hughes is one of the most important influences in my life, especially his illustrations for the fairy tales of George MacDonald.

"I love immaculate, rigid, antiquated forms where every bit of fat is cut off, so tight and perfect you couldn't stick a pin in it, but within which you can be as free as you want. And I'm not an innovator—that's not my talent. I've just taken what's there and tried to show what else you could do with it. Like the picture-book form, which requires an extraordinary condensation of feeling and words. It should last just a few minutes for the child, since most children have very short spans of interest. But I personally love the art of condensation, squeezing something big into its pure essence.

"I'm an artist who does books that are apparently more appropriate for children than for anyone else, for some odd reason. I never set *out* to do books for children—I *do* books for children, but I don't know why. And, to me, the greatest writers—like the greatest illustrators—for children are those who draw upon their child sources, their dream sources—they don't forget them. There's William Blake, George MacDonald, Dickens . . . that peculiar charm of being in a room in a Dickens novel, where the furniture is alive, the fire is alive, where saucepans are alive, where chairs move, where every inanimate object has a personality.

"There's Henry James, whom I would call a children's book writer, why not? He would have dropped dead if you had said that to him, but his all-absorbing interest in children and their relationships to adults creates some of his greatest stories. Just the way he allows children to stay up and see what the grown-ups are really doing. In *What Maisie Knew*, children are constantly mixing in the most deranged adult society, and they're permitted to view and morally judge their elders. It's like a fantasy come true. It's like Mickey not wanting, to go to sleep in order to see what goes on in the Night Kitchen. James' children stay up at night, too. Maisie hardly says anything, but we all know what she knows, and we see her know it.

"Finally, there's Herman Melville. I wanted to write something that had the same title as a book by Melville, but I couldn't call it *Moby Dick* or *The Confidence Man* or *Typee*. It had to be something a little vaguer. Finally I hit on *Pierre*. I needed a rhyme for the name, and that's how I came up with Pierre's favorite line: 'I don't care.'

"It's the two levels of writing—one visible, one invisible—that fascinate me most about Melville. As far down as the whale goes in the water is as deep as Herman writes—even in his early works like *Redburn*, which is one of my favorite books. The young man coming to England for the first time . . . I swear, I'll never forget that walk he takes in the English countryside. There's a mystery there, a clue, a nut, a bolt, and if I put it together, I find me."

INSIDE
AND OUTSIDE:
THE MEADOW

"There's a theme that appears in much of your work," I say to Maurice on my last visit to Connecticut, "and I can only hint at it because it's difficult to formulate or describe. It has something to do with the lines: 'As I went over the water/The water went over me' [from *As I Went over the Water*] or 'I'm in the milk and the milk's in me' [from *Night Kitchen*]."

"Obviously I have one theme, and it's even in the book I'm working on right now. It's not that I have such original ideas, just that I'm good at doing variations on the same idea over and over again. You can't imagine how relieved I was to find out that Henry James admitted he had only a couple of themes and that all of his books were based on them. That's all we need as artists—one power-driven fantasy or obsession, then to be clever enough to do variations . . . like a series of variations by Mozart. They're so good that you forget they're based on one theme. The same things draw me, the same images. . . ."

"What is this one obsession?"

"I'm not about to tell you—not because it's a secret, but because I can't verbalize it."

"There's a line by Bob Dylan in 'Just like a Woman' which talks about being 'inside the rain.' "

"Inside the rain?"

"When it's raining outside," I explain, "I often feel inside myself, as if I were inside the rain . . . as if the rain were my *self*. That's the sense I get from Dylan's image and from your books as well."

"It's strange you say that," Maurice answers, "because rain has become one of the most potent images of my new book. It sort of scares me that you mentioned that line. Maybe that's what rain means. It's such an important ingredient in this new work, and I've never understood what it meant. There was a thing about me and rain when I was a child: if I could summon it up in one sentence, I'd be happy to. It's such connected tissue. . . ."

The connecting tissue in the work of Maurice Sendak is the continually experienced awareness of the deepest child-self. "I don't believe, in a way, that the kid I was grew up into me," he once told Nat Hentoff. "He still exists somewhere, in the most graphic, plastic, physical way. . . . I communicate with him—or try to—all the time. One of my worst fears is losing contact with him. I don't want this to sound coy or schizophrenic, but at least once a day I feel I have to make contact. The pleasures I get as an adult are heightened by the fact that I experience them as a child at the same time. Like, when autumn comes, as an adult I welcome the departure of the heat, and simultaneously, as a child would, I start anticipating the snow and the first day it will be possible to use a sled. This dual apperception does break down occasionally. That usually happens when my work is going badly. I get a sour feeling about books in general and my own in particular. The next stage is annoyance at my dependence on this dual apperception, and I reject it. Then I become depressed. When excitement about what I'm working on returns, so does the child. We're on happy terms again."

A little boy once wrote Maurice a letter that read: "How much does it cost to get to where the wild things are? If it is not too expensive my sister and I want to spend the summer there. Please answer soon."

The "wild things" are, of course, the feelings within us, and if we lose contact with them and with our childhood being we become defenders of the Social Lie and the forces of death, as we mouth platitudes about "reverence for life." But life demands us to defend not denatured human beings but rather transformed and transforming boys and girls, men and women. The psychoanalyst Wilhelm Reich knew this when he wrote his great visionary oration in *Cosmic Super-imposition*:

"Outside on the meadow, two children in deep embrace would not astonish or shock anyone. Inside on the stage, it would immediately invoke police action. Outside, a child is a child, an infant is an infant, and a mother is a mother, no matter whether in the form of a deer, or a bear, or a human being. Inside, an infant is *not* an infant if its mother cannot show a marriage certificate. Outside, to know the stars is to know God, and to meditate about God is to meditate about the heavens. Inside, somehow, if you believe in God, you do not understand or you refuse to understand the stars. Outside, if you search in the heavens, you refuse, and rightly so, to believe in the sinfulness of the natural embrace. Outside, you feel your blood surging and you do not doubt that something is moving in you, a thing you call your emotion, with its location undoubtedly in the middle of your body and close to your heart."

About the Author

JONATHAN COTT, who lives in New York City, received his B.A. from Columbia College and his M.A. in English from the University of California, Berkeley. He studied children's literature and contemporary poetry on a Fulbright at the University of Essex in England. He has worked in radio (for KPFA in Berkeley and WNYC in New York), television (Granada TV in England), and publishing (for Stonehill Publishing as executive editor). He is the author of *Stockhausen: Conversations with the Composer*; *He Dreams What Is Going on Inside His Head* (a collection of essays, interviews, and reviews); and a collection of poems called *City of Earthly Love*. He has also edited *The Roses Race Around Her Name: Poems from Fathers to Daughters*; *Beyond the Looking Glass: Victorian Fairy Tale Novels, Stories and Poems*; and the forthcoming five-volume *Masterworks of English Children's Literature: 1550–1900*. His poetry has been widely anthologized and has appeared in such places as the *Paris Review* and the *American Poetry Review*. He is an associate editor of *Rolling Stone*, and his articles have appeared there for the last ten years, as well as in the *New York Times*, *American Review*, and *Ramparts*.